Life In The Land of IS

A Memoir

The Amazing Story of Lani Deauville
The World's Longest Living Quadriplegic

As told to
Bette Lee Crosby

BENT
PINE
PUBLISHING

Cover Design:
Michael G. Visconte
Creative Director
FC Edge
Stuart, FL

This is a memoir and is as accurate as memory softened by years
will allow. All of the events and people portrayed in this book are
as I remember them. I have however changed a few of the names
to protect the privacy of the innocent and the reputation of the
guilty.

ISBN #978-0-9838879-4-2

Bent Pine Publishing
Port St. Lucie, FL

First Edition

To Boogs

I Love You Infinity

One

I believe in IS. It's the singular moment that takes you from what was, to what will be. 'IS' is the face of reality. At times it's as warm and comforting as the summer sun against your skin; then without warning it can grow ugly beyond definition, a thing you'd turn away from if given the choice, but the truth is you don't have a choice. Nobody does. We don't get to choose the 'IS' of our life. 'IS' simply shows up on our doorstep and says *here I am, so deal with it.* In all probability, I should have died fifty two years ago; but after seventeen years of hanging onto the tail of the tiger, I wasn't quite ready to let go.

You might expect that a woman born into a family with turn of the century steel money and an aristocratic heritage would be plunked down on the pathway of plenty, but you'd be wrong. I grew up fatherless, crammed into a one room cottage with Mother and two siblings born of a different father. At times I could envision my half-brother, Scott, a valiant protector. Other times he became my tormentor. With our sister Dorothy Lee, there was no such question—she hated me from the moment I was born. Perhaps I could fault Mother for the haphazard choices that forced us into such a situation, but why lay blame on her when in some ways I'm as reckless and irresponsible as she ever dreamed of being. The likelihood is that she and I both inherited an errant gene, one that burrows its way into your soul and causes you to fly in the face of tradition, deny impossibility, and forge a pathway through this briar patch of life. If such a gene exists, it probably originated with Grandmother Alice Paul, a suffragette who marched herself down to Washington demanding the right to vote; then with two suitcases and three little girls slipped away in the dark of night, leaving her husband behind. Long before I entered this world I'd been infused with Grandmother's sense of defiance and my father's passion for unbridled freedom. Little wonder I grew up a tomboy, a daredevil, a latchkey kid who neither knew nor understood the meaning of fear.

The life I'm now living began in Southern Florida on a sweltering summer day, when the air was thick with humidity and my skin prickled with restlessness. It was June 2, 1958; two days after I'd strutted across the stage, a finalist in the New Smyrna Beach Beauty Pageant, and three days before I'd planned to wear the new prom gown hanging in the closet. I was seventeen, the age when sitting still is impossible, boredom worse than death, and a new adventure lurking around every corner. After spending over a year in New York, I'd returned to Daytona searching for something—freedom perhaps, or that magical stimulus that would quicken my heartbeat and send challenge pulsing through my veins.

At the age of fifteen, I had been allowed to go to Manhattan to attend the Semple Finishing School for Girls; but after a month of rather ridiculous curfew restrictions and listening to the same etiquette lessons Mother had preached from the time I was born, I moved out. My first thought was the Barbizon Plaza, an exclusive hotel for women. For a while it looked as though I might be accepted, but once they discovered I was not yet sixteen, I received a polite no. It was the same story with several other women's hotels; apparently a fifteen year old girl was something no one wanted as their responsibility. In desperation, I turned to my brother Scott, who was married to a Jewish woman. She pulled a few strings and got me into a Jewish Women's Hotel. If I were to stay in New York, it seemed to be my only option.

After being told repeatedly that I should work as a model, and equipped with few marketable talents other than my good looks, I decided to give modeling a shot. It was at a casting call that I met the three gay men, also models, who would ultimately become my best friends and protectors. We struck up a conversation and when they learned my age, Sam said, "Fifteen! What's a girl your age doing in New York alone? Do you even realize the dangers of this business? Some agencies issue a call for models, but they're not really looking for models! Get involved in something like that, and you could end up in serious trouble." The other two agreed. "We've got a spare room," Robert said, "You can move in with us and we'll get you to the legitimate agencies." Within the week, I left the hotel and moved in with my new friends.

True to their word, they guided me to the right places, recommended me to the agencies they knew, convinced me to 'fudge' my age and helped me find a reasonably steady stream of work which I supplemented with a job at a Greenwich Village coffee house. Day after day I slid my body into the latest fashions and smiled at the camera, a picture of serenity on the outside, but inside the seed of restlessness was starting to sprout. I smoked, I drank, I dated young men who were sometimes older than was appropriate, and I partied, all while my gay friends watched over me like mother hens. New York was fun, but it was a city—the streets crowded with people, remnants of trash tossed about, the only trees brass-potted saplings struggling for survival in front of luxury hotels. Dogs that should have been free to race across endless stretches of grass were forced to pee in the gutter. The handful of horses that clip-clopped through Central Park seemed weary of both tourists and traffic. On days when I wasn't working, I'd be lying in the grass in Central Park, looking up at the clouds and wishing I was back in the Tomoka Game Reserve. I knew New York wasn't the place I wanted to spend my forever. Modeling for the Macy's Catalog and for a wholesale furrier was not the glamorous life I had anticipated. Somewhere there was a real life waiting for me, a life with an exciting career and freedom poking out of its pockets. It was out there and my name was written on it, but it was going to be up to me to find it.

I was seventeen when I left New York City and returned to Daytona. That summer I breezed through job after meaningless job—car hop, secretary, hostess, lifeguard, cocktail waitress—jobs that asked nothing of me and gave nothing back. After New York, those jobs seemed infinitely boring. I wanted to feel alive, to shiver with the excitement of a new challenge, to reach out and grab the gold ring that was there for the taking. Since I'd already gobbled up all that Daytona had to offer, I thought maybe it was time to get to know my father, the evil-doer, the man my sister and brother hated with a passion. He'd been gone for well over ten years, but now he'd returned and was living in New Smyrna Beach. After some time with him, his new wife and his girly-girl stepdaughter, I was close to going over the cliff of boredom. When the telephone rang that fateful Monday, I jumped at it.

It was Johnny, the piano player at the Hollywood Bar in Daytona, and judging from the laughter in his voice, he and his pals had already been drinking.

"Sounds like you're having fun," I said, a bit envious that I wasn't with them.

"Not as much as we're gonna have," he answered. In the background a radio blasted Sheb Wooley's *Purple People Eater*. "Mike just bought this bitchy new hard top convertible," Johnny said, "The convertible hardtop folds into the trunk if you can believe that! We're taking this fancy machine on a ride to Jacksonville. Wanna come?"

"That's your idea of fun? Driving to Jacksonville, on a day that's as hot as this?"

"We got a real party going. Mike's pal rented a garage apartment in one of those fancy-schmancy joints on Atlantic Beach. The owner's away so we're gonna hang there."

"Big deal, we've got plenty of beaches right here in Daytona."

"Maybe so, but on the way to Jacksonville we're gonna stop at every gin mill we pass and have ourselves a little drinkie-poo."

At seventeen, I was too young to be drinking but too reckless not to. The thought of such a trip dangled in front of me like a juicy apple. "And I suppose you want me to drive?" I asked.

"Yeah," Johnny answered, "We're already wasted and you can drive okay even when you're sloshed."

"Pick me up in five," I replied and that was it. A single stone had been dropped into the river of life and it began a series of ripples that circled round and round creating the pattern that would ultimately become the 'IS' of my life. Minutes later, Mike beeped the horn and I dashed out the door to slide behind the wheel. I pressed my foot to the pedal and came alive as we careened down Route One, raucous laughter echoing in my ears and the wind ruffling my hair. The first bar we came to was The Roadhouse. "Pull in," Mike shouted. We scrambled out of the car, knocked back a quick scotch then continued on our way. That was the first of Heaven only knows how many we had before finally arriving in Atlantic Beach.

That day was everything summer was supposed to be— freedom, a fast car, hot sun, ice cubes swirling through a sea of scotch—it didn't get any better than this. My skin was tan, my body taut; I looked good and knew it. So once we reached Atlantic Beach I stripped down to my underwear; poised myself on the edge of the seawall and dove in. I was strong, athletic, invincible, and determined to impress my buddies with a perfect 10 dive. I was also drunk.

As I struggled to open my eyes, I sensed the smell of murky water and the movement of arms circling my body, but everything else was foggy. My brain felt like it was swimming through pea soup. I didn't know where I was or how I'd come to be there.

"We need an ambulance!" a voice screamed.

Ambulance? The athlete inside of me wanted to protest, to say I'd simply had the breath knocked out of me but, before I could say anything, I started losing consciousness.

"Hang on Lani," a voice said, "The ambulance will be here in just a minute."

With the fading of those words, came nothingness. When I finally regained consciousness, I was on a stretcher being rolled toward a black hearse, the kind that often did double duty as an ambulance. For a moment Johnny's face hovered over me, creased with worry and slackened from too much whisky, "You're gonna be okay," he mumbled, the words slurred in such a way that they bumped up against one another, "They're taking you to the hospital." He stepped back from the hearse into the blinding glare of sunlight. Then with a fierce finality the metal door clanged shut.

Moments later the engine roared to life and the siren began to wail.

As we rumbled through the streets, Ross, a young first-year ambulance attendant held a stethoscope to my chest and listened intently. He wrinkled his brow then leaned across and spoke to Al, the driver. "We better stop and get a doctor to take a look at her," he said, "She's barely breathing."

"There's no stopping," Al grumbled, "our job is to get her to Emergency."

"She may not make it to Emergency," Ross whispered back.

"Stopping is just gonna waste time," Al argued.

The discussion went back and forth a few times, and then the hearse suddenly screeched to a stop in the parking lot of a small clinic. "Thanks," Ross said as he pushed the door open and stepped out, "I'll get the doctor to come take a look at her."

I was drifting in and out of consciousness, listening to bits and pieces of their conversation through a thick gray fog.

Moments later, the door swung open again and the man I had to believe was the doctor climbed into the hearse. I remember the shapeless shadow hovering over me, but most of all I remember the voice. Angry. Agitated. "Why in hell did you bother to stop here?" he said, "This is a *clinic*! Not a hospital!"

"I thought maybe you could do something to help her breathing," Ross apologized, "she's having trouble..."

"She's got a *broken neck!*" the doctor snapped, "She probably won't make it to the hospital alive!"

Despite the fog in my head I tried to speak, but to that doctor I was nothing more than a body waiting to die. He ignored my effort and turned to the ambulance driver, Al. "You're the senior member of this team," he said angrily, "You should know when a patient is critical, they go straight to Emergency!" With that, he climbed out of the hearse and banged the door shut.

A sound finally came from my mouth. " Wha...happen?"

Ross, the youthful ambulance attendant who would eventually become a treasured friend, lowered his face over mine. "Don't worry, you're going to be fine," he said in an effort to negate the doctor's prediction, "Just hang in there, we're on our way to the hospital."

I felt as if I were trying to wake myself from a dream—where was I? What had happened? Was there some kind of accident? I'd been in accidents before, I'd had the breath knocked out of me, why was it so different this time? At that moment I remembered nothing and saw little beyond the dimpled chin of Ross's face. "You're gonna be okay," he repeated over and over again, his words soft and comforting.

Realization came to me in slow motion and I began to understand that it was me the doctor had been talking about. I could barely breathe, but somehow I squeezed the question from my chest. "Was...he...talking...about...me?"

Instead of answering, Ross again said, "Just hang on, you're gonna be okay." Then, he ever so gently explained how I had been injured in a diving accident. "That seawall's deceiving," he said, "the water there is real shallow."

"But...who...?"

Ross understood my question without additional words. "He's a doctor, a local clinic doctor; we stopped there because I was concerned about your breathing."

"He...s...ass...hole..." I gasped.

Ross nodded.

Although I was teetering on the edge of consciousness, I knew Ross's unspoken answer had been yes. Anger flared inside me, anger at the thought of a stranger handing me a death sentence without a moment's hesitation. Me, a seventeen year old, who for want of summer excitement drank too much and recklessly dove into shallow water. Me, Lani Verner! The rebellious gene passed down from Grandmother Alice Paul swirled through my body; it circumvented my broken neck and settled in my head. *I'll show that asshole!* I thought. *I'm not going to die! I'm not! I'm going to...* before I could finish that thought I'd slipped back into unconsciousness.

I don't remember arriving at Baptist Memorial Hospital nor do I recall the brightly lit emergency room. When I finally came to, I was in a dark room and somewhere in the distance I heard a voice calling, "Mo...ther ...Mo...ther...ple...ase..." The sound of that cry was followed by a hurried rush of footsteps and a second voice telling me to calm down that a nurse was on her way. Only then did I realize the earlier voice had been my own. Before I could clarify my thoughts, a nurse jabbed a needle into my arm and I drifted into nothingness.

I can't say how many minutes, hours or days passed before I opened my eyes again, but when I did, it was daylight and the pain in my head was excruciating. Mother and Carl, her third husband, the man I called Pappy, were beside me. "Thank God, you're awake," she sighed, "we've been sick to death with worry."

Sick to death with worry? Where was I? What had happened? "Wh...wh..." It felt as though an elephant were sitting on my chest. I could barely breathe and a single syllable had to be sandwiched in between shallow wisps of air. There were so many questions to ask, but each effort to speak brought more pain—pain that raced through my body and settled in my head, pain so intense that it was impossible to think beyond it.

Ever so slowly Mother began to peel back the layers of what had happened, "The water at that seawall was far too shallow for diving," she explained, "When you dove in, you hit your head on the bottom and it caused a form of paralysis, but mind you, it's only temporary. You'll probably be on your feet again in a matter of weeks."

Pappy, still looking shell-shocked, nodded.

Mother, having known me all my life could read the questions in my eyes. "Pa...in," I gasped, "Pa..."

"I know," she said sympathetically. "It's what the doctors call spinal-shock. When a spinal cord is injured, and yours was, it causes temporary paralysis and considerable pain throughout the whole body. It needs time to heal, Lani dear—rest and time."

I had so many more questions, but neither the strength nor the perseverance to push them out so I lowered my eyelids and drifted off.

For the next few weeks, I was only vaguely aware of my surroundings. Faces came and went—Mother, Pappy, Johnny, Ross the ambulance attendant, Al the driver, nurses, doctors, and orderlies who attached an iron frame to my bed and flipped it over periodically. I was now in a Stryker frame—the flapjack flipper of hospital beds, designed to prevent pressure sores on immobile patients. When I was on my back, I counted the ceiling tiles. When they flipped the frame over and I was on my stomach facing downward, I counted the floor tiles. And when I wasn't drifting through my mysterious world of oblivion, I thought. I tried to look back on the accident but remembered nothing—the drinking, the drive to Jacksonville, the blistering sun on my back as I arched my body and dove from the seawall...even the cracking of bones that brought me to this time and place—all of it was gone from my memory. The only thing I remembered was *The Purple People Eater* echoing in the background as Johnny laughed into the telephone.

At first it seemed there was little difference between night and day. The light was on during the day and off at night, but that was my only indicator. There was neither a clock nor television in the room and my roommate was an elderly woman who arrived comatose and remained that way. At times I heard the murmur of voices in the distance and sensed the movement of nurses who went about their tasks wordlessly, but most of the time I floated in and out of a colorless haze that offered a welcome escape from the reality of 'IS.' For a while Mother and Pappy remained in Jacksonville and came to visit every day. At first they'd simply stand alongside my bed and keep watch. They'd step aside when the orderlies would show up, fasten an iron frame to the top side of my bed and flip it over with me sandwiched in the middle. Given the semi-conscious state I was in, it made little difference whether I was right side up or face down, but I grew increasingly aware of the scraping and clanging of metal when this process took place.

As my periods of consciousness grew longer, I learned to communicate with single syllable words and facial expressions. I had lots of questions, but only a few words with which to ask so I would wait until Mother came—she, it seemed, could decipher my question by the expression accompanying those jumbled words. First she explained the Stryker frame, how it worked and why I was in it. "People get pressure sores when they are lying in one position for a long time. Remember how you used to make pancakes for me?" she asked, then not expecting an answer she moved ahead, "Well, this bed works rather like that. When you've been on one side long enough, they flip you over to the other side. It's a temporary thing, once the paralysis goes away you'll move into a regular bed."

"Can't... move...head...?" The why was in my expression.

Mother glanced over at Pappy as if to ask 'what am I supposed to I tell her?' He gave a slight shake of his head and shrugged. The apprehension bouncing back and forth between them was obvious, I stammered, "What's...wr...ong?"

"Nothing's wrong," Mother said, "...but they had to shave the hair on the top of your head to insert the Crutchfield Tongs that hold your neck and head in traction. It will take time to heal, Lani, and your head has to remain stable so you can't expect—"

"I want...to...see..."

"Dear, I don't think that's a very good idea. It's a silly thing that might upset you and why aggravate yourself with—"

I could feel my breath quicken, "Give me...mirr..or!"

"Lani really, do you think—"

"Mirr-or...now!"

When there was no mistaking the anger in my eyes, Mother grudgingly reached for the mirror and held it above my face. I took one look at myself and began to laugh. My bald head was wedged into an iron frame and attached to tongs like the icemen once used to carry chunks of ice. "Looks...ri-dic-u-lous."

"Yes, dear," Mother gave a sigh of relief, "it does look ridiculous."

It was during those early days that I began to understand what happened. Piece by painful piece the picture came together. "Thank God you thought to call me before you started for Jacksonville," Mother said, but being Mother, she had to add, "I told you to be careful, but of course you didn't listen. That's always been one of our problems, you *never* listen."

A prisoner in that strange rotating bed, unable to move a muscle or to feel anything from my neck down to my toes, I could do little more than listen. So, I listened while Mother talked. She filled the empty hours with words of encouragement and memories of our life together—memories she somehow managed to twist into being about her. "I suppose this could be considered my fault," she sighed, "When I worked at the Bath and Tennis Club, I was the one who encouraged you to dive off of the high board..."

I loved it there, loved the Banyan tree in the center of that huge greenhouse, the pecky cypress walls, built-in aquariums...the bluer than blue water...

"You were only four years old, but when you went flying off of that board, people clapped like crazy. 'Have her do it again, Dorothy,' they'd say. So I'd give you a nod, and you'd march your little self right back up that ladder..."

You used me to entertain the restaurant's customers...and I loved it...

"You certainly were a little daredevil and such a tomboy. Why, you'd take on boys twice your age and send them running home to their mother. I'd look out in the yard and you'd have that little boy next door dressed like Jane while you played Tarzan."

I remembered, oh how well I remembered. *Kent and his little cousin David were my best friends. He was okay with being Jane to my Tarzan, Dale Evans to my Roy Rogers...he was my friend, the sort of friend who accepts you for who you are, the kind of friend who doesn't try to change you.*

"You got along so well with those other children; I could never understand why you and your sister couldn't get along.

Every other word was some sort of argument. I think you deliberately tried to provoke her every chance you had and she..."

She hated me from the day I was born! Have you forgotten that's when my father started molesting her? She told you Mother...she told you but you chose not to believe her.

In time, I would grow weary of Mother's stories and drift off to sleep and when I woke another face would be beside me. Another face, another version of what had transpired.

"I was the first one to dive in," Johnny said, "...it was a helluva belly flopper." He laughed and I smiled, not remembering the moment, but imagining it. "I saw you standing on the seawall, but I never dreamed you'd dive. Not a real dive. I figured you knew how shallow that water is..."

I was drunk... I grew up in Daytona Beach where the beach was so wide that cars could race on it. The water never got up to the seawall.

"I was in the water when you hit bottom, and swear-to-God, I felt the earth shake. I knew you was hurt bad, so I grabbed onto you and started yelling for help. Man, you were so out of it, your eyes were all glazy and..."

I began to remember the rough water, Johnny's arm circling my body. I'd been a lifeguard and knew what to do, I tried to put my arm around his shoulder so that I wouldn't be dead weight, but nothing happened. I've come to believe that I remember the water sloshing up against us, the weight of my body being lifted from the water, the people screaming...but I guess I'll never know for certain if the recollection of those moments is truly mine, or just a memory of what I've been told.

As I listened to Johnny talk, I saw it the way one watches a movie, where an actor is going through the motions of your life, the story's right, but the character is robotic, unrealistic in a strange indescribable way.

Like Mother and Pappy, Johnny's face came and went. I listened, pushed out a few words and slept again. My life had become the Groundhog Day that kept repeating itself over and over again.

Oddly enough, I remembered Ross the first time I was conscious enough to see his dimpled chin. With the position of my head stabilized, a person didn't come into view until they were standing beside my bed, so I first heard his footsteps. "Remember me?" he asked.

"Yes..." I grunted and returned the smile.

"You gave us quite a scare," he said, relaxing into a more natural stance. "This is my first year working the Emergency Response squad, and I never had a patient die on me."

"I...wasn't...going to..."

"I worried you'd give up after you heard what that jerk-face doctor had to say, but he had the exact opposite effect."

My expression asked the question before my mouth could expel the words. "What..?"

"Instead of giving up, you got mad and cussed that doctor all the way to Emergency. The adrenaline kept your heart pumping and that's what probably saved your life. You could barely breathe, but you still managed to come out with some cuss words I've never even heard before!"

After a year in New York, I guess I knew quite a few doozies. "Sorry..."

"Don't be," he chuckled. "But with this being a Baptist Hospital, I figured it'd be doing you a service to skip over those words in my report."

Later that afternoon Mother and Pappy showed up with a look of concern on their faces. "I hope you know how much I hate to do this," Mother said with the sound of tragedy dripping from her words, "but, Pappy and I have to leave tomorrow. We've got to get back to Daytona. We both have jobs and...well, you understand. Of course, I'll be coming back to see you. Often! Not every day mind you, but often."

"It's...o...kay," I answered.

"No, it's not..." she sighed tragically. "I know I should stay here. This whole thing is probably my fault and now here I am leaving you to struggle through this on your own."

"Not...your fault."

"It most certainly is! I should never have encouraged this diving business. I should have never suggested you become part of that high school swim team. If I'd have let well enough alone, you would have never gotten involved with this diving nonsense."

"I like… doing it… would… have done… it any…way."

"You liked getting up at the crack of dawn to practice? You liked spending every minute of your time diving into a pool, climbing out, and doing it over and over again for hours on end? What for?"

"So I… could win…State Cham…pion…ship. You prom…ised if I did…"

"I know, I know. It's that horse thing again. I know I promised to buy you a horse if you won the State Diving Championship, but I didn't really think you'd win."

"Why not?"

Mother shrugged, "You only had six months to get ready, nobody becomes a diving champion in six months—it takes years of practice, years of training, a coach…"

"But, I did win."

"Yes dear, I know you did. But, you should have realized I didn't actually have the money to buy a horse. Anyway, I made it up to you. You know I did. I spent my hard-earned money to buy Dusty just so you could ride in that quarter horse race."

"You paid… seventy-five dol…lars for Dusty… but… an hour later… I gave… you… one hun…dred dol…lars. I won…that race. The horse did…n't cost you a nic…kel, you made a profit… on her the ve…ry first day!" The pain of losing Dusty was far from gone, and Mother had reopened the wound. "When I won… you said Dusty… was my horse…you said it…I re…mem…ber. But… it was just… another empty promise… wasn't it Mo…ther? If you… had let me… keep Dusty, I would have… found a way… to feed her—but no…"

Mother heaved a gigantic sigh, "Lani dear, let's not spoil our time together by talking about that horse. It's over and done with. History. Why bother thinking about it now?"

It was too late to stop, I was already picturing Dusty. It was so like Mother to stir up memories of the best and worst times of my life...

Two

Every breeze that blows through your life leaves something behind—the lingering scent of jasmine, a grain of sand stuck to your toes, memories that become part of who you are. In a moment of passion, my father dropped a seed of his being and it blossomed into my overwhelming love of animals and this land we inhabit. My father was an Apache, a man whose ancestors treasured these things long before Europeans came to America—and although I am neither my father nor my mother, I was born with the ancestral heritage of both.

Perhaps that's why animals so often filled the voids in my life. You might think that after all these years I've forgotten a few and allowed them to drift into faded memories, but that hasn't happened. Each of those wonderful creatures has become a part of me, a memory easily resurrected, an emotion that continually warms my heart. My first love was Bucky, the squiggling bundle of brown fur that my brother Scott gave me for my ninth birthday. "I'm off to join the Marines," he said handing me the puppy, "and I figured this little guy could keep you company while I'm gone." Bucky gave me something I seldom had—unconditional love. With Bucky it was always there and it came with tail wags and a generous amount of face licking.

With my father long gone and Mother always working, I was generally left at home alone. Scott had little time for me and Dit unquestionably resented me—something for which I blame

Mother. She was crazy in love with my deadbeat father and I was their love child. My arrival brought joy, whereas Dit's arrival brought disgrace along with Mother's banishment from the Verner household. Regardless of the reason, no parent should obviously favor one child over the others. But Mother did—and I was the child she favored. Scott never measured up to her expectations so, in time, he quit trying and left home to join the Marines. Dit fared even worse. Mother could find nothing good to say about my sister, despite the fact that she did all the cleaning, grocery shopping and cooking. So Dit, in turn, treated me the way Mother treated her. It's little wonder that my sister married the first man who happened along—she did it because she was hoping for a better life.

The passion Mother had for my father always amazed me because he was a violent, mean-tempered man who mortgaged our house to the hilt then skipped town taking every last cent of her inheritance money and our car. The most vivid memory I have of my father is one where he is pummeling his fist into Mother's face. Although I was only four years old, the sight outraged me in such a way that I ran between them and, with my hands on my hips, demanded he stop hitting her. "If you don't stop," I threatened, "I'll throw you into the bushes!" I don't recall what happened at that point, but with things being as they were, the likelihood is he gave me a pretty sound beating. I suppose that was the first instance of my protecting Mother, but rest assured it wasn't the last.

After my father took off, Mother learned that he'd left her with a house, a huge mortgage payment and no money. Although she had paid for our house upfront, he took out the biggest mortgage he could get, pocketed the money, then withdrew every dollar they had in the bank and closed the account. He slipped out of town in the dark of night, leaving us penniless.

Mother did what she had to do to survive. She rented our beautiful big house to strangers and the four of us moved into the tiny one-room guest cottage out back. Our bathroom consisted of a stand-up shower and toilet built into the closet. The kitchen was another closet equipped with a two burner hot plate, icebox, and small lavatory. Our clothes were kept in suitcases beneath beds that were pushed up against the walls. It was during the Second World War so work was plentiful. Mother was able to hold down two jobs; working at the department store during the day and the club in the evening. Scott helped out with a morning and evening paper route, while Dit did the cleaning and cooking. Since I was only four years old at the time, my primary responsibility was taking care of me.

We lived in that one room cottage for almost three years until Mother began earning more money and found a boyfriend willing to help out with expenses. We were then able to move back into the big house. Well, sort of move back. Mother, Dit and I slept in one bedroom, Scott slept on a cot in the dining room, and the remainder of the rooms were rented out to new strangers.

Once Scott had gone into the Marine Corps and my sister was married, Mother decided she could save money by selling the house, paying off the mortgage, and moving us to a small garage apartment. When the last of our belongings were loaded into her boyfriend's pickup truck, I picked up Bucky and climbed into the back of the truck.

"The dog can't come," Mother said, "this apartment doesn't allow pets."

I felt as though she had taken my head off with a machete. "I'm not going to leave Bucky," I screamed, "He's my best friend!"

"I'm sorry dear, but we have no choice." Mother took the dog from my arms, unceremoniously set him on the sidewalk and drove off. As she pulled away from the curb and sped down the street, I saw Bucky darting in and out of the cars, trying to follow us.

"Noooooooooo!" I screamed, then jumped out of the truck and ran back to scoop him up. "Go without me," I shouted angrily, "I'm not letting Bucky get killed because of you!"

If it was up to me, I would have followed my heart. I would have somehow found a way for us to survive. But a kid is not given those choices; life is what it is, so Bucky was taken from me.

With tears streaming down my face, I sat beside Mother as we drove to the Humane Society and I watched her hand my dog over to a total stranger. "I'm sorry," she said to me, "but things can't always be the way you want." To my ten-year-old mind, it seemed as if they were never the way I wanted.

Once we moved into the new apartment, it was only Mother and me. Since she was working, I took over the daily household chores. I did laundry, ironed our clothes, vacuumed, dusted, did the dishes, did the grocery shopping, and cooked the meals. My friends often asked why I had so much work to do and my answer was always the same. "I have just as much time to play as you do, but I also have responsibilities."

After losing Bucky, my next best friend was a parakeet named Turk. I trained Turk to do a dozen different things and he grew so tame that his cage door remained open. Turk's fate was no better than Bucky's, because one day Mother's one-time cleaning lady saw him on the screened porch and opened the door thinking he wanted to go out. Turk wasn't Bucky, but he was all I had.

After Turk flew away, Mother said, "That's it! No more pets. They're nothing but trouble!" Knowing that she would stand firm on this resolution, I quasi-adopted Duke, the German Shepherd puppy that belonged to a couple who lived down the street. Duke was a big dog, with a loud bark and ferocious appearance. Neighbors crossed the street when they saw him pacing the yard, but with Bucky and Turk both gone I needed a friend. Armed with a box of Milk Bone biscuits that I'd bought with part of the grocery money, I approached the dog. Duke growled and bared his teeth. "I'm trying to be your friend," I said and tossed a biscuit. He growled again then gobbled the treat. I tossed another, and then another, each time a bit closer to where I was standing. Within days, I was rolling in the grass with this dog that terrified the neighborhood. My mother worked and his owners worked, so Duke and I spent the days playing together. He became my best friend, my replacement Bucky—that was until Mother discovered the 'For Rent' sign on the caretaker's cottage of a mansion. The cottage was larger than our apartment and it overlooked the water. When the owners of the mansion went away every summer they hired someone to water the lawn, a huge expanse of grass that stretched down to the river—Mother conveniently suggested that for a reduced rental rate, I would water the lawn daily.

"I don't want to move," I said, "I like it here. And, what about Duke?"

"He's not your dog, so he'll stay where he belongs—with his owners!"

"But Mother…"

"Lani," she groaned impatiently, "I am not going through this discussion every time you come across some stray looking for a home!"

We moved and once again, the dog I loved was left behind. They say love overcomes many obstacles and I have to believe it's true, because Duke did eventually become my dog. His owners were moving to a place that didn't allow pets and they would be there for one year. They called to ask Mother if I'd be willing to take care of Duke for that year. Apparently trying to avoid a scene, the magnitude of which we'd had with Bucky, she replied, "No. It's unfair to Lani. She already loves Duke and after a year I'm certain she won't want to give him up." Mother paused a moment as if to let the thought sink in. "Of course," she said, "If you're interested in *giving* her the dog, then I suppose I could allow her to take him." I'd listened to the entire conversation and couldn't believe my ears—Mother was actually going to let me have a dog! The couple delivered Duke to our house the very next day, and the moment he saw me, he leaped from the window of the car and came bounding across the lawn. As we rolled and tumbled in the grass, the wife gave her husband a sly look and said, "We obviously made the right decision." At that moment I thought Duke would be with me for as long as either of us lived. Of course, I also thought the same about Dusty. But as Mother said, "Things can't always be the way you want." I was destined to have and then lose the animals I loved, animals that were in many ways more of a family than I'd ever known. I may not have had Duke or

Dusty for as long as I wanted, but for the short while they were a part of my life, I was gloriously happy.

My hospital bed was turned to face the floor when I heard footsteps, and a voice brought me back from my reverie. "Are you sleeping?" he asked.

"Hi Ross," I answered. Spending so much time in that upside-down position had taught me to recognize feet as well as faces.

"How're the pressure sores?" he asked.

"The nurses seem to think they're pretty bad, but I can't feel anything."

"Have the orderlies been turning this frame every two hours?"

I laughed. "When I'm upside down all I see is speckled tile, and there is no clock in the room."

Ross's feet disappeared from view and I heard him shuffle out the door. The next thing I heard was the sound of voices coming from the hallway, one of them was Ross. There was a heated exchange of conversation which ended when Ross said, "NOW!" Moments later two orderlies appeared and flipped my bed. I was now looking into Ross's face.

"Nice to see you," I said laughingly.

Ross could make me laugh when few others could, and he could also settle into an intelligent conversation and answer the questions others avoided. "I've been here a few weeks," I said, "Probably about a month. Don't you think I should be seeing some movement by now?"

Ross shrugged, "Your spinal cord is badly damaged, the fourth, fifth and sixth vertebrae in your neck broken, and your lungs paralyzed. With all that, it's a miracle you're breathing as well as you are."

"I don't know if I'll ever regain movement without some big-time surgery," I sighed. "Doctor Byrd says I'm lucky to be alive and he doesn't think I should put myself through another surgery."

I paused for a minute then added, "...but I'm beginning to wonder if C. A. Byrd is the right doctor for me anyway."

Ross gave a half-grin and nodded.

Over the years I'd been through numerous injuries. I was a daredevil tomboy. As a kid I'd suffered two fractured skulls within a three month period. As a teen, I'd entered a race on the back of a quarter horse too wild to be ridden and ended up with fractured vertebrae in my neck, a broken shoulder, broken wrist, and several broken ribs. Okay, I won the race and came away with one hundred bucks, but I had more broken bones, bumps and bruises than I could count. Despite all of those mishaps, I'd always bounced back. I'd done it before and I knew I could do it again! "To hell with Byrd!" I said, "That old jerk is not really interested in helping me to get better; he figures he'll keep me comfortable and wait for me to die. Well, that's not good enough for me! I think a really good orthopedic surgeon could fix my broken neck. If the vertebrae in my neck were repaired, at least I could sit up in a wheelchair. I could move around and do things."

Ross nodded, "You're probably right," he said, "Let me look into it. I'll ask around and find out who the top guys are. Then, we'll take it from there."

"Maybe with the right surgeon, I'll be able to walk again..." I mused.

Ross laughed, "I gotta hand it to you kid, you got gumption!"

I knew, and he knew that I knew, the likelihood was I would never walk again—but hey, hope is free and it comes in all sizes.

After Ross left, I returned to my thoughts of Mother. I was fourteen years old when she dangled the promise of my own horse in front of me—I remember it only too well. Mother had raided the last of our inheritance so we could join the Elinor Village Country Club; a club with round after round of parties, elegant dining, a golf course, tennis courts, an Olympic-sized pool and a very handsome lifeguard. I became Mother's tag-along companion. She'd clip a pair of rhinestone earrings on my ears, outfit me in a dress far too sophisticated for a girl my age, and off we'd go. When we were partying in public I was allowed to both smoke and drink. "You can order a Rum Collins," Mother would say, "but make sure you tell the waiter, to go light on the rum." Dressed as I was, I looked years older so the waiter always took my order without question. After he'd set our drinks down in front of us, Mother and I would laughingly light up our cigarettes and spend the evening waiting for some wealthy tourist to ask us to dance.

It was at the club pool that Mother made the promise. I'd been doing dive after dive from the board, when two girls from my new school approached me. "You're a pretty good diver," Caroline said, "you ought to join the swim team."

"Yeah," Patty agreed, "Right now I'm the only diver on the team. We've got some good swimmers, but if we had another diver we might be able to win the State Championship."

Mother was lying on the chaise leafing through the pages of *Vogue.*

"I'm not that good a diver," I said, "and I'm not sure I really want to…" Diving, swimming, partying at the club—those things were okay, but what I really liked to do was spend time at Colonel Moon's stable in back of the country club.

"Think about it," the girls said and strolled off across the veranda.

Seconds later, Mother came walking over to me. "You should do it," she said. "Those girls are from wealthy families and it would be quite a feather in my cap if my daughter was part of their team."

"I'm not really interested in diving and swimming, I do it for fun, but…"

"I know, I know," Mother sighed, "you're interested in horses." She hesitated for a second then made the offer. "Tell you what," she said, "you join the swim team and if you win the State Diving Championship, I'll buy you your very own horse."

I turned toward the girls and ran across the pool deck yelling, "Hey, wait up Patty!"

That was it. I spent the remainder of the summer practicing, learning the basics of competition dives from our handsome lifeguard and perfecting my form, or so I hoped.

When school started I met my new swimming coach, a wonderful woman who unfortunately had no experience with coaching divers. She handed me a copy of the Amateur Athletic Union handbook and I was on my own. At that point, I only knew how to do two dives—a jack knife and a swan dive—and as I studied the drawings of the different dives, I began to realize how much more I had to learn if I wanted any hope of winning the competition. I began leaping out of bed as soon as the sun crossed the horizon. I'd wash my face, hurry over to the club pool, scramble across the wire fence, and start practicing. I'd do dive after dive after dive, until there was barely enough time to rush home, drive Mother to work and make it to school. The instant class ended, I headed for Welsh pool where our team practiced. Patty Lucy and I were still the only two divers, and there was no one capable of coaching us, so we worked together trying to perfect our technique. As the months went by, it seemed that despite long hours of hard work, I was still limited to the basic dives required for the competition.

"I'm not feeling any too confident about this," Patty said.

"Me either," I admitted. Then I thought about Mother promising that a win meant I could have my very own horse. "I'll stick to the basic dives," I suggested, "but make them absolutely perfect. That way maybe we can score high enough to win."

"Maybe," Patty replied and we locked pinkies to seal the deal.

Shortly thereafter I met the woman who would not only help me perfect my dives, but also provide the inspiration I needed to win the competition. The National AAU Swimming and Diving Championships were to be held at Welsh Pool, so our team practice was suspended for two weeks to give the participating athletes a chance to practice in the pool where they would be competing. Being the diehard I am, I went to the pool anyway.

That's where I met Pat McCormick, a woman who'd won the AAU Diving Championship numerous times and then went on to win several Olympic Gold Medals. After hours of my sitting there watching her dive, she swam over to me. "You seem pretty interested in what I'm doing," she said, "are you a diver?"

I grinned sheepishly, "Not like you, but I'm trying to win the State Championship so my Mother will get me a horse. Winning the championship is the only way I'm ever going to get my own horse, so if I don't win, I'll absolutely die!"

"Well, we can't have that can we?" Pat laughed this great big happy laugh, "Jump in," she said, "and let's take a look at what you've got."

After my first dive, I swam to the side of the pool to hear the verdict. "You're not bad," Pat said, "but your approach needs work. You look tentative and if you want to win you've got to look confident. Even if you're scared to death, you've got to step on that board acting like a winner. The judges can sense fear, and to them fear is the same as failure."

For the rest of that afternoon and several afternoons following, Pat coached and encouraged me. During that time Pat told me her own story—she had missed being on the 1948 Olympic team by $1/100^{th}$ of a point, then came back to win two Gold medals in the 1952 games. "So you see," she said, "give it everything you've got. You may not be the very best, but maybe you'll be a fraction of a point better than the next guy."

Long before the competition took place, my competitive nature kicked in. I became part of the diving team in the hope of getting my own horse, but it wasn't just about the horse anymore, suddenly it was about winning. Much to my amazement, as the year moved along I managed to place first in every diving competition. And, with each win, my confidence increased.

The Championship Meet was ironically enough held in Jacksonville. On Saturday, our Swim Team outperformed the competition and, if we took a couple more events and the diving, Seabreeze High could win the State Championship—an unprecedented event since Seabreeze was a relatively small school with students in grades 7-12. It was up to Patty Lucy and me. Patty did far more difficult dives than I did, but her form was sometimes inconsistent. Throughout the year I had been practicing dives with a lower degree of difficulty, reasoning that if I did them as perfectly as possible, my points for quality would be high enough to offset the lower degree of difficulty. Hopefully I was right.

On Sunday, I watched as the other divers took on challenge after challenge, going for the more difficult dives and then losing points for less than perfect execution. *If I do everything right, maybe I've got a chance...* As the loudspeaker crackled my name, I could swear I heard Pat McCormick's voice in my ear...*confidence,* it said, *confidence.* I stepped to the end of the board, turned to smile confidently at the judges, and then did a near perfect front dive in a layout position, entering the water without a ripple. Although the judges sat looking stone-faced, my lowest score was 9.0 and my highest 9.7—*Okay, maybe I've got a shot at winning this!*

My second dive was the jackknife, a front dive in the pike position and again I aced it with 9.5 being my lowest score. I was starting to breathe easier.

Patty Lucy began to fall apart, although she was doing much more difficult dives, her scores were lower. Suddenly Seabreeze High's Championship hopes were resting on my shoulders, and the half-gainer dive I had coming up was my weakest. I tried to look confident as I stepped onto the board, but Pat McCormick's voice was nowhere to be heard. I dove, and as I arched my body into the back half somersault, I knew the dive was off. I went into the water with a splash and knew it was bad, not just bad, but really bad— horrible to my mind. My lowest score plummeted to 7.6 and my highest was a mere 8.3—that was it. I'd probably lost the team's championship along with any hope of ever owning a horse. As I climbed out of the pool, I saw the sadness in my teammates faces. "I know," I said, "It was horrible."

"Not your best maybe, but not all that bad," Inger said. Several Seabreeze swimmers agreed and gave me seemingly bright smiles to bolster my confidence. Unfortunately, I'd already seen the disappointment in their eyes. They knew, as I did, that my dive probably cost our team the State Championship.

I had one last dive to do—a back summersault dive in layout position, not the easiest, but even with its high degree of difficulty, it was one of my best dives. I no longer had anything to lose. Gone was my hope of a horse, but maybe I could help the team salvage second or third place. I forced myself to remember Pat McCormick's advice and tried to look confident. I dove and entered the water straight as an arrow, no splash, no ripple. My balance was absolute and the execution as perfect as I could hope for. *Maybe we can get second place.* I swam to the side of the pool and, before I could climb out, I was swarmed by my teammates, "You did it!" they screamed. I looked at the scoring cards the judges held in the air...10,10,10,10, 9.8—with the lowest score thrown out, I had achieved a PERFECT 10...definitely enough for Seabreeze to win third place, maybe even second.

I wrapped a towel around my shoulders, stood alongside my teammates and waited.

First they would announce the winning divers, then name of the Championship School. The loudspeaker crackled, "The third place award for diving goes to Penny Proctor from Bolles High School." I was beginning to feel a bit more nervous. Penny had done some pretty fancy dives and if she got third place, where was I going to end up? The loudspeaker crackled again, "Second place goes to Patty Lucy of Seabreeze High." A breath whooshed from my chest. Patty had helped the team edge its way into second or third place, but I'd done nothing. After all those months of hard work—no horse, no medal, nothing. I turned and walked back toward Mother, happy for my team, brokenhearted for myself. The loudspeaker crackled one last time, but with the noise around us, it was barely audible. "Ladies and Gentlemen, our Gold Medal Winner and new Florida State Diving Champion is Lani Verner! And, this year's Swimming and Diving Team Championship goes to Seabreeze High!"

Suddenly I was surrounded by teammates, friends, well-wishers—"Did I win?" I asked.

"Yes," Mother screamed, "You won!"

Tears of joy began to cascade down my cheeks. Not only had I helped my teammates to victory, but now I would have the horse I'd wanted for so long. After months of hanging around a stable I'd discovered on the seedier side of town, I knew exactly which horse that was going to be. I'd whispered my secret in her ear numerous times. "Dusty, I'm going to win this," I'd say, "I'll win the championship and I'll tell Mother you're the horse I want."

You might wonder why it would be Dusty I wanted; she was fast, really fast, but she was also the wildest and scrawniest-looking quarter horse in Blake Frederick's riding stable. There was nothing majestic about Dusty, she was borderline ugly and blacker than the devil's shadow. More often than not, she'd bite or kick if someone tried to saddle her. She was considered unmanageable and mean, so nobody wanted to ride her, and the few that did, did so with a vengeance that bordered on animal cruelty. Still, her contrariness only made me love her more. "We've got plenty of nice horses," Mister Frederick would say, "Why in the world do you want to ride *that* one. She's dangerous, unpredictable and mean as they come." To me, Dusty was none of those things. Yes, she was spirited and willful, but truthfully speaking, so was I.

Months earlier Mother watched me ride Dusty, so choosing her for my horse should come as no surprise. I knew Mother was none too fond of this particular horse, but she'd only seen me ride Dusty once and it happened to be one of the times I was thrown into a clump of wet grass. For weeks I'd been asking her to come and watch me ride, but Mother argued that if I absolutely had to ride horses, I should be doing so at the stable located in back of the Country Club. "Colonel Moon's stable charges a dollar-fifty an hour to ride," I'd explained, "Mister Frederick only charges a dollar, and sometimes he lets me ride free."

On the afternoon Mother finally came to watch me ride, Dusty had saddle sores and rather than making them worse by tossing a saddle on her, I decided to ride bareback, which I often did.

"Watch how fast she can take off..." I shouted, digging my heels into Dusty's boney ribs. The horse sprang forward and to avoid falling off, I grabbed hold of her mane. Mother raised an eyebrow and gave me her standard look of concern, but I moved on, cantering around the pasture, maneuvering Dusty in and out around the barrels set up for barrel-racing practice. Dusty was moving well, and hopefully, Mother was impressed. As we flew by the last barrel, I saw Mother still watching and I yelled, "Watch how fast she can stop!" That's where I made my mistake, because when Dusty planted her hoofs and came to a sudden stop I kept going—sailing over the horse's head and plopping down at Mother's feet.

Even Mother had to laugh. "This ugly horse is the one you want?" she said still chuckling, "I don't doubt she's a lot of fun, but wild as this horse is, I'd be petrified that you'd kill yourself."

"I won't," I answered, "it's just that today I was riding bareback. When Dusty's got a saddle on, I never fall off!"

Mother shook her head and gave me that look of doubt she'd honed to a new level of expertise. "Enough about the horse," she said, "Now hurry up so you'll have time to clean up for dinner. Tonight the Club is having a lobster buffet and the band...."

After the Championship festivities and Gold Medal Ceremony were over, we climbed into the car and started for home. I began thinking back to the day that Mother saw me ride Dusty and said, "I can't believe I'll finally have the horse of my dreams...and I've already decided, Dusty is the one I want."

Mother let out a deep sigh, the kind of sigh that generally preceded some devastatingly tragic announcement. "Oh Lani," she said, "I wish you would forget about this horse thing. You know we can't afford a horse. I mean, it's not only the cost of the animal, there's boarding, food, veterinary bills..."

"You promised!" I snapped bitterly.

"Don't speak to me in that tone of voice young lady!" Mother said sharply. "I realize I promised, but I didn't think you'd win."

"Then why..."

"Because I thought if you were on the swim team you'd associate with the right kind of people and possibly even qualify for a college scholarship. I honestly thought that once you developed an interest in diving you would forget this ridiculous obsession with horses." She shook her head as if to acknowledge the tragedy of it all, and then said, "I suppose with you being your father's daughter, I should have known better."

The tears began to gush from my eyes, "How could you?" I sobbed.

Mother was not normally what one would consider a tender-hearted person, but she turned to me and spoke with an earnest sadness. "I'm sorry," she said, "I truly am. I know how it feels to have someone you love destroy your dreams and I hate myself for having done it to you." She reached across the seat and took my hand in hers. "I love you Lani," she said tenderly, "more than anything else on earth. I promise to make it up to you. Somehow, someway, I'll…"

"I understand, Mother," I sniffled, "I understand." The truth was, I didn't understand—I hated my father for robbing my mother of her dreams and I hated her for robbing me of mine.

From that day forward, whenever I had a dollar in my pocket, I gave it to Blake Frederick and rode Dusty for one wonderful hour. When I didn't have the money, I spent the day mucking her stall and brushing her down. In moments of fantasy, I imagined Dusty to be *my* horse—then some skilled rider would walk through the door looking for a high-spirited horse and Blake Frederick would send them off astride her back. When that happened, the truth smacked me squarely in the face. I'd stand at the gate, my eyes glued to the trail, watching and waiting. Eventually horse and rider would come into view; Dusty heaving and out of breath, having been ridden too hard and too long. With my heart thundering in a beat that coincided with hers, I'd unsaddle the tired horse, walk her to cool her down, and then sponge her down with cool water. "Don't worry Dusty," I'd whisper in her ear, "One of these days, I'll find a way to take you away from here, and I won't ever let anybody be mean to you again."

When I could no longer stand being away from her, I began coming to the stable almost every day. Eventually I asked, "Blake, you want me to clean out those other stalls for you?"

"For how much?" he replied dubiously.

"Nothing. I'm not looking for money. I just like being around horses."

"You like cleaning up horseshit?"

I nodded.

He gave a big belly laugh, "Go ahead then, make yourself happy."

Since I was on a roll, I figured I might as well go ahead and ask about the other thing I had on my mind. "I know Dusty doesn't get ridden as much as the other horses," I said hesitantly, "...if you want her to get more exercise, I could ride her once in a while. I wouldn't mind doing that either."

He laughed louder than the first time. "Yeah, I suppose that mean-ass horse could use some exercising. Just make sure you check with me first. Now go on, get to work..." He walked away laughing like a department store Santa Claus.

I may not have owned Dusty, but she certainly owned me. For the duration of that summer, I'd be at the stable the minute it opened. I worked like someone getting paid fifty-dollars an hour. If a trail guide was needed, I'd be a trail guide. If a groom was needed, I'd be a groom. By late afternoon, I'd be finished with anything and everything that could be done. "Is it okay if I ride Dusty for a while?" I'd ask. Then off we'd go. In time, Blake Frederick even allowed me to bring Duke to the stable. That summer, Dusty, Duke and I discovered the nature trails of the Tomoka Game Reserve. We'd amble slowly through game trails overhung with branches of decades old oaks, bay trees, pines and mossy cypresses. When the sun was low in the sky, we'd return to the stable.

Just when I'd reached the point where I didn't believe things could get any better, Blake told me about the Cracker Day Race. "If you're up to it, you can ride that mean-ass horse in the Quarter Horse race," he said.

"Dusty?" I asked, leaving my mouth hang open.

He nodded, "If your mama don't mind."

"She doesn't mind at all! But Blake, I have to tell you, she really doesn't like to be called Mama. She says it's undignified for children to call their mother anything but Mother."

"Oh is that so..." Blake gave one of his belly-bouncing laughs, "Well, I'll call her whatever she's a mind to be called, long as she don't come down on me for letting you ride in that race."

"Wow, thank you," I gasped, hardly believing my good fortune.

"Yeah, sure," Blake answered in a way that made me think he was proud of handing out so much happiness. "You know," he said, "they've also got those Gymkhana Games at the Cracker Day Fair. You might want to ride Dusty in those as well."

"That would be great," I replied, even though I didn't yet know what the Gymkhana games were. Whatever they were—if I was riding Dusty, what could go wrong?"

That Saturday morning was bright, clear and blazing hot. When Mother and I arrived at the fair, I discovered that Blake had entered Dusty and me into three races: the barrel race, the flag race, and the grand event of the day—the quarter horse race.

The barrel race came first. When we practiced in the pasture I ran Dusty through obstacle courses, but that was simply for fun. I never dreamed that one day I'd be participating in such a race. I swallowed the apprehension in my throat and watched as the first five entrants ran through their paces. The pattern of the race rapidly became obvious. When the starter's gun went off, horse and rider had to weave between the barrels at a gallop, circle the last barrel and weave their way back without knocking any barrels over. Fastest time won. I knew Dusty was fast and she could turn on a dime, but riding right after me was a blue roan that looked like trouble. Before I had time to worry about it, the starter's pistol sounded a bang. Dusty and I took off, weaving through the barrels, a sharp right, a sharp left, another right, another left, circle the end barrel, reverse the pattern. We were back at the starting gate in what seemed like a heartbeat. I asked about the time—ours was the best so far. The blue roan moved to the starting gate. When the pistol went off, the blue roan bolted out of the gate and went through the barrels like a summer breeze. "Oh no," I sighed, "they're going so fast!" Then it happened. The blue roan circled the end barrel and knocked it over. Had it not been disqualified, that horse would have won the race, but we were declared the winner because skinny little Dusty had edged her way through the barrels without touching one. The prize was a case of beer, which I knew Mother would put to good use. She loved her warm, flat Schlitz. *Yuck!*

The second race was the flag race, a similar event with one exception—I had to carry a small flag, deposit it in the last barrel and retrieve the one that was already there. Dusty beat the blue roan by two seconds and I won a keg of nails.

"Nails?" Mother said, "What are we supposed to do with a keg of nails?"

The announcer told Mother he could auction it off for a tidy sum and we both smiled—I anticipated the money would be set aside so that someday I could buy Dusty, but Mother had other plans.

As we walked away, I noticed a woman on a beautiful black Arabian mare riding beside an olive-skinned man on a large chestnut stallion. The man's appearance was similar to the way I'd always pictured my father—ruggedly handsome, pitch black hair, muscular, with his back held straight and strong. They rode toward Mother and me. The woman spoke first, "Congratulations on winning those races," she said with a smile.

They introduced themselves as Fred and Mina Hanna from Holly Hill, Florida—a town right next door to Daytona Beach.

"You're quite the rider," Fred said, "How come we've never seen you at any of the other Gymkhana races?"

I swallowed hard then said, "I don't have a horse. Dusty isn't really mine, she belongs to Blake Frederick. He just let me ride her for the races."

Fred chuckled and Mina smiled. "Nobody would ever know Dusty isn't your horse," she said sweetly, "the two of you look as if you belong together."

I took that as a compliment. "Oh we do!" I answered enthusiastically. "I plan on buying her just as soon as..." I caught the look on Mother's face and stopped there.

The conversation continued on and before long Fred and Mina joined Mother and me so we could watch the remainder of the day's events together.

The quarter horse race was the last event of the day and it began with qualifying heats. I moved to the starting line and looked at the competition. They were real cowboys—men considerably older than me, riding horses much healthier than Dusty. Suddenly, as if she sensed the onset of danger, Dusty grew skittish and started moving about as if she were trying to throw me. I held on, leaned forward in my saddle and whispered, "Don't be nervous, Dusty, you're better than these other horses." I rubbed her neck affectionately and ignored the snickers of the cowboys. Within a few minutes, she'd quieted down. When the starter's pistol sounded, Dusty took the lead and we were the first ones to cross the finish line.

"Mother," I called out as we rode across to where she was standing, "Dusty and I are going to be in the finals!"

Blake Frederick walked over. "Afraid not," he grumbled with a grim-faced look.

"But, we won our heat..." I stammered.

"I know, I know. But that was pure luck. The truth is you're outclassed by a mile. Anyway, Dusty's too tired to run again. She'll collapse before she makes it to the finish line."

"No she won't," I pleaded, "Dusty can do it. She's not even tired."

"Forget about it," Blake said and turned away.

Mother grabbed onto his arm, "Hold on a minute," she said, "Lani won that race and she deserves a chance at the finals!"

"I'm not concerned about Lani," Blake answered. "...but I can't let a good stable horse drop dead just 'cause the kid wants to run her against a field of heavyweights."

"Please, Blake, please," I pleaded, "Dusty won that race easily, and she can win this one, I know she can. I've been feeding her lots of extra food and taking good care of—"

"No," Blake snapped angrily, "No. And, that's my final word on this!" Again he turned...

Mother opened her purse, "How much do you want for that flea-bitten nag?" she asked.

My mouth dropped open.

"One-twenty-five," Blake answered.

Mother raised an eyebrow, "You're kidding?"

"No, I'm not. She's a money-maker for the stable."

"That bag of bones is no money-maker! I'll give you seventy-five."

"No deal," Blake answered, "One hundred, maybe..."

"There's no way," Mother said and snapped her purse closed. As she turned away, Blake grumbled "Okay," and the deal was done. In the span of a few heartbeats, Dusty became my horse!

Mother gave me a sly wink and said, "Now get yourself over there and win this race."

The moment the starter's gun sounded, I knew this race was going to be different. Blake was right, we were outclassed. But there are times when heart trumps talent, and suddenly Dusty broke free of the slower horses and began to gain ground. It was as if she understood that she was now my horse and she was doing it for me. With her new owner on her back, skinny little Dusty ran like a champion and pushed through to cross the finish line neck-in-neck with two other horses.

The loudspeaker that generally announced the winner was silent. Three men in the judge's booth alternately nodded and shook their head. Horses and riders paced back and forth, still there was no announcement. Finally, after what amounted to a lifetime in my ownership of Dusty, the loudspeaker crackled, "It was a dang close race," the judge said, "but in the opinion of the judges, myself included, the winner of this race is Lani Verner riding the black mare, Dusty. Come on over here, little lady, and collect your prize."

Beer, nails...now what?

The round-faced judge handed me an envelope with one-hundred-dollars cash!

"See Mother," I said handing her the envelope, "Dusty's already paid for herself!"

Mother rolled her eyes and gave a shrug that was the equivalent of – *What now?*

To say I was ecstatic was an understatement! Dusty was really my horse and I had won enough money to pay for her! Over my short lifetime, I had loved and lost so many animals, but now my heart could rest easy. I owned my beloved Dusty and no one could take her away from me. It was too good to be true. I wondered if I would wake up and find this was nothing more than a dream? I pinched myself. No, I was awake and the pinch hurt. I couldn't recall ever being as happy as I was at that moment. I finally had a horse, not just a horse, but the horse I had loved for so long. I promised Dusty that I would one day own her and I did it—did it myself! Well, perhaps not totally by myself, I did have my lucky stars to thank for Mother's competitive spirit. Caught up in the excitement of the moment and a fervent desire to see me win, she'd opened her purse and her heart. Yes, I was happier than I could ever remember.

Three

As I lay there in the hospital bed, thoughts of Blake Frederick calling my mother Mama brought memories that stretched even further back in time. I couldn't remember when she was anything but Mother—it was a rule, a law almost, that she be called Mother. Looking back, I realize she clung to that title because it was her last thread of prestige, the only link to her aristocratic heritage and the wealth that was long gone, the inheritance my father had taken when he disappeared. Mother lived her life regretting what was, instead of accepting what is, and it brought her heartache after heartache. I knew that I didn't want to live a life of regrets.

It began the day my mother was born. Clarence Van Dyke Tiers shook his head in disgust, "Another girl," he grumbled. Three times he'd hoped for a male heir to step into the family's steel business and carry forth the Tiers name, and three times he had been disappointed. Mother was a red-faced, squalling bundle of disappointment; disappointment that caused her to forever regret she had not been born a boy. Finding it impossible to please a father of such mind, she eventually gave up trying and settled into being the black sheep of the family. In her senior year of high school she became pregnant and was forced to drop out of school to marry the baby's father, Morris Scott Verner. Morris was twelve years older than Mother and the son of a family only slightly more wealthy than that of Clarence Van Dyke Tiers. Mother, who had unquestionably been rambunctious, was then considered the most scandalous woman in Oakmont, Pennsylvania.

"A slut!" Morris' mother screamed, "You want my son to marry a slut?"

"It was your wayward son who led my girl astray!" Clarence Tiers responded, "He's considerably older and he should have known better!"

"A woman of decent morals would have kept her bloomers on!"

The argument went back and forth, each side defending their own and accusing the other, but in the end Morris Scott Verner and Dorothy Tiers got married and moved into the Verner house with Morris' parents. Although it was deemed the only feasible solution, the Senior Mrs. Verner's opinion of my Mother never wavered. She would have no part of Mother or the illegitimately conceived offspring.

"You will have nothing more to do with that woman," she told Morris. "You are not to sleep together, nor are you to invite her into our circle of friends! And if you dare disobey this order, your Father and I will disinherit you without a moment's hesitation!"

Morris, weak-willed and lacking any skills of his own, depended heavily upon his inheritance, but that didn't stop the burning desire he felt for Dorothy. He'd see her bending over Scott's cradle, or holding the child to her breast, and the fire in his groin would flare again. Ignoring the ultimatum, he'd wait for darkness to shroud the house then tiptoe down the hallway and slide into bed beside her. Dorothy, who lived in fear of Morris's mother's wrath, said nothing when she first discovered herself carrying a second child. But, as her stomach swelled it became obvious.

"It's not mine!" Morris swore, choosing wealth over honor. "I've had nothing to do with her! She's obviously been carrying on with someone else."

Despite the truth of how Morris had come to Mother's room most every night, Mrs. Verner, of course, believed her son. Morris was given a choice—divorce Dorothy or lose his inheritance. He chose divorce.

Long before the second baby was born Mother left the Verner household and moved in with her mother. She soon had two small children—Scott, the son who forced her into a loveless marriage and Dorothy Lee, the daughter who caused her to be exiled in disgrace. With her reputation now in ruins, her father, Clarence Van Dyke Tiers, sent Dorothy and a governess to Florida in a 1931 Packard. His instructions specified that she and the children were to live in the gatekeeper's cottage on a plantation still owned by her great grandfather, Jacob Paul. It was there that she met Cole Blease Jones, the man who would ultimately become my father.

I know very little about my Father. To me he was like a heavy fog that rolls in, covers everything, and then disappears in the blink of an eye. The things that come to mind are mostly memories metamorphosed through my brother and sister, ugly things that people seldom mention aloud, things the mind sweeps into a dark corner and tries to conceal. I do know that my father was deliciously handsome. He was a man of fiery passion with an insatiable appetite for sex, a ready fist and a low tolerance of children. He was also a drunk. Not a drunk who parties and puts lampshades on his head; but a mean drunk, inclined to kick aside anything that stood in his pathway. When the pathway grew littered with broken promises and empty whisky bottles, he turned on his children. My sister, Dottie Lee, suffered the worst of his rage. She was also the primary object of his sexual abuse. I know this, not because I witnessed it, but because it was written on my sister's face, in the anger of her eyes, and her obvious dislike of me from the moment of my birth.

One of the few memories I have of my Father is not actually of him, it's of my Mother mourning the loss of him. I was only four years old but I can still picture her clutching me in her arms as she creaked back and forth in the rocking chair; her sorrow was thick as maple syrup and she sobbed as if her heart would break. "He's gone," she moaned, "your father is gone!"

"Gone where?" I asked innocently.

"Just gone! He cleaned out our bank account, took the car and left." She pulled me closer and I could feel her heart thundering. "He mortgaged our house to the hilt, took every last cent we had, and left..." she sobbed, "and after all I've done for him..."

Sadly enough what Mother said was true. She had time and again financed his unsuccessful business ventures, tolerated his carousing, allowed him to abuse her and, although she denied any knowledge of it, allowed him to abuse her children—which was unquestionably the worst sin of all.

After Mother and Pappy left Jacksonville and returned to their jobs in Daytona, Ross became my most frequent visitor. Several times a week, he'd show up at the hospital and stay for a lengthy visit. I was reminded of an old Indian superstition claiming that if a person saved someone's life, they became responsible for their care. Ross seemed to be doing just that. Two days after I'd listened to the argument outside my hospital room, I was moved from the Stryker frame onto an alternating pressure point mattress. It was an inflatable bed that whooshed pockets of air in first one spot and then another to prevent patients from getting pressure sores— something the Stryker frame had failed to do. Ross was not only a caring friend, he was also the person who went in search of the most qualified orthopedic surgeons.

"Okay," he said sliding himself into the chair next to my bed, "I've narrowed it down to a few possibilities. Well, actually two. But, these two are the most respected orthopedic surgeons in the business. They've got a list of credentials big as your head."

"With or without the Crutchfield tongs?" I quipped.

Ross laughed, "With!"

"Keep talking," I said.

"Both of them are right here in Jacksonville. The first one has over three decades of experience. He specializes in the type of spinal surgeries most neurosurgeons shy away from. He's good, very good."

"Over three decades of experience," I repeated, "so, he must be in his sixties?"

"Something like that."

"What about the second doctor?"

"He's a lot younger, not as much experience but, according to everyone I've spoken with, he's brilliant. That's not just my opinion. I checked it out with Al, and several of the residents."

Ross was leaning toward this second suggestion and I was inclined to agree. "Given all the innovations in medicine over the past forty years," I said, "isn't the younger doctor more likely to be aware of current techniques for the treatment of spinal cord injuries?"

Ross nodded, "My thinking exactly."

It seemed as if things were looking up. "This has been a very good week," I told Ross, "The revolving torture chamber is gone, I'm lying on a real bed and before long this new doctor should have me up and around."

"Up and around?" Ross raised an eyebrow and gave me his comedic look of doubt. "The guy's a genius, not a magician." Suddenly he became serious, "You have no idea how far you've already come," he said, "The day I brought you in, I didn't think you'd live. I sat in the waiting room for six hours so I could be here to talk to your parents. And when the nurses shaved your head for surgery, I asked them to give me your hair. I honestly thought you'd die and I wanted your folks to have your hair so they could glue it on for the funeral."

I saw his eyes fill with water and at that moment I knew Ross was the dearest friend a girl could ever wish for. "That's the most thoughtful thing ever..." I said, and meant it from the bottom of my heart.

When you're held prisoner by the inability to move, time creeps by more slowly than you'd ever imagine possible. Minutes feel like hours and hours like days. You try to fall asleep thinking when you wake it will be a new day, a tomorrow when time speeds by and you've moved on to recovery. You close your eyes and hope, but when you open them everything is just as it was minutes ago. It was during those long days at Baptist Memorial that I first began to experience sensory deprivation; and, in my loneliest moments, I willed my spirit to leave my body and wander around the hospital visiting other patients. After so many years things like this have a tendency to grow fuzzy in your mind. But, despite the passing of time, I can vividly recall asking the hospital staff about other patients—patients I had never met.

"Is the rash on Edna Kennedy's stomach any better today?" I asked a nurse named Isabelle.

She stopped whatever it was she'd been doing and looked at me dumbfounded. "How did you know Edna has a rash?" she said.

"Yesterday I sensed she needed a friend, so I visited with her."

"Are you out of your mind?" Isabelle replied, "You can't possibly get out of this bed! You're in traction; you can't even sit up, let alone go somewhere to visit somebody…" she shook her head in disbelief. "Keep talking crazy like that and I'll have the doctor prescribe something for delirium."

I realized then—no one at Baptist Memorial was ever going to believe it was my spirit, not my body, that had gone to visit other patients in the hospital. How could I expect them to believe something like that? Most of those nurses had never even seen an Apache, let alone had one for a father. Cole Blease Jones was a terrible father, a mean abusive man, but he came from a people of wondrous abilities—a people who understood the movement of spirits.

The days continued to drag by ever so slowly and I continued to allow my spirit to go where it willed, but I said nothing more to the nurses.

Every weekend Mother and Pappy came to visit, and on Wednesdays Mother took the Greyhound Bus and rode up to Jacksonville to spend a few hours with me. But, it was the visits from Ross and the letters from my brother that brightened most days. Nothing would have given me greater pleasure than a visit from Scott; but he and his wife Lora lived in Pennsylvania and their first baby was due momentarily, so I had to content myself with words written on paper. Scott's letters were warm, loving and passionate, but at times they could be fairly risqué and since it was a Baptist hospital, I was rather selective as to which nurse I asked to hold them while I read. I was happy that it was Ross who was sitting beside me as I read the letter announcing the birth of Jordan, Scott's first daughter. When Scott likened the birth process to one of squeezing a watermelon seed between his thumb and forefinger and watching it pop out, we laughed uproariously. Gertrude, an ill-tempered nurse I had secretly nicknamed "Prune-Face," came rushing in to shush us. "Lower your voices," she said angrily, "we've got sick people here!"

"Don't I know it!" I quipped, and we laughed even louder.

When the letters were read, and my visitors gone, I found myself drifting back in time to those troublesome thoughts of Mother, and of Dusty.

After I had won the quarter horse race, Mother looked at me and said, "Now that you've got this horse, where do you propose to keep it?"

"Um...at Blake's stable?" I answered tentatively.

"That's impossible," she said setting her mouth in a grim straight line. "Do you realize how expensive it is to board a horse? I'm stretching it to make ends meet now, there's just no way we can afford..."

"I'll get a job," I volunteered. "I can earn enough money to—"

"Lani," Mother sighed, "you're fourteen years old. You need to be in school, and besides, there's no way a part-time job would cover the expense of boarding a horse."

Fred Hanna spoke up, "We don't have an extra stall, but we've got five acres of pasture land. You can leave Dusty with us until you make other arrangements."

"Yes," Mina added, "We've got plenty of room. I'd have to charge you thirty-five dollars a month for her food and she'd have to eat from a bucket, but she'd be real comfortable."

"I suppose that might be the best solution," Mother said flatly.

On the ride home from the Cracker Day Fair, Mother returned to the subject. "You do realize," she said, "this is only a temporary measure. When the weather turns bad, that horse will need to have a stall."

"I know," I answered, afraid of where the conversation might be headed.

"I was thinking…" Mother said, "Your sister and Joe have a lot of land out back…but it's covered with saw palmetto."

"I'll chop them down and clear out the area," I replied eagerly

"That's quite an undertaking," she warned, "…but if the palmettos were gone, I think Joe would be willing to let you have a paddock—"

Before Mother finished the sentence, I jumped at it. "I don't mind the work," I said, "I'll do it!" I knew it was going to be hard work. Clearing away saw palmetto was a task that generally called for a bulldozer—I'd be doing it with nothing more than an axe, a shovel, and some heavy duty work gloves—I figured it would take me three, maybe four, days.

"I'll speak to Dottie Lee tomorrow and see what she and Joe think of the idea."

Uh-oh, getting my sister to agree to anything I wanted could be a problem.

Dottie Lee resented me from the day I was born. She was the reason Mother had become an outcast. I, on the other hand, was Mother's love child. My sister was overweight and bore a strong resemblance to the weak-willed Morris, whom Mother hated. I had my father's dark eyes, his love for speed, his reckless thirst for adventure and, like him, I was a creature of the earth. To Mother, I was a souvenir of the lusty love she had chosen. Scott and Dottie Lee were simply remnants of the marriage she'd been forced into. On the day I was born, Cole Blease Jones began sexually abusing Dottie Lee and it continued until the day he disappeared from our house. Life was cruel to my sister and she in turn was cruel to me. No doubt she hated me, but it was with understandable reason.

Dottie Lee and I were half-sisters but we were born ten years apart and the only thing we had in common was our mother—a mother who showed unbridled favoritism and used her diabetic condition as a tool to manipulate all three of her children. During WWII, I was four when I learned that the Morse Code used by soldiers was comprised of dashes and dots that were called dits. Thinking this quite funny, I tagged my sister with the nickname of Dit. Although years later it came back to haunt me, at the time she seemed to enjoy it. That silly little nickname was probably the only thing Dit ever liked about me and now the fate of my horse was in her hands. I was prepared for a 'No' but to my surprise, she and Joe agreed to the plan.

The next day I began work. I arrived at their house before the light of day had breached the sky and I worked until almost dark. The palmettos bunched themselves together in an impenetrable mass that fought against my axe with razor sharp thorns protruding from the trunks. Many a night I was covered with cuts and bruises and too weary to lift my arm to wave goodbye, but when I left their house I'd head for the pasture where Dusty was waiting. I had no saddle or bridle, so I rode bareback and clung to her mane as she galloped around the pasture. At the end of each exhausting day I knew she would be there waiting—I was as much a part of her as she was of me. Together we were one.

After what turned out to be months of back breaking work, the palmettos were gone and the paddock area was ready. Joe hastily erected a wire fence with a gate and Dusty was moved to their backyard. We had yet to build a stall and feed room but, for now, she had a home.

I was there every day. When I wasn't helping Joe, I was riding Dusty or playing with Lee, my sister's two-year-old son. For the first time in our lives, Dit and I had something in common—our love for Lee. The boy had absolutely no fear of Dusty, so as I worked he trudged along behind me. At the end of the work day, sandy-haired Lee would be as exhausted and dirty as I was. Sometimes I let little Lee ride with me. Dusty was so spirited that she would playfully try to throw me sometimes, but when she had the toddler on her back she moved slowly and carefully, seemingly cognizant of the precious bundle astride her. Occasionally we'd ride Dusty to the local food store and when I went in to pick up whatever we came for, I'd sit Lee on top of a tall kerosene pump and tell him he was responsible for holding onto Dusty's reins. Lee took the job quite seriously and shoppers often followed me into the store chuckling at the size of the toddler who was in charge of a full grown horse.

With Dit now expecting her second child, she tired easily and walked with a heavy step; so I remained there for most of the summer. I worked at finishing Dusty's stall, but I also helped take care of my nephew, did housework and laundry—washing what seemed to be millions of diapers and hanging them on the clothesline to dry. My sister and I had spent most of our life as strangers, enemies actually, and while we still couldn't be considered 'friends' we'd reached a plateau of détente.

Dit gave birth to Larry shortly after Dusty's stall was finished. During her hospital stay, I lived at the house—mothering Lee and cooking dinner for Joe. I was still there a few days after she got back from the hospital and when she failed to get out of bed one morning, I looked in on her. Dit's face was blood red and she was thrashing about in some sort of delirium. "Where's Joe?" she screamed, "Where's Lee? Help! Help…"

I hurriedly pulled the First Aid kit from beneath the bathroom sink and began to rummage through it in search of a thermometer.

"Joe," Dit screamed, "Joe, come quick! I need help!"

I rushed back and took her temperature—it was 105. Joe was at work, so I called and left a message that Dit was sick and he should come home as soon as possible. I was only fourteen years old, but I was far more capable than most girls that age. For years

I'd been taking care of Mother whenever she went into insulin shock—I'd carried her down the stairs and driven her to the hospital time after time after time. Now Dit needed help and she couldn't afford to wait for Joe. I ran to the refrigerator, pulled the ice trays from the freezer, dumped the cubes in a bowl and poured water over them. Grabbing a stack of dishtowels, I headed back to the bedroom leaving a trail of splashes behind. Dunking the towels in the icy water and not bothering to wring them out, I covered Dit with cold cloths. For the moment I had to ignore the new baby who was awake, obviously hungry, and screaming like a banshee. I also had to turn a deaf ear to Lee, crying because he needed to have his diaper changed. I had to focus on Dit. As each towel grew warm, I replaced it with one that was icy cold. Eventually, Dit's temperature began to drop and she fell back into the pillow with an exhausted sense of calm. Once she was resting easily, I changed Lee's diaper and quickly scuttled him over to the neighbor's house. Hurrying back, I changed Larry, fixed him a bottle and fed him. I had to guess the ratio of water to formula powder because up until now Dit had been breast feeding the baby. When Joe walked in a half hour later, Dit was more or less resting comfortably, the baby had gone to sleep and Lee was back from the neighbor's house.

"I thought you said there was an emergency," he said.

"There was," I sighed wearily, "there was."

Four

Not long after we moved Dusty to the paddock at Dit and Joe's house, Mother scraped together enough money to buy me a used saddle and bridle. When Dit recuperated from the kidney infection that followed Larry's birth, I was free to ride Dusty for as far and as long as I wanted. It was what I had been waiting for and what I had dreamed of. It was the summer I came to think of the Tomoka Game Reserve as a universe of serenity and solitude. I'd saddle Dusty and we would ride off with Duke running beside us. I carried nothing but the hunting knife and small hatchet in leather sheaths on my belt, and an iron skillet. It was just my horse, my dog and me—together the three of us spent endless hours traveling the wooded game trails that ran through cabbage palms and wild banana trees. I learned to spear fish with a sharpened oak branch, discovered edible berries, wild banana trees, and tender white sprouts hiding beneath wild grasses. I found that cattails have an edible portion at the bottom and cabbage palms, when split open, yield a heart of delicious swamp cabbage. Visions of living off the land as my father's people once did, spurred me on. Hours stretched into days and the days linked themselves together keeping me where I belonged. My excursions grew into camping trips that lasted several weeks, and, I discovered the shack of an old man who poached feral cattle from the reserve. He sold beef jerky, and for fifty cents I could buy enough jerky to feed Duke for two weeks, maybe longer. In a clearing close to a fresh water spring, I built a lean-to of branches and palm fronds. This became my world—I now had a place to go and a family I could count on. Dit was feeling better and no longer needed me. Mother welcomed the opportunity to invite men into the house without having to explain herself to a teenage daughter.

On a grey and gloomy Sunday, when there was little else to do, I took Duke and Dusty for what I anticipated would be an afternoon outing. But the game reserve was a magical place, a place that drew me in and encouraged me to get lost in its beauty. The filtered light of day evaporated into nothingness before I realized that I'd gone too far and might not be able to get out of the reserve before dark. I had none of my tools—the hunting knife, the axe, the skillet—all of these things were with Dusty's saddle, hanging just inside the door of her stall. Even my lean-to campsite was not within reach.

With dusk rapidly settling around us and the dampness of rain in the air, I started down a trail that looked vaguely familiar. In the distance I saw a cypress swamp. *Okay, if I circle around this and it runs into the game trail, we might be able to get to the edge of the reserve before dark.* We ventured around the swamp, one of many in the game reserve, but darkness overtook us. I could no longer see my hand before my face. Duke became a glimmer of eye and Dusty, black as she was, seemed invisible. Like it or not, we would have to camp here. Heavy clouds obscured any stars or moonlight I might have hoped for and the night was now black as pitch.

I felt my way around until I came across a decent size clearing. Then I gathered small pieces of wood and dug the cigarette matches from my pocket. Still damp from the earlier rain, the wood spit and sputtered. I needed something dry to get the fire going. After a bit of searching, I uncovered some reasonably dry pinecones and with those I was able to coax the smoky mess into a small fire. With only a smidgen of light, I gathered a few more pieces of tinder and actually got a campfire going. Now I could see where I was, but it was a place I had never seen before. The blackened pine, the mossy slime, the tangle of briars strangling a thing that had once been a tree, all of it was eerily unfamiliar. Needles of apprehension crawled up my spine, slowly and methodically, the way a spider crawls along a drainpipe. In the unrelenting darkness, I was able to find the trunk of a broken pine tree angled about four feet above the ground. I climbed onto that and settled in to wait for the first light of dawn. Normally, I would have hobbled Dusty with one of her reins and let her graze in the surrounding grass, but this night something prevented me from doing it. Instead, I held her reins in my hand and kept watch.

A few hours into our wait, Duke jumped to his feet, growling ferociously, the hair on his neck and back standing straight up. Dusty began snorting, ears twitching, nostrils dilated, she was trembling so furiously I feared she would bolt and I would lose my grip on her reins. Suddenly, I heard what sounded like a woman's scream—it was close, so close that it pierced my ears like the thrust of a needle. Dusty began bucking and kicking wildly, making sounds I'd never before heard. She pulled at the reins so violently it was all I could do to hold on. "Let's get out of here!" I shouted, struggling to swing myself onto her back before she broke loose. The three of us tore through that perilous black forest as if the devil were chasing us. The animal eyes of Duke and Dusty saw the things I could not see, so they were the ones who prevented us from smashing into trees or running into cypress swamps. Our hearts pounding with fear, we ran until we were breathless and could run no more. When we finally stopped, I stood watch for the remainder of the night—my eyes fixed on a darkness that gave way to nothing. I listened and waited.

With the breaking of dawn, my anxiety eased and we moved out to search for a familiar game trail that would lead us to the edge of the reserve. Minutes later we came upon the smoldering campfire we'd abandoned in the dark of night. I realized then, like blind mice we'd run in a circle. We were right back where we started. A short distance from the fallen tree, the soft ground was covered with large paw prints. The prints were mixed in with Duke's, but unmistakably different. I'd seen these prints in the reserve before; they were the paw prints of a Florida panther. We were fortunate to get away unscathed! The hungry panthers in the reserve fed on small game, wild hogs and even feral cattle. A dog, a human or a horse would have made a very nice meal…luckily we didn't become one.

That summer I spent countless days and nights in the game reserve. I would spread my beautiful Indian blanket on the soft grass and lie there as I watched spectacular sunrises and sunsets. With my head resting on my saddle and Duke sleeping beside me, I counted stars. I also counted the dwindling number of days until my return to school. *Someday,* I thought, *Someday, I'll be free to do whatever I want, whenever I want.* I felt the reserve was where I belonged. I was one with nature and this was my world. The popularity, dances, cheerleading, swim team—none of it mattered to me. It was the country club world Mother loved, but it wasn't my world.

I was lost in those thoughts when I heard footsteps entering my hospital room and an unfamiliar voice said, "Hello good looking."

Unable to see the speaker's face, I had to wait until he crossed the room and stood closer.

"I'm Doctor Charles Meade," he said smiling, "mind if I get in bed with you?"

I laughed and he laughed. Then he sat down on the side of the bed and we began to talk. All of a sudden, I knew the handsome man I just met was going to change my life.

"I'm the orthopedic surgeon you called in for a consultation," he said, "I've already gone over your x-rays and we've got our work cut out for us, but I think it's doable." Step by step he detailed the situation and the solution. "You've broken the fourth, fifth and sixth vertebrae," he said, "but we can fuse them together which will give your spine stability. The fifth vertebrae exploded on impact and unfortunately there's nothing left of it but fragments."

"Oh," I hesitated, concerned of what was to come.

"So…what we'll have to do," he continued, "is harvest some bone from your hip to create a replacement for that fifth vertebrae. The surgery is called a laminectomy. It's a procedure where we remove the bone laminae to open up the space in the spinal canal and… "

I think I love you.

"Although there's no way to repair your spinal cord, this will give you movement of your upper body. You'll be able to sit up, and hopefully move your torso and arms…"

I know I love you! "How soon?" I asked.

"How soon can we do the surgery? Or how soon will you be able to move?"

"Both," I answered with a look of happiness that radiated from deep inside my heart.

"The surgery, we can schedule right away; the movement, only time can tell. At least you'll be able to sit up." He gave me a knowing grin and said, "You won't be moving around the day after the operation if that's what you think. Lani, this is very invasive back surgery and there's a lengthy recuperation period. Yes, I'm hopeful you'll start to experience miniscule increments of movement fairly soon, but it may not be anything more than a twitch. Just be patient and perhaps in time…"

I could be patient. I'd had a lifetime of being patient. I thought back to the summer I owned Dusty and how it came to an end all too fast. I had wished for the days to be weeks and the weeks to be months. I had hoped to ride into the Tomoka Game Reserve with my horse and dog, and find myself in a summer that stretched beyond eternity. But instead, I found myself tied to the sister who resented me the way one resents a blemish on the tip of their nose.

Once Dit recovered from that kidney infection, she was more irritable than ever. You might think she'd be grateful that I saved her life, but it wasn't the case. Everything I said or did was wrong and she snarled at me like a dog hovering over a bone. The worst was when someone said something that in any way flattered or complimented me.

With just a few weeks of summer left, we were sitting at the breakfast table when Joe said, "Dit, your sister's something else. The kid's only fourteen but when you got sick, she jumped in to take care of you and both kids."

I cringed, knowing what was coming.

"I wasn't all that sick," Dit snapped, her agitation obvious.

Instead of catching the irritation in his wife's tone, Joe continued on. "Have you noticed how little Lee follows her around? He said she's gonna teach him to ride soon as he's growed enough. She's damn good with that horse of hers, so I know she can do it."

Dit's eyes narrowed and she glared at Joe as she spoke "Lani's not that good," she said, "I can ride just as well as she can."

"Sure you can," Joe laughed. Then he stood up and walked out.

I could see Dit was seething, and I tried to smooth it over. "He's just teasing you," I said, "don't pay any attention to him."

She didn't bother to answer and I knew the fury of hell would soon be headed my way. It happened that same afternoon. I was out in the paddock playing tag with Dusty—that was our game. I'd smack her on the rump then she'd chase me until she playfully knocked me down. Of course, as soon as I got up I'd smack her again, and the game would continue. I was sitting on the ground when Dit called out, "Put a saddle on that horse, I'm going for a ride."

"That's not a good idea," I answered, "Dusty's so high strung, she tries to throw everybody who rides her."

"You ride her! If you can ride her, I can ride her!"

"But Dit, she even tries to throw me sometimes! She only lets me stay on her back because she trusts me. It took a long time before—"

"Who in the hell do you think you are talking to? I've been taking care of that horse for months and now you're trying to tell me that I can't ride her?"

I didn't want to get into it with Dit because I knew when she wanted to be mean, she could be two-fisted mean. Instead of reminding her that I had been the one taking care of her, the two kids, and the horse, I said, "I'm not saying that you can't ride her, it's just that I don't want you to get hurt. Dusty knows me and it's the only reason she—"

Dit looked at me with genuine hatred in her eyes, "I was riding horses before you were born," she snarled, "now shut up and saddle the horse so I can go for a ride!"

"Please don't. It's too dangerous. When Dusty doesn't like a rider, she'll scrape against a tree or take off running and…"

Dit didn't say a word, she just stood there looking like she'd rather run a knife through my heart than take another breath.

Grudgingly, and with a lump of fear settling into my chest, I began to saddle Dusty. First I brushed and coddled her, hoping to ease her into a good mood—the kind of mood where she was more docile. I stalled as long as I could, but once the horse was saddled, my sister climbed on her back and trotted off. "Stay with the kids until I get back," she called out and dug her heels into Dusty's ribs.

"Be careful," I mumbled woefully, although I knew she was already beyond earshot. I could almost see the events to come and I was dreading the thought of it.

As they disappeared from view, I saw Dusty prancing the way she did when she was trying to unseat me. Dit was hanging to the reins and looking none too steady.

Less than five minutes later, Dusty cantered up to the house without Dit, "I knew it!" I moaned.

Leaving the boys with a neighbor, I climbed on Dusty's back and tried to retrace the path they had taken. As I rounded the first corner I saw my sister on the ground beneath a large oak tree. She was moaning and holding her right arm. "I think my arm is broken," she said, "that damn horse deliberately ran under a low hanging branch and knocked me off!"

A few hours later Dit's broken arm was in a cast—but I was sentenced to spend the last few weeks of summer taking care of my sister and her children.

"Next summer," I'd whisper to Duke and Dusty, "Next summer the three of us will spend every night and day in the reserve. Next summer we'll be able to do what *we* want..."

The last days of summer were on the horizon when I finally got a chance to ride over to the Hanna ranch for a visit with my friends, Mina and Fred. "I think you might have a problem," Mina said eyeing Dusty.

"Problem?" Other than my impossible-to-deal-with sister and school starting again soon, I couldn't imagine a problem.

Mina shook her head regretfully, "I'm real sorry..." she sighed. "When Dusty was staying out in the pasture I'm pretty sure she was in heat, and it looks like Fred's Tennessee Walking stallion got hold of her."

"You mean she's..."

Mina nodded, "Yep, pregnant. Judging by the way she's starting to fill out, I'd say you're gonna have a foal come spring."

"Oh no," I cried. "Mother will never allow me to keep two horses!"

I knew it was the absolute truth—the instant I told Mother about Dusty's pregnancy, she would dredge up seventeen thousand reasons why we should get rid of the horse. My immediate answer to the problem was to say nothing, which was what I did. I waited until I saw the bulge in Dusty's belly and began to worry about her health and the health of the foal and then when I finally did tell Mother, it was just as I'd expected.

"Oh Lani," she said, "How could you..."

"Me?" I knew it was going to be a battle, so I immediately went on the defensive. "I didn't do anything! Things like this happen. She was in heat and Fred's stallion—"

"Don't bother to explain, I understand the process."

"Well, it's not my fault—"

Mother released a sigh that floated through the room like a melancholy echo. "Lani dear, I'm not blaming you," she said, "but given our financial situation, keeping a pregnant horse is absolutely unthinkable."

The image of Dit as a baby flashed before my eyes and I thought – *Getting kicked out because you're pregnant, isn't that exactly what happened to you Mother?* I was awestruck that she didn't see the similarities. "It won't cost very much," I said, "the foal will stay in Dusty's paddock until it's weaned, then I'll sell it. You'll get your money back in no time and—"

"Lani, you make it sound quite simple, but it's not. I've struggled with making ends meet so you could keep your horse, but now with this…" She gave another mournful sigh. "The hard truth is that Dusty is going to need veterinary care and I just can't afford to pay for it."

"I'll get a job, I'll do whatever—"

"We've gone over this before Lani; you are not getting a job, you're going to school. I will not even consider the thought of you sacrificing your education for the sake of a horse…"

"But…all I want is—"

"I'm sorry," she interrupted, "…truly sorry. I understand what you want, but the answer, unfortunately, is no."

"Why?" I insisted, "Why is it I can never have what I want?"

"Why?" Mother repeated, looking up at the ceiling as if she expected to find the answer written there. When she began to speak her words were slow and sad, "I guess it's because I've misjudged things. I misjudged Morris and he destroyed my reputation. Then I misjudged your father and he left us without…" Mother's eyes began to fill with tears.

"That was a long time ago," I said. "That was then, this is now. You can afford to belong to the country club, so why can't I—"

"The reason we belong to that club," Mother said, narrowing her eyes, "is so that you can meet the *right* kind of people. Maybe if you spent more time at the club—"

"I don't want to spend time at the club!" I shouted, "I don't enjoy being with people dressed up like peacocks. I like being with Duke and Dusty. I like going to the game reserve and being by myself. I like it when no one's around to frown at what I'm doing."

"I like a lot of things I don't have," Mother replied wearily. "You may not believe it, but I would like to be able to say yes you can keep the horse, but I can't, and that's that."

"I'm not going to sell Dusty!"

"Unfortunately, you have no choice." Mother turned and walked toward the bedroom. "That's my final word," she said, "and I don't wish to discuss it any further."

"You can't make me sell Dusty," I screamed, "...you can't! She's my horse!"

Mother closed the bedroom door behind her and there was no response.

"You can't do it!" I screamed, "It's not right...I love Dusty and she loves me."

No sound came from Mother's room.

"Please," I begged, "please don't make me sell Dusty!"

The bedroom door remained closed.

"Okay then, don't answer me. Just go hang out with your fancy country club friends, see if I care! I'm leaving and I'm never coming back!"

I stormed out of the house and slammed the door behind me.

"I'm not doing it!" I mumbled as Duke and I crossed the street and headed for the beach.

After leaving the house I walked along the sand all the way to Ormond Beach. When I could walk no further, I climbed onto a high dune and sat with my arm wrapped around Duke. He seemed to understand my anguish and snuggled himself so close that a breeze couldn't pass between us. "How could Mother do this to me?" I sobbed, "How can she make me get rid of Dusty?" I felt that a part of my life was ending, and in fact it was.

During the long night I thought about running away from home, but came to the sad realization that I had nowhere else to go. After the broken arm incident, Dit resented me more than ever.

Scott was in the Marines with no place for a kid sister; and my father was a mean, abusive drunk who apparently wanted neither Mother nor me.

Despite everything he was, my father lived inside of me. I thought back, not to him, but to the people and the places he had come from—a kinder, gentler nation, where families sat around a campfire at night and chanted songs of joy, where horses and dogs and children were never torn apart, where they were free to run across wide stretches of grass with the wind whistling in their ears. With all my heart I wanted to believe such a world existed and that somewhere there was a family with one empty place in their circle, a place that was rightfully mine. In the dark of night, when millions of stars crowd the sky, you allow yourself to dream such dreams. But when the pale pink rays of morning began to light the horizon, I knew it was a fantasy. My life was what it was—nothing more. I buried my face in Duke's thick fur and cried for a long while. When my tears were spent, we trudged home together. *I was no longer whole, but at least I still had Duke.*

The following week Mother ran a newspaper ad listing Dusty for sale. I prayed no one would respond and for a few days they didn't. I knew my time with Dusty was limited, so I rode her as long and as often as I could. During one of those long rides a woman took notice of Dusty and asked if I knew where such a horse could be purchased for a reasonable price.

"My daughter wants a horse so badly," the woman said, "but most of the stables are asking outrageous prices. I can't afford—"

"Dusty's for sale," I said sadly. I could have lied. I could have pretended to have no knowledge of a horse for sale; but the sorry truth was that I knew Mother was going to get rid of Dusty, one way or another. If I had to lose the horse I loved, I wanted it to be to someone who truly wanted her and would love her as much as I did.

The next morning the woman brought her daughter to see Dusty, and I found myself selfishly wishing this would be one of those days when Dusty would act mischievous and uncontrollable, but such was not the case. She behaved beautifully and as sweet and gentle as she had always been with Lee. The girl, who looked a little older than I, fell in love with Dusty. That afternoon the woman came back with a trailer, loaded Dusty into it and drove away without ever noticing the trail of heartbreak left behind.

I never saw my beloved Dusty again.

Five

Three days after I first met Doctor Charles Meade, he performed the surgery on my spine. Mother and Pappy arrived at the hospital early that morning and Mother was flittering about like a nervous butterfly. "Now don't be frightened, Lani," she said, "this is the best—"

"I'm not the least bit frightened," I answered. And it was the truth. I knew without this surgery, I would never be able to lift my head, much less have hope for rehabilitation. Moments later, I was wheeled off to the operating room, leaving a nervous Mother and Pappy to wait.

She later told me they waited for what seemed an eternity before Doctor Charles Meade strolled into the waiting room wearing a smile. "It went well," he told them, "Lani's fifth cervical vertebra was pulverized, so there were a lot of bone fragments that had to be dug out, but we were able to get them all. We've reconstructed the fifth vertebra using some bone from her hip and fused the three broken vertebrae together; that should give her strength and stability in her neck." He motioned for them to have a seat and continued talking, "This surgery should help Lani regain a limited amount of mobility in her upper body, hopefully she'll be able to sit up and have some use of her arms. But, given the severity of the damage to her spinal cord..." Suddenly he was no longer smiling, "...Lani will never walk again."

"Perhaps with another surgery…" Mother stammered.

Doctor Meade shook his head, "I'm afraid not. But Lani is a very brave, and very determined, girl; I haven't known her for a long time, but I believe she'll do amazing things once she starts to sit up."

For several days following the surgery, I was in severe pain and heavily sedated; so it mattered little who was there or what bed I was in. But when I started to come around, I was furious to find myself back in the dreadful Stryker frame. "How could you…" I said to Doctor Meade, who I had now begun to call Charlie.

"It's an absolute necessity," he replied, "You have to remain motionless until those bones knit together and form a strong bond. I know you don't like it, but the alternative is to remain flat on your back for the rest of your life!"

"You can be unbelievably convincing," I groaned. Grudgingly I agreed to remain in that torturous bed with twenty pounds of sandbags hanging from a pulley attached to the Crutchfield Tongs which now felt as if they had become a part of my head.

"However," Charlie added, "I will instruct the nurses to make certain you're turned every two hours; I don't want those pressure sores getting any worse than they are."

Although I believed myself to be on the doorstep of recovery, my condition was still listed as 'critical.' Little by little everyone settled back into the routine of the previous month. Mother and Pappy came to visit on weekends, Mother came by herself on Wednesday, Ross would pop in and out almost every day, letters came from Scott, and I remained in the Stryker frame, counting ceiling tiles, counting speckles on the colorless tile floor and allowing my spirit to wander free visiting with other patients. On one occasion, a silver-haired woman who leaned heavily on her cane, hobbled into my room; "I just wanted to thank you," she said, "for visiting my Tommy. He passed on a few minutes ago, but he said your visits made his last few days far more bearable."

Prune-face, a ill-tempered nurse who justified the nickname I had secretly given her, turned and looked at the woman, "Visits?"

she said, "Not from this one, she can't even lift her head up! You sure you've got the right room?"

"Oh I'm quite sure," the woman answered and hobbled out.

When Mother came to visit she chatted on nervously, repeating over and over again how I would soon be up and walking around. "Any day now," she'd say, "any day now you'll start to see movement in your arms and next thing you know you'll be walking."

I knew that was not true. Charlie had been very up front in telling me there was no surgery that could enable me to walk again. I would however, be able to sit up in a wheelchair and move around; which to me, was a gigantic improvement. That was a life I could deal with. The only problem was Mother. For weeks she'd been talking about how I'd get up and walk out of here, so I was nervous about her reaction to the truth. Mother was a drama queen, a woman who could turn a bee sting into a life-threatening illness. Even if the bee stung someone else, Mother found a way to make it all about her. "I was standing right there and saw it happen," she'd say, "When that bee landed on your Aunt Eleanor's arm, I nearly fainted! She is highly allergic to bee stings, you know."

When I began to feel a tinge of movement in my left forearm a few weeks later, I knew it was time to tell Mother the truth. On Saturday she and Pappy arrived earlier than usual, and it was Pappy who noticed the slight movement of my left forearm. After a few minutes of jubilant celebration, Pappy darted out the door claiming he had to get something from the store. While he was gone, I took advantage of the opportunity to talk to Mother.

"There's something I have to tell you," I said, "...but Mother, please don't overreact."

"Lani dear, I do not overreact," she replied, pulling a hankie from her purse in preparation for the tears. "I'm a strong woman and I can handle anything you have to say."

"I know you're strong," I repeated, "that's why I'm going to trust you to handle the truth about my condition bravely."

"Oh no, don't tell me..."

"Mother!" I hesitated for a moment and she stopped sniffling, so I went on. "The accident broke my neck and severely damaged my spinal cord; it's more damage than is repairable. The surgery Doctor Meade did should enable me to sit up in a wheelchair, possibly even have some mobility in my arms, but please understand, I will never be able to walk." The way Mother was looking at me made it seem as though she could see words chiseled into chunks of stone tumbling from my mouth, but still I continued. "I'm a quadriplegic and that's not going to change. It is what it is. I've done a lot of thinking about it and I'm okay with it. It wasn't my first choice, but I've come to grips with the fact that I'll be spending the rest of my life in a wheelchair. Mother, I hope for both of our sakes, you'll be able to do the same. Everything is going to be okay, being a quadriplegic will not stop me from making something of my life."

Mother burst into a torrent of tears. *Drama Queen.* "I know, Lani, I know," she sobbed, "I've known since the day of your surgery, but I didn't think you knew and I didn't want to be the one to discourage you." We began laughing uproariously at how we had worked so hard trying to hide the truth from one another.

Moments later, Pappy burst back into the room. He was a bit winded, but wearing a smile that stretched from ear to ear. "Guess what I got you from the gift shop downstairs..." he said gleefully. Before I could venture a guess, he reached into the bag and pulled out a black leatherette case that read 'Timex.'

"You're always asking what time it is," he said, "...now all you've got to do is lift your arm and you'll know!" Pappy stood there with his chest puffed out and his face filled with pride.

"I can honestly say I've never received a more wonderful gift," I replied, my eyes filling with tears of gratitude.

Pappy leaned over, kissed my cheek and buckled the new Timex to my wrist.

Even though it was a wonderful afternoon, some things are never forgotten and once I was alone in the room my thoughts drifted back to those earlier days...

After Dusty was gone, I could no longer control my anger toward Mother. Our relationship was never wonderful, but suddenly it bordered on adversarial. I argued that the money from the sale of Dusty rightfully belonged to me since I'd given Mother the one-hundred dollars I won in the quarter horse race, and, I'd won the State Diving Championship. She argued that it was money needed to keep the household running and since I was living there, I should be willing to help out. She asked me to sell the saddle and bridle she'd bought for Dusty. I flatly refused. "As soon as I get enough money I'll buy my own horse," I snapped back.

"We've gone through this fifty times Lani and I haven't changed my mind! I will not even consider the possibility of allowing you to leave school for some flunky job where you'll end up working like a dog and earn peanuts for the rest of your life. You're going to remain in school and get an education—like it or not!"

"I don't care about making a lot of money! All I care about is—"

"Oh, you don't care about making a lot of money? Well guess what? If I had the money I once had, this horse thing wouldn't be the problem it is!"

"It's a problem because you made it a problem! You made me sell Dusty and I'm never going to forgive you!" The arguing went on and on, there was no end to it. The only moments of respite were those when we failed to speak to one another.

By the end of the year, my grades had started to deteriorate. I had little interest in school, cheerleading, or social clubs—and I had absolutely no interest in partying at Mother's Country Club. I missed Dusty more than anyone could possibly imagine, and although I bumped my way through the days with a 'who-cares' attitude, inside my heart felt as if it was riddled with holes.

I hung around anywhere and everywhere there were horses, perhaps expecting that one day I'd run into Dusty. I dreamed that if she saw me in the midst of a crowd, she'd come from behind, nose me to the ground and challenge me to a game of tag. I made friends with Ruth Ann, the girl who'd ridden the blue roan in the Gymkhana barrel race, and she introduced me to her dad, Bert Faircloth, a well-known horse trader. It was Bert who taught me about 'green-broke' horses and, much to Mother's chagrin, it was Bert who sold me the honey-colored filly that soon put me in the horse trading business.

One Saturday, I was perched on the fence watching Bert try to run a grey colored quarter horse through the barrels. Whenever Bert tried to turn left or right, the horse went straight. "What's the matter with her?" I asked.

"Nothing," Bert answered, "she's just green-broke. She's trained for a saddle and rider, but she ain't got the hang of cutting yet. That's what I'm tryin' to teach her."

I laughed, "It doesn't look as if she wants to learn."

"Well, she's gonna have to. A cutter's gotta respond to the neck rein," he gave the rein another swift jerk and smacked his riding crop across the horse's neck. After three tries, she eventually veered right. "Horse's worth a lot more once it's trained for cutting," Bert said, "Florida's cow country."

I sat and watched for nearly an hour as Bert yanked and slapped at the horse. Maybe it had to be done, but, it seemed to me, there might be a kinder, gentler way of doing it.

When Bert climbed down from the horse, he walked over and sat next to me. "You interested in a green-broke horse?" he asked.

"I might be," I answered, "it depends on the price."

Bert laughed out loud, "For a kid, you got a pretty good head for business."

I followed Bert over to the pasture and he pointed out a honey-colored filly, "She's a real good quarter horse," he said, "but she's just green-broke. Think you can train her to cut?"

"It depends on the price," I repeated.

Bert laughed louder than before, "Okay, since you're a friend of Ruth Ann, I'll let you have her for a-hundred-twenty-five."

"I'm Ruth Ann's very good friend," I answered, "...so how about I'll give you seventy-five?"

"How about one-hundred?"

"Nope, best I can do is eighty-five, and that's only if you throw in free pasture space where I can keep her."

Bert laughed so hard his belly jiggled. "How about eighty-five and on weekends you help out with a few chores around here to pay for the pasture space?"

"Done." I stuck out my hand to shake his, but Bert, still laughing, wrapped me in a big old bear hug. "You're one helluva kid," he said, "Yes sir, one helluva kid!"

Without saying a word to Mother, I took my money from the sale of Dusty and bought this new green-broke horse. "Honey," I whispered in her ear, "I'm going to call you Honey, and someday you'll be the best cutting horse in the Gymkhana."

Oddly enough, once I began training Honey my relationship with Mother grew less adversarial. I set aside my anger because I was too busy working with the horse. I had figured out another way to train green-broke horses and so far it was working like a charm. Yanking on a horse's rein and smacking her with a whip seemed too cruel, so I came up with an inexpensive alternative. Purchasing two packages of thumbtacks and a strong metal file, I used the clamp in Bert's tool shop to hold each tack and filed it down so that when the tacks were pushed through the outside of Honey's rein they protruded just a fraction of an inch—not enough to hurt her, just enough to make it uncomfortable. When I gave the rein a gentle tug, Honey felt the tacks' prickling and turned immediately. Without my ever striking her with the riding crop, she was turning sharply in a matter of days. No blood, no smacking with a crop—just a gentle prickling to remind her to turn. It worked perfectly!

When Bert spied Honey cutting back and forth through the practice barrels, he said, "You got a real talent for training horses kid, yes sir, a real talent!"

"Thanks Bert," I yelled as I picked up the pace and circled Honey through the obstacle course a second time.

I waited until a few days before the Gymkhana race and then told Mother I'd spent the money we got for Dusty and bought another horse.

"You did what?" she said angrily.

"I didn't spend it all," I answered defensively, "This one's a green-broke horse, they don't cost as much. I didn't spend half of what we got for Dusty." I could see Mother's obvious annoyance, but went on to explain how I'd trained the horse and was entered into the upcoming Gymkhana. "Honey can win this," I said, "I know she can."

I suppose Mother had simply grown tired of arguing, she rolled her eyes and gave a sorrowful shake of her head. "I just don't understand this obsession with horses," she said wearily, "but if you're determined to do it there's nothing I can do to stop you. I should have realized that a long time ago."

"Will you come and watch?"

"Of course. Just because I don't approve of the choices you make doesn't mean I don't love you. Regardless of what you do, I'm always very proud." She turned and mumbled under her breath, "I guess I'll never understand why it has to be horses instead of something at the Country Club...but Lani is Lani...and that's how she is."

That weekend Honey won every race we entered. After her third straight win, several people gathered around asking where I'd gotten such a good cutting horse. "I trained her myself," I answered proudly.

"You interested in selling?" the foreman from the Circle R asked.

Honey was a good quarter horse; I liked her well enough and I'd had a lot of fun training her, but Honey was not Dusty and she never would be. "It depends on the price," I answered.

"How about one-seventy-five?"

I shook my head, "How about two-fifty?"

"Too high," he said. "I'll go two-twenty, but that's my limit."

I hesitated a minute then answered, "Okay then, two-twenty it is."

He reached into his pocket, counted out the bills and handed them to me. I looked over and saw Mother smiling.

After Honey, I bought another green-broke horse, trained it and sold it. Then there was another and another and another; the long string of horses came and went without my ever shedding a tear. They were simply horses—fun to work with, fun to train, fun to ride horses—but they weren't Dusty. I've come to believe losing Dusty closed up a small corner of my heart. It's a place where she will be with me forever, a spot that's hers and hers alone. When one of my green-broke horses walked away with a new owner, I could feel glad about it. I knew they would perform well as cutting horses working with cattle on a ranch, but I also hoped they'd find a cowboy to love them as I had loved Dusty.

I was in the eighth grade that year. For the first time in my life I wasn't just a tomboy, I was one of the girls; and a popular one at that. Although last summer I dreaded any thought of not being with Duke and Dusty in our wonderful game reserve, I now welcomed the social activities with my new friends. I enjoyed the parties, the dates, the dances. I even enjoyed the notoriety I got from driving to school in Mother's brand new Buick Century.

Never one to miss an opportunity to have things her way, Mother finally hit upon something that would get me out of the horse training business. One evening as we were having dinner, she mentioned that she'd seen a beautiful baby blue convertible for sale. "A nineteen-forty-seven Chrysler," she said, "...a real fun car!" She dropped that thought on the table and allowed it to sit there for a few minutes before she spoke again. "Seems to me," she mused, "a girl your age would prefer zipping around in a car like that rather than wasting time with horses."

"What do you mean?" I asked apprehensively.

She gave a shrug, "Nothing really, I just thought maybe you'd like to take the money you've made selling horses, and buy yourself a snappy little car."

"You'd let me have my own car even though I don't have a driver's license?"

"Why not?" Mother said, "You've been driving mine since you were eleven."

We went to look at the car the next morning. The moment I saw it I could picture myself behind the wheel—driving my friends downtown for lunch, everybody piled in together for a day at the beach and me dressed in my cheerleader outfit heading to the football game with the other cheerleaders. That afternoon I withdrew my earnings from the bank and bought the car, which ultimately ended my career as a horse trainer.

When I opened my eyes, I was no longer whipping around town in my blue convertible. I was lying rigid with my head locked in the grip of the Crutchfield Tongs. Just when I'd come to believe nothing worse could possibly happen, something did. The nurses at Baptist Memorial were trying to abide by Charlie's instructions that my Stryker frame be turned every two hours, that's what led to the disaster. On a Tuesday, when one of the orderlies normally assigned to the task failed to show up for work, a young nurse jumped into help. "I'll lend a hand so we can get this done," she told the orderly. Together they began to flip the Stryker frame. It went well enough and they were in the process of releasing the straps when the inexperienced nurse removed the bottom rod and sent the bottom frame—the head of the bed—crashing to the floor. With the bed no longer supporting me, my head was left dangling from the twenty pound pulleys attached to the Crutchfield tongs drilled into my skull. All hell broke loose and suddenly there were more orderlies and nurses in my room than I could count. With the delicate bones in my neck recently fused and still healing, everyone feared the worst—me included. Fortunately, a series of x-rays indicated that the fall had not created further damage. For the remainder of my stay at Baptist Memorial, two and sometimes three orderlies were always on hand to flip the Stryker frame.

Although there were no further mistakes, they seldom turned the bed every two hours.

I'd like to say it was smooth sailing from then on but, shortly thereafter, different complications began to surface. First, it was a very severe kidney infection. Next, the bedsores took on such proportion that they burrowed into my bones. And ultimately, my breathing took a turn for the worse. I developed a raging fever, and began to see death as a realistic possibility. Struggling for every breath, I found myself wondering if death would be an unkind fate or a blessing in disguise. In some ways, slipping away from this life was a tempting solution, a peaceful respite, rather like the serene moments of solitude I had found in the Tomoka Game Reserve. But I was only seventeen years old and there was so much more I wanted to do, so many more mountains to climb and so many more worlds to explore. The same resilience that time and again brought me bouncing back from adversity, took hold and in my ear it whispered a strange little quote from Henley's Invictus...*It matters not how straight the gate, how charged with punishment the scroll, I am the master of my fate, the captain of my soul.* I suddenly laughed aloud. I knew I was not going to die—I wouldn't allow myself to do it.

That night I began experimenting with breathing techniques to make my heart beat. I concentrated on sucking air as deeply into my body as possible and then expelling it with a forceful push. Yes, my lung muscles were paralyzed, but I could force my diaphragm to work! *Breathe in, breathe out...breathe in, breathe out...feel your heart beating...MAKE IT BEAT! Don't stop! If you go to sleep you may not wake up...*

By morning, the fog that had been closing in on me was beginning to clear and a streak of red sun was lifting above the horizon. I had lived through the night and I would go on. I would go on because there were a million reasons to live, too many for me to ever let go. For days my heartbeat had been thready and irregular, but now it was growing stronger. I had looked death square in the eye and said, 'No, I'm not ready yet!' I had kept myself alive with my own determination to live.

That near-death experience was a time of learning and dramatic insight. Death was not the terrifying thing we all fear. It was warm, friendly and inviting. I had not trembled in fear of death, but neither was I ready for it just yet. I had a life waiting for me, a life that offered challenge and reward, love and laughter. There would come a time when I would be ready for death and when it came, I would no longer fear it…but that time was not now. I knew that during the long night, I had truly become the master of my fate!

If I were to single out the turning point in my life, it would be that night. I was reborn with the intention of completing my rehabilitation, going on to college and ultimately working in a field where I could care for other people as they had so tenderly cared for me. That would be my IS, and I knew it was a good one. I thought about the nurses who watched over me, the orderlies, Ross, Mother and Pappy, Scott with his wonderful letters, my caring friends, and the incredible Doctor Charles Meade. They had all worked so hard to support and encourage me. Now it was time for me to pay it forward, to give others the love and care they had given me. With Mother's recurring insulin shock comas, I had always been a caregiver of sorts, but now I would do more.

That night, I vowed to spend the rest of my life, regardless of how long it might be, working to make the world a better place, a more loving place than it had been before I entered it. Unlike Prune-face, who had no love to give, I discovered that I had an abundance of it and I was determined to use it to help others.

Six

In the weeks that followed, the movement in my arms became gradually more pronounced. I was reclassified from critical to poor condition and, while that may not seem like much, it had been a life and death struggle for me. Despite the fact that I was growing stronger, my urinary tract infections continued to be a problem. On a number of occasions, my fever soared to one-hundred and five and I was again listed as critical.

"You've got to consume more liquid," Charlie said, "or else these infections will continue to get worse."

"Drink more?" I replied doggedly, "I can't stand the thought of forcing down more water and the lemonade and iced tea this place serves is putrid."

"You still need more fluid," Charlie explained, "Tell me what you think you would like to drink and I'll prescribe it on the medicine chart."

"Hmmm," I hummed playfully, "I'd really enjoy a nice cold Budweiser."

"Budweiser Beer?" Charlie laughed.

"Exactly." I was picturing the cool amber liquid pulled up from a tub of ice and served with an overload of friends and laughter. I can't say for certain whether or not I thought Charlie would actually prescribe such a thing, but he did.

"Okay," he said scribbling a few notes on my chart, "it's done. Anytime you want a cold Budweiser, tell the nurse and she'll get you one." As Charlie left the room he looked back and gave me a wink, "Of course you may have to drink an awful lot of Budweiser to get rid of that urinary tract infection!"

"Okay," I laughed. The thought of having a beer in a Baptist hospital was delightfully wicked and made me feel as if I was beginning to live again. I didn't really like beer, but this would be fun! Mischievous to the core, I waited until the next morning when grouchy old Prune-face was on duty. When she walked in with the medicine tray, I said, "I'd like something to drink," stifling a chuckle.

"Water or juice?" she replied impatiently.

"Neither. Doctor Meade suggested I drink Budweiser Beer whenever I'm thirsty. It's supposed to help me get rid of this urinary tract infection. He said there would be a supply in the refrigerator and I should ask the nurse to bring it."

"Beer?" Prune-face stammered, "For a seventeen year old kid?"

"Yes, he wrote it on my medication list." I gave my words the sound of childish innocence, but inside I was laughing uproariously. Prune-face said nothing more; she simply turned and stormed off. After a considerable amount of time she returned with the frosty Budweiser on a medicine tray, a blue hospital straw sticking out of the top of the can.

"This is illegal!" she snarled, "But if it's prescribed as medicine, you're going to take it like medicine! Drink!" The nurses were supposed to make sure patients took the medications they delivered, so she stood there with an angry glare and watched as I chug-a-lugged the beer.

It had been many months since I'd had anything as tasty and I wanted to stretch it out, take little sips and allow the pleasure to last longer—but Prune-face was determined not to let that happen. Every time I paused, she commanded, "Drink!" So I did...and truthfully, I enjoyed every gulp. After she stomped out with the empty can, I nodded off and it was the best sleep I'd had in ages.

After only two short weeks of torturing Prune-face with my daily request for a Budweiser, a solemn-faced Charlie Meade came walking into my room. His shoulders were hunched a bit more than usual and he wasn't smiling. "We've got a problem," he said. Then he went on to explain how my insurance coverage had reached its maximum, "Baptist Memorial won't let a patient without insurance stay here, so we're going to have to find a new place—a hospital that doesn't require insurance."

My mind was instantly flooded with the fear that I would end up in some kind of nursing home, flat on my back forever, with no hope of rehabilitation. The expression on my face probably reflected my thoughts. Charlie sat down on the edge of my bed, "Don't worry," he said placing his hand over mine, "I've already located another hospital. It's right here in Jacksonville."

"A hospital that takes people without insurance?"

"They'll take you because you're only seventeen."

"What kind of hospital is..."

"Hope Haven, it's a children's hospital, you'll get good care and—"

"A children's hospital?" I echoed in disbelief, "I'm not a kid! I haven't been since I was nine. For the past eight years I've led the life of an adult and—"

"I realize that, but without insurance coverage our options are pretty limited. Hope Haven is a good hospital and although you've made some improvement, you're not ready to go home. You need to be in a place where you'll get nursing care and help with rehabilitation."

I couldn't argue with that.

"I've spoken with the folks in admission," Charlie said, "and they've assured me you'll be placed in a private or semi-private room." He paused a moment and gave me the mischievous grin I'd come to love, "If it's a private room, maybe you can find a nurse willing to sneak you an occasional cigarette or beer."

Two days later I was to be moved to Hope Haven. I was in my room waiting for the transport team when a new orderly poked his head in my door and asked, "Are you Nancy Lynn Jones, the patient scheduled for radiation?"

"I haven't been a Jones for over ten years," I answered laughing out loud. He moved on and I heard him repeat the question at the doorway of the room next to mine. *Jones...now that certainly brings back memories...*

On the first day of school, mothers generally send their children off with new shoes, freshly scrubbed faces and a handkerchief tucked into their pocket. Mine scooted me out the door without my name. Once the teacher settled the children into their seats, she began roll call. "Tommy Brown?"

"Present," a voice called out and the boy's hand shot up.

"Sara Jean Foster?"

Another answer, another hand shot up identifying a tall girl wearing glasses.

I waited as the teacher called name after name. For every name there was a voice and a raised hand, except when she called out Barbara Jones. "Barbara Jones?" she repeated a bit louder. Still no response. "Is there a Barbara Jones present in this classroom?" she asked with obvious annoyance. We all looked around the room waiting for a girl named Barbara Jones to raise her hand. Still there was no response, so she moved on to the last few names. Somehow she had forgotten to call my name—Lani Verner.

Shortly before the dismissal bell rang, the teacher handed me a folded piece of paper and said, "Please give this to your mother." Moments later my first day of school ended and I scampered out of the building with the other children.

Once I rounded the corner and could no longer be seen, I unfolded the paper. The teacher had assumed that like most of the other children I could not yet read, but I had been reading ever since I was four. Inside the note was a single sentence, written in heavy black script—'Why does your daughter not know her own name?'

Dummy... I thought as I refolded the note, *you're the one who doesn't know my name!*

That night, Mother and I talked for a long while. She told me Barbara Lani Jones *was* actually my name, a name she'd given me in case I chose not to be called Lani. "Lani is such an exotic name," she said, "I was afraid you might someday resent it, and that's why I added the Barbara." She laughed, "I guess it was a mistake because you're obviously not a Barbara! And, as for the Jones..." her face was lined with regret, "well, that was your father's name; after he left I went back to using Verner and just called us all Verners." Once the story was told, Mother's eyes grew watery and she gave a mournful sigh, "Lani dear, that silly name wasn't my only mistake, I've made so many... Blease Jones, your father, did things..." Mother's voice faded into nothingness and she sat there for the longest time without saying anything more.

The next morning she took me down to City Hall and filed an application to legally change our names to Verner. I would then and forevermore be Lani Verner. With a few strokes of a pen, I had taken on the Verner name held by my sister Dottie Lee and my brother Scott. In my childish mind I thought perhaps this would make us a family—a family woven together like a single bolt of cloth, seamless end to end. But Cole Blease Jones had left too much heartache behind, so we remained a patchwork quilt—mismatched remnants of people placed side by side and stitched together with threads too fragile to ever repair broken lives.

As a child, I couldn't understand why my sister seemed to resent me as she did. It was not just the sibling rivalry or the bickering commonplace in many families, but a hard-edged anger that slammed into me with a heavy hand. In time I came to realize it wasn't me she hated, it was my father. I was simply the spawn he left behind.

My sister was ten years older than I, so by the time I was nine, she was married and a year later she and her husband moved out of the house and were gone. Although my heart carried the scars of her hatred, she left me with few other memories. Scott was eleven years older and sometimes tried to play the part of my big brother or father, but a household with an abusive father and a self-absorbed mother doesn't offer much in the way of role models.

I carried all those memories with me when I was transferred to Hope Haven. Just as Charlie had promised, I was given a large private room—which might sound luxurious, but was actually so lonely I wanted to scream. Since Hope Haven was a state-run facility—a Shriners' Hospital, there were far fewer nurses bustling from place to place and at times I could go for hours without seeing a living soul. Before a full day had passed, I was bored and lonely; so lonely I would have welcomed a visit from my Baptist Memorial nemesis, Prune-face.

The physical therapy I had so eagerly anticipated turned out to be one or two trips a week to the therapy room where I was lifted onto a tilt table which put weight on my leg bones to prevent the loss of calcium. For the remainder of the week, I spent endless hours alone in my room. There were very few visitors, no television, no radio, and I was not yet capable of holding a book or turning the pages.

Being alone was nothing new, I'd learned to cope with it as a kid. After we moved from the big house into the one room guest cottage, I was almost always alone. Mother was generally working, and Scott and Dit were busy with their friends or school. Barely four years old with nothing else to do, I pulled a box of books from beneath the bed and began sounding out words until I could eventually read a story from start to finish. That opened up a whole new world, a world of fantastic places and exciting friends, a world I could visit anytime I wanted—a world without anger, resentment or limitations. With all the books I'd read, I had never come across the term Astral Projection; but locked in the loneliness of that private room, I found myself lifted into it.

I discovered it was possible to close my eyes and will my spirit to travel far and wide, to other countries, and other times. How many of those travels were resurrected memories is impossible to say, but I wasn't limited to the times and places I had read about. On days when the hallway was silent, I'd drift away to find my spirit self standing among the veiled women in the marketplace of Algiers, or painting pictures on the wall of what I knew to be the inside of a pyramid. I heard the roar of lions in the Roman Coliseum, and saw myself navigating the canals of Venice. Although I had no previous knowledge of the monasteries of Tibet, I saw myself kneeling in silent prayer, and tasting strange foods served in earthenware bowls as I sat alongside the cave dwellers of Mexico and Peru. I learned to fly like an eagle with the wind lifting me to heights I'd never before imagined and looking down I saw the earth as a borderless universe of forests and oceans. I wasn't psychotic. I was simply filling the empty hours of the day in the most exciting way I could envision. One of my favorite travels was a return to Cuba, the place where Mother and I had once taken a vacation...a time filled with fun instead of the controversy that so often clouded our relationship.

It was the summer of 1953, Batista was the President of Cuba and Havana was the glittering center of nightlife. Grandma Jones, my father's mother, had recently passed away and left me a small inheritance, money Mother viewed as ours, money she decided to spend as she saw fit since I was only twelve at the time. Her first priority was a trip to Cuba, "A vacation is exactly what we need," she said, and booked us on the next boat to sail from Miami. In Havana, I saw my first strip tease dancer, learned Spanish from a Chinaman, and helped Mother pick a number of winners at Jai Alai and the Greyhound Races. With the money she won at the races, Mother chartered a small plane and shuttled us off to the other side of the island and the luxurious Hotel Internationale at Varadero Beach. It was there that I encountered Lucky Lucciano. Looking back, I realize what a naïve kid I really was, and fortunate, I suppose, to have made it back in one piece.

It started with a simple swim. Mother and I were sitting on the beach when I noticed a beautiful mahogany yacht anchored off shore. "I'm going to swim out to that boat and back," I announced. Mother glanced up for a moment then, unconcerned, she turned back to her magazine. "Okay," she said, "just don't be gone too long."

In the water distance has a way of tricking you, things look close, but as you start swimming toward them they move farther and farther away. That's precisely what happened with the yacht, and by the time I reached it, I was thoroughly exhausted. Attached to the side of the ship was a floating dock with two small outboard motor boats. I climbed onto the dock and sat there to rest. I had barely caught my breath when an angry voice yelled, "Hey, what the hell are you doing here?" I looked up and found myself staring into the barrel of a very large gun.

"Me?" I said trembling, "I'm not doing anything. I'm just taking a rest." My words were popping out faster and faster. "If I'm bothering you, I'll leave right now. I don't mind, I can swim back to the beach. I didn't mean to—"

"Cut the lip kid. Stay right where you are and don't move a muscle! I'll be right back."

As he turned and disappeared from view, I thought about diving in and making my getaway, but I knew bullets could whiz through water and no matter how fast I was, his bullet would be faster. So I sat there, barely breathing and not moving a muscle. After what seemed like a very long time, he came back looking no friendlier than he had before.

"Get up here kid," he snarled.

I'm no dummy and, although I had never had a gun pointed at me before, I didn't need to be told you don't argue with a man holding a gun. I obediently scrambled up the stairs from the dock onto the deck of the ship. The first thing I saw was a group of ladies strolling around in their altogether— high-heel shoes and sunglasses were the only adornments they wore. On the chaise lounge there was a heavy-set dark-haired man smoking a cigar. He was not naked, but seemed to be the main focus of the ladies' attention.

He eyeballed me for a few seconds, then waved me over to the chaise. "So kid," he said, "What are you doing here and who sent you?"

"Sent me?" My eyes were the size of saucers, "Nobody sent me. My mother's on the beach waiting for me to come back. She'd be furious if she knew I swam out this far; but the thing is I didn't know it was this far. I started swimming and—"

"Okay, okay, I got it." He gave a gusty laugh. "So, you thirsty? Want a Coca-Cola or something?"

"Yes sir," I answered for fear of offending him, "I would love to have a Coca-Cola."

He slapped one of the naked ladies on the behind, "Charlene, get the kid a Coca-Cola."

"Sure thing," she toddled off in her high heels with her behind wiggling side to side.

Compared to the guy who'd ordered me off the dock, the cigar man was actually quite nice and while I stood there drinking my Coca-Cola we talked about where I came from and how my mother and I were enjoying our stay in Cuba. When I finished the soda, he asked if I was okay to swim back. I answered yes and he told me to get going so my mama wouldn't be worried. I was going to tell him that Mother never allowed anyone to call her Mama, but then I figured some things are best left alone.

When I arrived back at the beach, Mother said, "You were gone a long time. Did you have a nice swim?"

"Yes," I answered and said nothing more for fear of being given a lecture.

On the way to dinner that evening, I slipped away from Mother long enough to ask the clerk at the front desk who the mahogany yacht anchored in the harbor belonged to.

"Lucky Lucciano," he answered reverently, then he whispered a hushed warning, "I wouldn't go anywhere near that yacht if I were you."

The following morning, we started for home and I was a bit relieved to be leaving the mahogany yacht behind. I never did tell Mother about my encounter with the man reputed to be the Mafia kingpin who had brought American financed gambling to Cuba.

With little else to occupy myself, my spiritual trips through time and space became a favorite pastime. I could go anywhere I wanted to go. I could walk, I could run, I could fly. Traveling through time and space, I was able to turn my isolated room into a reasonably pleasant environment but, unfortunately, not one where my rehabilitation could move forward.

Eventually, I was transferred downstairs to a large ward with over forty beds, every one of them occupied by a small child. With me completely bedridden and most of the children fairly mobile, I was reminded of a comic strip where the sleeping giant is captured and tied down by the little people of Tiny Town. But blessings come in many types of disguises, and it was there among those miniature people that I found Smitty—the nurse destined to become my angel of recovery and newest best friend.

I continued to be plagued with bedsores and they grew consistently worse. Charlie, still overseeing my care, called in a plastic surgeon for skin grafts to repair them; but it was Smitty who eventually found the cure. She reached into her own pocket, bought high-potency vitamin C pills and began feeding them to me. Suddenly the bedsores began to improve. She then convinced Charlie I needed to get into a bathtub. Hope Haven had a special device for lifting severely disabled patients into the tub. Once that happened, the bedsores started to heal even more rapidly. "She's got potential," Smitty told Charlie, "...but she needs more aggressive therapy."

Doctor Meade nodded thoughtfully, "You're right," he said, then he walked out without a word of what he was planning to do.

Smitty had her own plans, and luckily those plans included treating me like the adult I was. When the ward had quieted down and most of the children asleep, Smitty would sit by my bed and hold a cigarette for me. I came to view Smitty as an angel of mercy, yet she terrified many of the children in the ward—which to me seemed rather funny. Perhaps it was because Smitty had been an Army nurse, she could look and act tough when tough was needed.

On the eve of my eighteenth birthday, I thought back to the partying I'd done for my seventeenth, and began to dread the next day. Smitty, who had her finger on the pulse of everything that happened, didn't say a word about my birthday, but that evening she had the kids in bed earlier than usual. "Lights Out," she commanded, then silently rolled my bed down the hall toward the medication room. *At least I'll get a cigarette.* When Smitty pushed open the door and wheeled me in, there was Lucy McDaniel, my swim team pal, and on the table—a six pack of Budweiser, a full pack of cigarettes and a pizza. We spent the evening laughing about old times, eating pizza and drinking beer; and that, I can honestly say, was one of the most memorable birthdays I have ever experienced. It's odd how falling to the bottom of life's pit enables you to appreciate things so much more—the thing I had learned to appreciate was not a thing at all, it was people. Although I once longed for the solitude of the Tomoka Game Preserve, I now knew that I liked people. I liked them much more than I did before my accident. The people didn't change, I did. I took time to see them, to listen to what they had to say, to feel their joy and sometimes their anguish within the stillness of my own body. The truth is that without the strength and physical capabilities I had been born with, I was growing into a bigger and more complete human being.

Not long after my birthday, Smitty began to get me up and into an old-fashioned wooden wheelchair—the kind of chair that reclined so far back you could almost believe you were lying down. Even with the chair in a fully reclined position, it was too much for me. After being flat on my back for nearly a year, my heart had lost the ability to pump blood into my head when it was elevated; so every time Smitty put me in the wheelchair, my eyesight blacked out. I could not see a thing. Not light, not people, not my own hand in front of my face, yet I was still conscious. Ignoring that, Smitty still insisted on getting me up and into that wheelchair. She would show up with the chair every few days and insist we go for another outing; and every time we did, we had the same conversation.

"This is ridiculous," I'd insist, "My vision is totally blacked out when I'm sitting up."

"You're not sitting up, you're sort-of reclining!"

"I still can't see a thing," I'd say laughingly.

"You will in time. Work on it."

Once Smitty got me into the chair, she'd wheel me outside for some fresh air and sunshine. "Just look at that glorious sun!" she'd say, knowing full well I couldn't see a thing.

"I can't see the sun."

"Try harder." She'd push the chair a few yards further along the walkway, "Okay, now do you see those beautiful red flowers?"

"I still can't see anything but black."

"Open your damn eyes and look," she'd laugh.

I'd insist that my eyes were open and she'd stop pushing the chair long enough to come around and check, "Yep, they're open," she'd say, "So when the hell are you gonna admit to seeing those damn red flowers?"

It was a game—a game where we'd tease each other so fiercely that we'd often return from our walk laughing hysterically. Sometimes when she asked about the flowers, I'd tease back and say, "Oh yes, now I see the red flowers and they are absolutely beautiful."

"Do you really see them?" Smitty would ask excitedly, and I'd shake my head no then we'd both crack up laughing. "I thought you were putting me on," she'd say, "because those flowers are yellow!" For me it was so much more than therapy or a game, it was a portion of the day when I laughed, when I felt human, when I could look ahead and see that somewhere down the road there was a life for me. I had moved past the torturous Stryker frame and the Crutchfield Tongs with sandbags hanging from my head, my bedsores were healing beautifully and although everything remained black as night when I was sitting in the wheelchair—I had progressed to being in a wheelchair!

One afternoon Charlie walked in with a grin that was a mile wide. "Good news," he said and plopped down on the side of my bed. "I didn't want to tell you this until I determined whether or not we had a chance at it, but things are looking good."

"What's looking good?" I asked excitedly.

"I've been talking to the people at the Florida State Office of Vocational Rehabilitation, trying to get them to provide funding for you to go to the Rusk Institute in New York. Outside of the Veteran's Hospitals, the Rusk Institute is the only facility that offers specialized programs for people with spinal cord injuries."

"Are they going to do it?"

"There's a good chance. This department has never before accepted a quadriplegic into the vocational rehabilitation program, so this would be a first for them."

I waited for the other shoe to fall.

"Don't look so apprehensive," Charlie said, "I think they're pretty well convinced that you're a special case and well worth the cost of rehabilitation, but they want to send a counselor over to interview you."

"So when this counselor shows up, am I supposed to say I see the flowers?" I asked, winking at Smitty who was standing within earshot and laughing uncontrollably.

"I don't get it," Charlie said looking confused.

"A personal joke," I answered and gave Smitty another wink.

A few days later the counselor arrived and spent several hours taking me through various aptitude, personality and IQ tests—questioning, I suppose, whether or not I was mentally and intellectually worth rehabilitating.

A few weeks later, Charlie told me I'd been accepted and would be transferred to the Rusk Institute the following week. I accepted the news with both joy and sadness. I was thrilled to be moving to what, hopefully, would become the next rung on my ladder to rehabilitation and yet I was heartbroken to leave Smitty behind. She was a gruff old army nurse with a heart of gold, a person the little kids saw as fearsome, but someone I knew to be the best friend I ever had...excluding perhaps my beloved Duke and Dusty.

That night sleep was a long time in coming as I lay in bed thinking about the trip to New York and remembering the last time I'd been there...

Seven

I suppose you might say my fascination with New York began five years earlier in Philadelphia. It happened the summer I was thirteen years old. Mother booked a compartment for me on the train that ran from Miami to New York. Duke and I boarded the train in Daytona and stepped off in Philadelphia. This was a new world, a world bigger than any I'd known before. I could feel the door to my life opening wide. I was there to spend the summer with my big brother—the brother I continually tried to see as the heroic champion of my tangled up life. There was no question Scott looked the part of a champion. He was tall, blond, handsome, charming and successful—but, he was also married. Instead of accepting his wife Lora as the quasi-tolerant sister-in-law she was, I saw her as competition for my brother's attention. I was thirteen years old. My father had abandoned me, my sister hated me, and my mother's life seemed to be one long search for a man to replace her lost love. Scott, it seemed, was my last hope—for what I wasn't sure—perhaps to find myself, or the place in life where I belonged.

Lora was a special needs teacher in the Philadelphia School System. Since she worked with children from foreign countries, she was often preoccupied with her students and studying other languages. That's when Scott and I would take the train into Manhattan to see a Broadway show or wander through the antique bookstores of Greenwich Village. I didn't feel like a kid when I was walking beside my brother, I felt grown-up and important. But then there were those other evenings when Lora was at home; she and Scott talked about the things of their life, things that did not include me. When Lora was there I felt like a kid again, and the thought of her being as intellectually intimate with my brother as I imagined myself to be sizzled through my blood and caused me to turn moody and resentful. I was lonely and desperate to connect with someone, to be a part of a family. I wanted a meaningful relationship of some sort, but of what sort, I had no idea. When they began nuzzling noses or whispering secrets, I'd hook the leash to Duke's collar and off we'd go. We walked through Rittenhouse Square, listened to musicians in the park and spent endless hours at the Café Rodin, a coffee house where people who were bright and articulate like my brother sat and discussed the failures of the world. I loved the coffee houses, the folksinging, the people and their stories; but perhaps most of all I loved the way being there made me feel. Although I was barely a teenager, I looked and acted much older so I was accepted as one of them. I belonged! I was like a finger in a glove, warm, cozy and comfortable just like all the other fingers around me. I fit! In school I was a cheerleader, one of the popular kids, a girl with a number of different boyfriends; but that life circled around me and never quite settled in or became part of who I was. It wasn't that I considered myself better than my classmates; I was just different, I was the plaid shirt in a laundry load of pastels. This new world, this world of coffeehouses and intellectuals, this was my world, I was certain of it.

The year I turned fifteen, was the last year I'd spend my summer in Philadelphia with Scott; and to say it was turbulent would be a gross understatement. Mother and I were constantly at odds with one another and having my own car only served to make me more independent than ever. I had little patience for school, and hated the classes. From the age of four I'd been self-taught, so the slow pace of classroom learning was boring and frustrating. In the midst of a social studies class, I'd find my thoughts wandering back to conversations overheard at the Café Rodin. Classrooms, it seemed, were for learning about the past, but I was busy thinking about the future. With every passing day I became more disenchanted and my number of truancies grew. By the end of my eighth school year, I barely had the one hundred and eighty days of attendance required to move on to the ninth grade. When Duke and I boarded the train for Philadelphia that summer, I was like a ripe persimmon waiting to burst open.

More than ever, I wanted Scott to spend time with ME. I wanted him to see me as a mature adult, a partner who could join in the philosophical conversations at the coffee houses, someone who appreciated the theatre, museums, fine art, sculpture, and literary works. I wanted Lora to disappear, so it could be just my brother and me. Of course that didn't happen. Instead they snuggled together on the sofa with me sitting in the chair alone. One night, we were sitting in those same positions when Lora stretched her arms above her head and yawned, "I'm a bit sleepy," she said, nudging Scott playfully, "perhaps we'd better go to bed early."

"That's a great idea," he answered, curling her into his arms.

She stood and then he stood and as they walked toward the bedroom, Scott glanced back at me, "Help yourself to whatever you want," he said, "Lora and I are going to practice making babies." He laughed and closed the door behind him. It was a lighthearted comment that floated through the air and landed on me like the blade of a guillotine.

For a long while, I remained in the chair feeling sad, neglected, and orphaned almost. "You're the only one," I told Duke, "you're the only one who truly cares about me." I nuzzled my face into the thick fur of his neck and sniffled. But I was fifteen years old, and at fifteen you have an extremely wide range of emotions—what began as anguish, suddenly changed to defiance. "To hell with them all," I whispered to Duke, "If they don't want me, I don't want them!" Watching them walk away, I began to realize I hated the thought of marriage and babies. I especially hated the thought of their marriage. I'm never getting married, I told myself, never having babies, no sir, that's not for me! Suddenly, I knew I had to leave, get away from there, and move on. What had once been an open door was now a stifling box. I no longer belonged!

It was almost three AM when I eased open Scott's bedroom door, reached into the top dresser drawer and took all of the cash he had hidden there. I lifted his car keys from the tray atop the dresser then tiptoed from the room closing the door behind me.

I left the apartment with Duke, a small bag of clothes and one-hundred and thirty dollars. I had no idea where I was going, but I knew I had to go. Since we'd had so much fun in New York, I figured that was as good a place as any. The coffee houses beckoned to me. Unfortunately, I arrived in town at the height of the morning rush hour, when the city was jam-packed with horn blowing cars and pedestrians who haphazardly marched themselves into oncoming traffic. I inched around Manhattan for a maddening two hours, realized it would be impossible to park or go back to revisit the places I found so interesting—the coffee houses and the museums— so I circled around and backtracked through the Lincoln Tunnel. When I surfaced on the other side of the Hudson River, I headed south and passed Philadelphia without giving it a second glance. I drove south, hoping to eventually find an east-west highway that would take me to California. Even though I'd never before been to California, I began to think maybe that was where I was meant to be.

As I sailed past town after town, my thoughts drifted back to Scott. Once he discovered I was gone, he'd probably have the police out looking for me. If he did, they'd spot me in a minute—a deeply-tanned sun-bleached blonde with a large German shepherd in the back seat of a Volkswagen convertible didn't exactly blend into the environment. I thought about what needed to be done, pulled off the highway and started searching for a hairdresser. Three hours later, my own mother would not have recognized me. I left Philadelphia with long blond tresses and emerged from the beauty shop with jet black hair chopped into a pixie cut—I vaguely resembled Audrey Hepburn in the movie Roman Holiday. Satisfied that I was no longer recognizable, I climbed back into the Volkswagen and took to the highway.

Halfway through Delaware, the car sputtered, gave the gasp of a dying elephant, and rolled to a stop. Duke and I climbed out of the car and before I could determine what my next move would be, a young soldier in a green Ford pulled up in back of us. "You need help?" he asked stepping out of his car.

I recognized him as the fellow who had been flirting with me along the highway. He would speed up, pass me and smile, then he'd slow down and I'd pass him—another smile. It was a game I'd been enjoying because he was rather cute.

"Thanks, I sure could use some help," I answered.

"Name's Ted Conway," He said and smiled.

"Lani Verner," I answered and smiled back. "Thanks for stopping. I have no idea what's wrong with this thing, I was driving along and then all of a sudden it made this wheezing noise and stopped dead."

"Well, let's take a look," Ted popped open the back end of Scott's Volkswagen and peered in at the motor. "When's the last time it was serviced?" he asked.

I shrugged, "I have no idea. It's my brother's car."

"A wheezing noise, huh?"

I nodded.

"Could be it's just out of gas. I'll drain a little out of my car and try to prime the carburetor." He shook the last few drops of Coca-cola out of a paper cup and then filled it with gas he siphoned from his tank. "Okay, maybe this will do it—you try to start the car while I prime the carb." As Ted was pouring gas into the engine, it exploded. He fell to the ground with burns on his face and both hands.

"We've got to get you to a hospital," I screamed and in typical Lani fashion started moving. I eased the soldier into the passenger seat of his car. Duke then jumped into the back and off we went.

"I'm stationed at New Castle," he groaned, "Get me to the base, there's a hospital there."

Instead, I stopped the first passerby I saw and asked for directions to the closest emergency room. Whizzing through two red lights, I pulled up to the entrance minutes later. Ted was quickly examined by an emergency room doctor who bandaged the burns. "What you really should do," the doctor said, "is get this soldier back to his base in New Castle. Some of these burns are serious. He needs to see a doctor at the base hospital."

I drove like a maniac, but in less than an hour we pulled up in front of the base hospital. He was taken immediately. I parked the car, left Duke to guard it, and followed the soldier into the emergency room. "I brought in Private Conway," I told the nurse, "how's he doing?"

"The doctor is with him now," She motioned to a row of plastic chairs, "Have a seat and I'll call you as soon as we know anything."

I sat and waited. As I waited I remembered Scott's car—if the police thought it was abandoned, they'd search out the owner. Once they found Scott and told him where his car was, he'd come looking for me and he wasn't going to be happy. I went to a telephone booth, called a local garage and asked them to pick up the car and store it until I could get there. Then I returned to the plastic chair and continued to wait. Daylight drifted into darkness, and about ten-thirty, the nurse called out, "Is there a Lani here?"

"I'm Lani," I answered. She led me through a maze of rooms to where my soldier friend was resting. His hands and face were heavily bandaged.

"Looks like I'm gonna be here for a few days," he said. "Can you take care of my car till I get out?"

"It's the least I can do," I said, "I'm so sorry to have—"

"It's not your fault, I was showing off. The truth is I didn't have a clue what was wrong with your car, but when a guy sees a girl like you..."

We both sighed.

That night I found an inexpensive motel and checked in as Lani Jones in case anyone came looking for me. I felt safe with Duke so when I crawled into bed I fell into a deep sleep. Using

Ted's car I went back and forth to the base hospital three times a day visiting him. "You could have taken my car and left me there," he said, "Thanks for not doing that."

"You've got to be kidding," I smiled, "I would never do a thing like that! You're such a nice guy and kind enough to stop and try to help me."

A week later, he was released. I handed him the keys to his car, thanked him again, and gently kissed him goodbye. For that whole week I had held tight to my anger; I'd sworn to never again see my family since they considered me so inconsequential. But after a week of walking in and out of a hospital, I began to realize that every life has meaning and Mother would no doubt be worried. Yes, I felt neglected and all too often ignored, but the sad truth was we were still a patchwork family, each of us connected to the other by a few loose stitches. Scott was my brother, but he was never really my champion. I had created an image that was impossible for him to live up to. It was the same thing Mother had done to him. For a week I tried to tell myself no one loved me, but all the while, I knew in my heart it was not true. Mother loved me; in her own strange unconventional way she more than loved me, she depended on me. Scott loved me too, and he tried to help me find my way in life; but truthfully speaking, my brother spent most of his life in search of himself, so there was pitifully little he could do to give me the guidance I needed.

I picked up the telephone and dialed home.

"Hello Mother," I said apologetically, "I'm sorry I haven't called before this, I know you must have been really worried..."

"Of course I was worried! Worried to death! Scott's been frantic! You have no idea of the anguish you've caused all of us! Where in the world are you? Are you okay?"

"I'm fine. I'm in Delaware, but Scott's car quit on me."

"I'm thankful that it did! Stay right where you are," Mother said, "I'll call Scott and have him come and get you."

"I don't think that's a good idea. You see there was this problem with his car..."

"I don't give a damn about his car! I've been worried sick about you Lani, and if your brother knows what's good for him, he'll get down there and get you, immediately!

After filling in a few sketchy details, I told Mother I was at the New Castle train station and agreed to wait there for my brother. "One thing he should probably know," I said, "is that I look a bit different."

"Different?" Mother replied with a nervous twitter in her voice, "Different how? Lani, what have you done now?"

"I —uh—colored my hair. It's black now. And short."

"Oh dear," Mother sighed, with that all too familiar tone of frustration.

Several hours later, Scott arrived at the train station to rescue me. Because I had Duke and did not now have the luxury of a compartment, we had to ride back to Philadelphia in a boxcar loaded with bales of hay and sacks of mail.

Mother arrived in Philadelphia two days later and after a series of lengthy discussions and an enormous amount of negotiation, everyone agreed that I should go back to New York City and attend The Semple Finishing School for Girls. Mother considered it a reasonable compromise and the most appropriate place for me to finish my schooling. *Hello, New York!*

The evening before I was to be transferred from Jacksonville's Hope Haven to the Rusk Institute in New York, Mother arrived at the hospital. "Since you'll be traveling on a commercial airline," she said, "I'm going to fly up with you."

"A commercial airline?" I gasped, "I thought I'd be on a stretcher."

"There's no medical transport available, but Doctor Meade has assured me that you'll be just fine on a commercial flight."

"Fine? How can I be fine? I black out every time I sit up!"

"The flight attendants are aware of that Lani, and they're going to recline your seat as soon as you are on board."

After an emotional goodbye with Smitty, Mother and I were loaded into an ambulance and taken to the airport. I was lifted onto the plane by stretcher, and then moved to the seat where, even though reclined, I immediately blacked out. For the remainder of the trip I saw nothing, but Mother and I spoke at length about my forthcoming rehabilitation.

When we arrived at LaGuardia, I was loaded into a second ambulance which whizzed along East River Drive and deposited me at the Rusk Institute on First Avenue. Even from my stretcher I could see the building was large, modern, and very impressive. It differed from Hope Haven in a multitude of ways, but the first thing I noticed was how the nurses scuttled from place to place with snappy steps and little conversation. After the trip I was totally exhausted and had no interest in seeing much of anything. Once in my bed, I wanted nothing but a long and blissful nap. Before I could close my eyes, a nurse came through the door pushing a modern straight-backed wheelchair with horizontal pegs circling both wheels. "Someone will be here in a few minutes to help you into the chair," she said and bustled out.

I wanted to explain it had been a long trip and I was much too tired to get up now, but, before I could suggest tomorrow might be better, she was gone.

When the orderly arrived to lift me into the wheelchair, I begged, pleaded, and cajoled him into allowing me the afternoon to rest. "It's almost five o'clock," I said wearily, "Can't this wait until tomorrow?" After a fair bit of wheedling, he gave a shrug and sauntered out. Moments later the nurse stormed back in; "What do you think this is—a rest home?" she said sharply. "Tomorrow morning you will get up and there will be no more excuses!" *Smitty's concept of tough was nothing compared to this!* Minutes later I was sound asleep.

It seemed as though I had barely closed my eyes when I heard a voice say, "Hey there sleepyhead." I opened one eye and saw

Scott standing there. Beside him was Lora, holding Jordan, their new baby daughter.

"Scott planned to surprise you at the airport," Mother said, "but they got delayed—"

"We started out early enough," Scott added apologetically, "but by the time we'd packed the car...and then at the airport we couldn't find the correct gate."

I looked at my brother and smiled. Perhaps for the first time in my life I saw him exactly as he was—no longer my champion, but a husband, a father, and a son who unfortunately disappointed Mother all too often.

The next morning, before breakfast, a nurse and orderly arrived to lift me into the wheelchair—not the reclining wheelchair Smitty had used, but the wheelchair they'd brought in the night before; a straight-backed chair that would force me to sit absolutely upright. Before I had a chance to explain my problem, everything went black. Hoping to catch the nurse before she hurried out again, I blurted, "I black out when I sit up!"

"That's not uncommon," she answered calmly, "You have orthostatic hypertension, it's a blindness caused by the drop in blood pressure when a patient goes from lying down to sitting up. In time you'll regain your vision, but for now, you'll have to work with what you've got."

I heard the clatter of trays and caught the smell of bacon. At first I thought 'working with what I've got' meant she would feed me breakfast then wheel me through the garden for a bit of fresh air and sunshine as Smitty had done. That vision was rapidly dispelled when she said, "Breakfast is on your table, so wheel yourself over and get ready to start eating."

"Wheel myself over? How? This is the first time I've ever been in a real wheelchair! You've got to show me what I'm supposed to do and how to do it! Right now I can't see a thing. How am I supposed to eat when I can't hold a spoon?"

I felt her slip a strap over my hand, "This device," she said, "will enable you to feed yourself. The spoon handle fits into it and you lift the food to your mouth using your arms." I felt her slide something into the device she had fastened to my hand.

"I can't see the table, the tray or the plate," I said turning panicky, "If I can't see where the food is, how am I supposed to feed myself?"

"You'll be amazed at what you can do once you put your mind to it," she answered, and then I heard the flip flop of her feet leaving the room.

For a few moments I sat there dumfounded, more confused than afraid. The situation was, in my mind, ridiculous. Did the nurse actually expect me to find the table where that breakfast was? Even if I could follow the scent of food, how was I supposed to get it from the plate into my mouth? I had never even seen whatever strange device she'd fastened onto my hand. Still, like it or not, this was where I was and I had to deal with it. I was hungry and alone. I found myself wishing Mother was there. She could have explained the device on my hand. She could have guided me to the table. And, at the very least, she could have encouraged me. But Mother wasn't there. She was in New York but not with me. At that moment, when I could have used her help, she was at Aunt Polly's Greenwich Village apartment—no doubt sipping cream-laden coffee and reveling in the stories my Broadway actress aunt had to tell.

If I wanted to eat, I had to feed myself. I thought back to the night before and tried to picture the set up of the room—the head of the bed was against the back wall, the bed in the right rear corner of the room, the window to the right, the door behind me, and my night table on the right hand side of the bed. But, there were four beds in the room. I stretched out my arm trying to get a sense of where I was, but there was nothing within reach. I lowered my arms and pushed those strange looking pegs forward using my wrists. It took all the strength I could muster, but after a few moments, the wheelchair actually rolled forward. For the first time in over a year, I had moved myself from one spot to another. It was an incredible experience, an achievement that far outpaced anything I had ever done before. I could feel a huge smile creasing my face. I can do this, I thought, I can and I will!

Following the smell of bacon, I edged my way toward the bed and kept going until I found the night table. I felt around trying to locate first the tray, then the plate and finally the food. Once I knew the dish was directly in front of me, I began to clumsily spoon food into my mouth, spilling more than I swallowed. After what seemed like an eternity of struggling to eat, I was exhausted, but I had done it. Although I had never wheeled myself anywhere before, I had found the table, located the food, and even managed to get a portion of it into my mouth. With a certain sense of achievement, I pushed myself back from the table and waited for someone to come and lift me back into the bed.

"Well, I see you found your way to breakfast," a voice finally said. "Evidence of it is splattered all over you and the table." She laughed, "Did you manage to get anything into your mouth?"

I recognized the voice as that of the nurse. "A little bit," I answered sheepishly, "but it was exhausting, I'm ready for a nap."

"Nap?" She laughed, "There's no napping. You've got your first therapy class coming up, and you've got to wheel yourself down there."

"I can't wheel myself anywhere," I said, "I can't see!" I waited for her to volunteer to take me but there was nothing but silence. "I'm not trying to be uncooperative," I explained, "but I've been totally immobile for over a year. I can't see anything at all when I'm sitting up. I'm totally blacked out."

"I know that," she finally answered.

"Well then, how can you expect me to wheel myself somewhere when I can't even see where I'm going?"

"That's just an excuse. At the Rusk Institute there are no excuses. You're going to have to learn to wheel yourself to wherever you need to be," she replied unsympathetically, "The purpose of rehabilitation is to teach a person to do things without assistance."

"But I can't see…" I argued, "This is all so new to me. How can a blind person go somewhere when they can't see where they're going?" I gave a slight giggle, "Have you got a seeing eye dog I can use?"

"I've already explained this, the blackouts are temporary. In time you'll regain your sight. Until then, just wheel yourself into the hallway and wait there." This was a no-nonsense nurse who was firm in her resolve. She made it perfectly clear that I was not going back to bed and was expected to wheel myself out into the hallway—even if it meant my bumping into things and possibly even people.

Inching forward along the wall with a protruding elbow and trying to feel my way with my hands, I maneuvered the wheelchair into the hallway and sat there; listening to everything, seeing nothing, and hoping I did not look like an idiot parked in the middle of the hallway. The morning seemed endless as I listened to people whizzing past me. They had things to do, places to be, and no time for chit-chat. Oh how I wished I could return to my bed, drop my head onto the pillow and go to sleep.

When lunchtime finally rolled around, the breakfast routine was repeated. I gobbled the food as quickly as possible then pleaded for time to take a short nap. "This is all so new," I told the nurse, "I haven't sat upright for over a year, in one day I'll never be able to…"

"I'll allow it this once," she finally said, "but after today…"

Rehabilitation was nothing like I expected; but then the move to rehabilitation had happened so quickly, I'm not certain what I had actually expected. Once I was back in my bed, I began to think—other people have gone through this exact same experience, other people just like me. If they can do it, I can! My competitive nature was starting to rear its head. I closed my eyes and drifted off, imagining how I would one day, roll down the long hallway and out the front door of the Rusk Institute.

The rehabilitation day ended at four o'clock and visitors were not permitted until then. When Mother arrived a few minutes after four, I was sound asleep and continued to sleep until six o'clock when the nurse woke me and said it was time to get back in the wheelchair.

"Lani dear," Mother said, "I understand you're sitting up for meals now. That's wonderful, darling. You're such a strong little soldier..."

At that precise moment, I knew I wasn't strong. I was still weak and vulnerable...but that was going to change. 'Don't be a wimp,' the nurse had implied. She'd thought of me as a wimp— me, Lani Verner, the girl who was afraid of nothing. I knew my hard work was just beginning. I was facing a long and very difficult road—but at the end of that road, an Olympic torch burned brightly, it was up to me to get there. I looked at my mother's face. It was lined with years of hard work and struggling, yet somehow she had forged ahead and carried her three children with her. She was a survivor and I would be also. Moments later I was moved into the wheelchair and she faded to black along with everything else.

My vision eventually returned, not in a blazing flash of light, but in tiny increments of filtered glimpses, and only after days of sitting alone in the hallway, fumbling with food and blackness— terrible, endless blackness. As I sat there with my eyes veiled, I listened to the faceless voices and in time I came to know them. Once I could see, I began connecting faces with voices and recognized some of the people to whom I'd spoken. Some looked exactly as I'd imagined, while others were totally different than the image I'd created in my mind. One of the people who had passed my chair each day, a person who'd taken time to stop and ask how I was doing, was Doctor Howard Rusk, the man who founded the Institute of Physical Medicine and Rehabilitation. I was astounded to learn that Doctor Rusk knew every single patient by name. What a remarkable man. He had given birth to the concept of Rehabilitation Institute and was still involved in every facet of its operation. During that first week I accused the nurses of being thoughtless and lacking in compassion when they left me to sit alone in the hallway. But, as the days passed, I came to realize it was their way of forcing me into a faster and more effective rehabilitation program. Rehabilitation was definitely not for sissies!

Eight

The day after I regained my vision I was handed a different schedule of rehabilitation classes to attend. The hospital staff apparently "re-evaluated" me as I sat in the hallway blind as a bat and feeling foolish. *I may not have accomplished anything else, but I had learned to feed myself as a blind person… if blindness was ever added to my list of problems.* The classes began at eight o'clock in the morning and continued until four in the afternoon with only one scant hour for lunch. Although I'd been at the Institute for less than a week and was totally unfamiliar with the building, I was charged with wheeling myself from one class to another all morning, wheeling myself back to my room for lunch, then repeating the process for a different set of rehabilitation classes in the afternoon. It may not sound like much, but for someone who hadn't moved a muscle in over a year, it was absolutely exhausting. When lunchtime rolled around, I gobbled my food as rapidly as the contraption attached to my hand permitted and then unsuccessfully suggested the nurses allow me to use the remainder of my time for a nap. Prior to the accident, I was always on the go, living life, having fun, chasing another new adventure, but now the thought of plopping my head down on a pillow was deliciously desirable. I had to wonder if tough-gal Lani had indeed been replaced by a wimp.

The individual rehabilitation classes were one hour long and I managed to be late for every single one of them. My peg-handled mode of transportation was big, heavy, and hard to push—I was dealing with muscles that had atrophied from lack of use, so I struggled for every inch of ground gained. Plus, I was unfamiliar with the layout of the six story building and the dozens upon dozens of classrooms. "I'm late for my next class," I'd say to an orderly passing by, "would you mind wheeling me down there?"

But, their answer was always the same, "Sorry, the rule is patients have to get themselves to therapy classes." The orderly would move on and I'd be left to continue pushing those blasted pegs around and around until I finally got to where I was going.

"Sorry I'm late," I'd mumble and Sam, the range of motion therapist, would generally laugh. "You're making progress," he'd say, "Today you're only a half-hour late, yesterday it was forty minutes."

Only one person took pity on me and offered a smidgen of help and that person was Hank, the elevator operator. I'd roll into his elevator looking exhausted after a day of pushing pegs from place to place; then when the elevator came to a stop on the fifth floor, kind-hearted Hank would step out and give my chair a running shove that sent me sailing five or ten feet down the long corridor. "Thanks Hank," I'd call back, "You're wonderful!" When the chair slowed I'd go back to pushing the pegs. In those days, that was what I called a free-ride!

Mother remained in New York for the first few days and each day she came to visit at precisely four o'clock, but by the time she lowered herself into the chair alongside my bed, I was fast asleep. I generally slept straight through until suppertime. Then Mother and I would talk as I gobbled my food. Still learning to work with the cumbersome spoon attached to my hand, I spilled and splattered food all over myself and the table. "And to think of all the years I spent teaching you proper table manners," Mother said laughingly rolling her eyes. A moment later I managed to get one of those squishy green peas on my spoon and since I was still learning to maneuver my way through the feeding process, I inadvertently flipped the spoon backward and sent the pea arching through the air to land with a plop on Mother's beautiful white blouse. Ordinarily, I would have been mortified at doing such a thing to

Mother, but this time I laughed hysterically and oddly enough she saw the humor of it and laughed with me.

After two weeks at the Institute, I was getting around reasonably well. I could wheel myself from physical therapy to whirlpool and be less than ten minutes late. The therapies started with reasonably simple exercises where my arms and legs were lifted and stretched to work through the muscle atrophy and gain greater range of motion. After I had been flexed, extended and rotated in a multitude of directions, I wheeled myself off to occupational therapy class and learned to write using another strange, but equally appreciated, device constructed of fiberglass and molded to fit the shape of my hand. Once this glove-like gadget was on my hand, a pen was inserted into it and I could use the muscle in my arm to move the pen across the paper and shape words. Admittedly I'd never win any penmanship awards, but making a mark on paper once I had lost the ability to grip the pen with my fingers was something I considered only marginally less than awesome.

With each progressing day, the therapies became more rigorous and expansive. Before long, I was fitted with a metal brace that extended from my upper chest to the tips of my toes. The brace enabled me to stand, something I never dreamed I would do again. "Putting weight on your legs," the therapist said, "will prevent the loss of calcium in your bones." I guessed it was true because I felt myself growing stronger every day. I counted the hours until I was rolled into the brace and allowed to stand in a specially designed cubicle that prevented my toppling over. After endless months of lying flat on my back and looking at a waist-high world, standing for one single hour was a thrill that rivaled sky diving.

In just a few short months I had gone from counting ceiling tiles to seeing a future filled with wonder. I was learning to live again. I made friends with people throughout the Institute—nurses, doctors, therapists, people with many other types of disabilities, and other quadriplegics, some of whom had injuries worse than mine. One of the people I met was the famous Brooklyn Dodger catcher Roy Campanella. He'd broken his neck in an auto accident. With my newly acquired pen-hand, I wrote about these adventures in scribbled letters to Smitty, Mother and Scott. I ate meals without spilling food on myself, and I fell in serious like—I say like, not love, because I've only had one true love and that came about years later.

One day, a handsome young black orderly lifted me into my wheelchair and the attraction was instantaneous. "I don't think we've met before," he said allowing his hand to brush across my shoulder and linger there.

"I know we haven't," I answered, smiling.

From that moment on, he made it his business to be where I was. We'd pass in the hallway and he'd give me a mischievous wink. When it was time to lift me into my wheelchair, he'd happen to be passing by; and, at the end of the day he always found his way to my room. At first we simply talked about things of mutual interest—the theatre, art, music. He was studying at the University, working as an orderly and singing backup for Dion and The Belmonts. "In the music industry," he said, "that's where I really want to be." He was bright, articulate, gentle, and compassionate. He made me laugh…and, he made me feel desirable again. His name was Prentice, but I nicknamed him Prince, because to me that's what he was—my Prince Charming. He made me feel alive and beautiful. When my four o'clock rehabilitation programs ended, we would often sneak off for a few moments of privacy, moments to cuddle, kiss, and caress one another.

"Lani, I've fallen in love with you," Prince said, "I'd like to bring you home to meet my mother and the rest of my family. I want to marry you."

"You know how I feel," I answered, "but right now I'm in no position to consider marriage. I've still got a tremendous amount of therapy ahead of me and I haven't even begun to figure out what I'll do as far as a career is concerned…" I let my words trail away without ever mentioning the ugliness staring us in the face. It was the 1950's and the concept of a white girl marrying a black man could start a race riot in places like Florida. I knew it and Prince knew it, but we were in New York, not Florida, so our affair continued without any further mention of marriage.

In one of my scribbled letters to Mother, I mentioned that I had a boyfriend, but also said it was someone of whom she would not approve. Mother immediately guessed he was black and, as expected, she did not approve. Scott, on the other hand, deemed it wonderful, and when Prince's birthday rolled around, my brother helped me purchase a gift—a silver medallion engraved "To My Prince Charming, Love Lani." Prince clasped the chain around his neck and wore it for as long as I knew him.

Day by day, I was pushing myself back into life, but with every step forward, there seemed to be two steps backward. As my mobility increased, so did my muscle spasms. They began shortly after the surgery to fuse my spine. While I was at Baptist Memorial, lying motionless and making no demands of those muscles, the spasms were mild, barely more than a twitch in my hand, forearm or leg. Once I started to work the muscles, the spasms grew violent. When they hit, my body became rigid and unmanageable, not just unmanageable for me, but for the attendant trying to dress me in the morning or undress me at night. After a while, three attendants were assigned to the task. Two held me down, controlling my body as it launched itself into a spasm, and the third struggled to put on or take off my clothing.

As the weeks went by, my rehabilitation progressed, although more slowly than I'd hoped. The muscle spasms often made my range of motion exercises painful and if one occurred while the therapist was fitting me into my brace, my body became so rigid I could virtually stand alone. Of course once the spasm subsided, I would collapse. But I was determined to outpace the spasms, so I continued to wheedle the therapists into letting me stand in the parallel bars without my braces. I was hoping as my muscles became stronger they would send a message to my nervous system, eventually enabling me to stand on my own as I did in a spasm. Unfortunately, my efforts always ended in collapse. The therapists, concerned that my stubborn attempts would end in injury, eventually stopped the standing experimentation. *One step forward, two steps backward, another step forward*...I wheeled myself to class after class and with each passing day I felt the renewed sense of independence bubbling up inside of me. Whirlpool baths improved my circulation. ADL classes taught me how to cope with the Activities of Daily Living. And lifting weights helped to strengthen my muscles, such as they were. But my favorite therapy session was the volleyball game I'd jokingly nicknamed "Kill the Quad." A therapist stood in the center of a circle of people like me—quadriplegics in pegged wheelchairs—and when the therapist tossed the ball to one or the other of us, we were to bat it back to him. It was an exercise designed to improve eye/hand coordination, but the games often escalated into fun-filled challenges of batting the ball past the therapist and bonking another of the 'quads' in our circle. It was during one of these games that the worst of my muscle spasms occurred. I had just pounded a shot to the far side of our circle when an extensor spasm hit. It stiffened my body with such a jolt that it lifted me out of the wheelchair and catapulted me across the room.

The therapist called for orderlies and a flurry of activity ensued. Within minutes, I was whisked off to x-ray. After flying across the room like Superwoman, I was fortunate to escape without any broken bones. That was the good news. The bad news was that the doctors ordered me to be strapped into the wheelchair to prevent the recurrence of such a violent event. *A giant leap backward!* Thick leather straps were affixed to my wheelchair and I was all but imprisoned again. One strap fastened across my chest, another across my lap, a third across my knees and the last one circled my ankles. The wheelchair that had given me a sense of liberation, now felt like a straight jacket. I was miserable. Strapped into the chair, I began to feel as if I were losing bits and pieces of the precious independence I had gained.

Sensing my frustration, Scott made a decided effort to visit at least twice a week. Rehabilitation patients were allowed to leave the Institute for excursions when we weren't in therapy, so Scott and I did just that. At first I expected it to be like the old days, when we'd tromp around New York together, seeing shows, and meandering through the Village—but, although New York was the same city, I was a different person and things change when you're in a wheelchair. On our first night out, we went to a neighborhood bar and forgetting that I was trying to train my bladder to function without a Foley catheter, Scott and I downed a pitcher of beer. I hadn't had a beer since I left Smitty, so I felt flighty as a kite as we giggled our way back to the Institute and I shamelessly left a trail of urine behind. After that incident, we switched to double martinis which, although far more potent, constituted of less liquid volume. More often than not, our outings were as theatergoers. We saw any number of Broadway shows, but to this day one stands out in my mind and that was when I saw a young Paul Newman in the Tennessee Williams show *Sweet Bird of Youth.* The moment Newman walked onstage, I leaned over and whispered in my brother's ear, "He's got the most beautiful blue eyes I've ever seen!" In many ways that was a good summer; a summer when I came to realize that Scott and I could still laugh and have fun together. I learned to see Scott as himself, my often imperfect brother—not the hero I'd so foolishly imagined, but a brother who truly loved me and tried to ease my rehabilitation.

With every week of therapy, I grew stronger; and the stronger I grew, the more powerful the muscle spasms became. In the ADL class, I focused on transferring myself from the wheelchair to the bed and back again, but partway through the endeavor a spasm would slam into me and I'd fall to the floor. I was becoming increasingly more frustrated and the therapists began to question whether or not I could be rehabilitated to a level of independence or occupational effectiveness.

When they gave voice to such a thought, I'd emphatically reassure them that such was not the case. "I can do this!" I'd say with a lot more conviction than I actually felt.

One day, after a particularly discouraging therapy session, a rather ordinary looking gentleman appeared at the door of my room. I recognized him right away because I'd seen his picture in numerous news articles. "You're Doctor Cooper," I said with astonishment. "Irving Cooper, the doctor who operated on

Margaret Bourke White, the photographer for Life Magazine! You stopped the tremors she had from Parkinson's disease!"

"I suppose you could say that," he replied smiling, "may I come in?" Brilliant though he may have been, Irving Cooper was not a man to waste time with idle chit-chat. "I'll get right to the point," he said, "I believe I can stop your muscle spasms."

I was flabbergasted, "How?" I gasped hopefully.

"As you know, there's a surgery I've used on people who have tremors associated with Parkinson's disease; and I think that by utilizing the same strategy in a different type of surgery, I can alleviate your muscle spasms."

After a day of falling to the floor every time I tried to transfer myself into the wheelchair, I jumped at it. "I'm all for it—"

"Not so fast, there's a downside to the surgery. Yes, I can probably stop the spasms, but in order to do it I have to sever the motor nerves causing them. Once I sever those nerves, that's it; there is no reversing the procedure." Cooper was not one to sugarcoat an issue, he went straight to the point, "…you'll never walk again," he said.

"I can't walk anyway."

"You can't walk right now, but even if the medical world discovers a method of repairing spinal cord injuries at some future point in time, you won't be a candidate for the surgery."

I hesitated for a moment and allowed the thought to sink in— the future was some faraway place that was little more than shadows and wishful thinking—I had to deal with today. I had to deal with the spasms preventing my rehabilitation. I had to deal with the IS of this moment in time. "I can deal with being in a wheelchair for the rest of my life," I answered, "and I'm actually okay with that. But, I'm not okay with being strapped down like a wild animal. Over these past few months I've seen how rehabilitation can normalize my life, so I'm willing to let the future hold whatever it holds. What I want to do is get on with this life— the life I'm living right now. So yes, Doctor Cooper, I do want the surgery!"

He gave me a wizened smile that implied he'd known all along what my answer would be. "You're eighteen years old," he said, "so legally you can make this decision, but I would feel better if your parents authorized it." He placed his business card on my nightstand, "Talk to them, and if they agree you should have the surgery, have them call me." He nodded and walked out.

I turned to one of my roommates, a young woman who had been hit by a bus and was now a double amputee, "Can you believe that?" I asked grinning ear to ear.

She shook her head in disbelief, "It sounds like a miracle," she said, "a real miracle."

I tugged the telephone from the nightstand and dialed Mother's number. After I'd given her the gist of my conversation with Doctor Cooper, I gasped, "Do you realize who he is? He's *the* Irving S. Cooper! He's the doctor who operated on Margaret Bourke White, the famous photographer for Life Magazine! After she got Parkinson's disease, she couldn't hold her camera still enough, but he did this operation and it stopped her tremors. Remember, we watched a television special about it? And, there was this feature article in Time Magazine..."

"I remember watching the show together," Mother sighed, "but to have such a famous doctor do this for you, why it sounds almost too good to be true."

Knowing Mother's penchant for manufacturing tragedy where none exists, I warned, "Now don't be concerned if Doctor Cooper tells you this surgery means I'll never again be able to walk— that's okay. The important thing is I'll be able to continue my rehabilitation, and one of these days, I'll be able to do things for myself. I plan on doing something with my life. I want to have a career, maybe even a career where I can help other people...but it will never happen if I stay strapped down."

"I know Lani," Mother said sympathetically, "I understand you better than you think."

That same afternoon, Mother telephoned Doctor Cooper and scheduled my surgery for the following week. I could barely contain my excitement, but when I shared the news with some of my fellow quadriplegics, they were considerably more discouraging. Alicia exclaimed, "Never walk again...man, I wouldn't go for that!"

"I can't walk now," I argued, "I can't even sit in the wheelchair without these God-awful straps tying me down. I feel like a prisoner. I can accept living life in a wheelchair but I can't accept being a prisoner. There's a huge difference! Using the wheelchair I'm liberated—I can go places, do things, go to school, have a career, and have a life. Being strapped down is not a life, at least not the kind of life I want. My life can be better than that!"

"Yeah," Alicia sighed, "but suppose they do find a cure, then where's that gonna leave you? Up the creek with no paddle, that's where!"

"I'd think long and hard about this," Marty said shaking his head sorrowfully.

After hearing those comments, my roommate decided perhaps this surgery wasn't such a miracle after all.

I listened and thought about everything I'd heard, but I was the one living inside my body—and somewhere in the back of my mind a tiny voice kept whispering, *Deal with the IS, Lani, deal with the IS!*

Mother arrived the day before my surgery. She met Prince and was actually polite to him—cool but polite. That afternoon I was transported by car to Saint Barnabas Hospital in the Bronx. My arrival brought a number of unexpected surprises, the biggest of which, was the advanced age of the patients. Hope Haven was filled with children; Saint Barnabas was filled with seniors, many of whom had passed eighty on the fly. As I settled into my room, I whispered to the nurse, "It seems that everyone here is so elderly."

She laughed, "Of course they are, this is a hospital for geriatric patients."

That evening, Doctor Cooper appeared at my door once again. "Are you ready for the surgery?" he asked. His voice was pleasant enough but totally void of emotion.

"I sure am," I answered brightly.

"And you do know," he said, directing his words to both Mother and me, "that once I do this surgery you will lose all hope of ever walking again."

Mother and I both nodded.

"Very well then," he acknowledged our acceptance, then turned and left.

"Serious little fellow, isn't he?" Mother said and we both laughed. In time, I realized Doctor Cooper was not at all emotionless—he was not setting a broken bone or curing a cold, he was dealing with problems so severe no other doctor would touch them and the only way he could do that effectively was to deal with just the patient and not the person.

Early the next morning, I was wheeled by stretcher into the operating room and there I saw a sign that read: *'Please be careful what you say, remember the patient is awake!'*

Fascinated by such a thought, I exclaimed, "Wow, Doctor Cooper—does that mean I can watch the operation?"

"I'm afraid not Lani," he answered, "That sign only applies to the surgery we perform on patients with Parkinson's disease."

Since quadriplegics almost always have breathing problems, I was to be kept in what was called a 'twilight' state of sedation. It was enough to render me unaware of what was happening, but not powerful enough to seriously hamper my breathing. The anesthesiologist inserted a syringe into my IV and said, "Count backward from one-hundred."

"One hundred, ninety-nine, ninety eight, ninety seven..." That's all I remembered.

I was turned over onto my stomach and the surgery began. Partway through the surgery, twilight turned into daylight and I awoke. There was a tube snaking its way down my throat and I felt as if I would gag. Using my lips and teeth, I painstakingly pulled the tube from my mouth and started to speak... "How's it going? "

"Oh my God!" the nurse exclaimed, "She's awake!"

Before I could finish asking my question, the plastic cone covered my face and I drifted back into the twilight from whence I'd come.

The next time I opened my eyes, Mother was sitting beside me. "Lani dear, thank goodness you're awake," she said, "How are you feeling?"

It was a good question. I hesitated a moment trying to gather a sense of how I was feeling. I waited, anticipating a sharp jolt of the spasms that had poked, pinched and pulled at me since my surgery at Baptist Hospital in Jacksonville—but the spasms were gone. "I feel wonderful!" I replied, astonishing myself as much as Mother.

When Doctor Cooper came to check on me the next morning, I asked if I could get up and sit in my wheelchair. I had grown accustomed to the fast paced days at the Rusk Institute and felt that I had already been in bed for too long.

"Up?" he repeated in amazement. "Do you really want to get up this soon?"

I nodded and laughed, "Yes, unless you're afraid I'll pop open because you didn't stitch me together well enough."

For the first and only time, I saw Doctor Cooper actually grin, "It's not that," he said, "but most of my patients are elderly and I've never had one ask to get out of bed the day after surgery."

Shortly thereafter, I was lifted into my wheelchair and we spent the afternoon traversing the beautiful gardens of Saint Barnabas. There were no more leather straps, none of the spastic pain I'd become accustomed to—I felt as though I could conquer the world. Chafing with impatience and ready to continue my rehabilitation, I asked Mother, "Do you think Doctor Cooper will let me go back to the Institute tomorrow?"

"Lani, he told you that you had to stay here for a week," Mother gave the weary sigh of tolerance she'd honed to perfection, "…but darling, I am certain you will badger the poor man until he agrees to let you go back earlier."

Mother was both right and wrong. I did badger Doctor Cooper about allowing me to return to the Institute earlier, but because the surgery had lasted a total of twelve hours, he stood firm in his mandate that I remain there for one week. He had only performed this particular surgery once before and wanted to make certain the results were as anticipated and there were no unexpected complications.

"But I feel fantastic," I argued, "So why do I have to stay here in bed?"

"You don't have to remain in bed," Doctor Cooper replied, "You're free to go anywhere you want, as long as you don't leave the hospital. The operation went well and I don't expect any complications—but, I still want you here so I can monitor your recovery." He turned and walked out of the room.

For the remainder of that week, I wheeled myself from room to room, enjoying visits with the elderly patients, telling jokes and delighting in their reactions as they chuckled at my scandalous stories. One week to the day, I was returned to the Institute—by car. Traveling by car is something most people take for granted, but to me it was a landmark of moving ahead with my rehabilitation.

In the week that followed, I worked harder than ever. Without the muscle spasms, I was free of the dreaded straps and could safely attempt to transfer myself from the bed to the wheelchair and back again. My spirits soared and I was bubbling over with energy and enthusiasm. Hank no longer had to give me a shove down the hall. I was moving on Lani-power and loving it. The muscle spasms no longer robbed me of my strength.

After one wonderful week of rehabilitation, I was notified that the Florida Office of Vocational Rehabilitation had run out of money. *One step forward, two steps back.*

"Run out of money?" I groaned, "How can they possibly run out of money?"

The admissions clerk who'd delivered the news simply shrugged, "Search me," she said and dropped the paperwork on my nightstand.

It was there in black and white—due to a lack of funding, the patient is to be released.

Three nights later, Prince and I found a quiet corner and tried to console each other. "This can't be happening," he said, "I love you Lani, and I know that once you leave here I'll never see you again."

"You don't know what the future holds…" I whispered, but in my heart I knew he was right. With the ugliness and violence of segregation gnashing its bloodthirsty teeth, I couldn't even invite him to come to Daytona for a visit. That night was the last time I ever saw Prince, but as he sadly walked away I caught a glimmer of the silver medallion that remained around his neck.

The next day I would return to Daytona Beach, under-rehabilitated and unsure of what the future held. I was certain of only one thing. My days would be spent in a spiffy little silver wheelchair with spokes on the wheels.

Vocational Rehabilitation had purchased the chair for me, but now I was on my own. I had to find a career that would enable me to support myself and a caregiver. And, I needed a college education to do it. *Back to School?* I had always hated school and dropped out of high school when I was still fifteen, so how, I wondered, would I cope with the challenges of college? Maybe this time would be different…this time had to be different! Here I was, not fully rehabilitated and carrying a lifelong hatred of school—yet, I knew with absolute certainty that I was going to need an education if I was ever to have the independence I craved. As much as I would have preferred other alternatives, I had to accept the fact that a good education was key to the freedom I wanted—the freedom I needed—the freedom I'd strived for my entire life. Like it or not, I had to return to school.

Nine

The idea of school boggled my mind and resurrected memories of two summers earlier when I was seventeen and had not a care in the world. I closed my eyes and allowed the picture of that summer to flood my thoughts. It was the summer I'd walked away from New York nightlife and returned to Daytona.

For years, Mother had breezed through what seemed to be an endless string of boyfriends and lovers. But that summer she suddenly developed an interest in settling down. "Carl and I are very much in love," she said, "We're planning to be married."

Oh no, not again!

When I first met Carl in the spring of 1957, I liked him, liked him better than anyone else Mother had ever dated. That evening, he'd come for dinner and I was struck by the way he and Mother seemed to fit together. They spoke easily, laughing and reaching out to touch one another time and time again. There were no harsh words flying back and forth, no tension. It was a hand in glove relationship where he'd pass her the salt before she even asked for it. Mother, busy cooking, turned to me and said, "Lani, I forgot to buy the butter I need for this recipe, will you and Carl run down to the store and pick up a pound?"

I'd had a number of experiences where Mother's boyfriends hit on me the moment she turned her back, and I wasn't ready for another one. "I can go by myself," I answered.

"No," Mother said, "Go with Carl. You know what kind of butter I always buy, but it will be faster if he drives."

I gave her that rolling my eyes look and repeated, "I can drive myself."

"Just go with Carl," Mother replied with air of exasperation. "His car is in the driveway."

At that point, there was no way to get out of doing what she said without a screaming match. Reluctantly I followed Carl to his car and got in, squeezing myself so close to the passenger side door that I could feel the handle poking my ribs.

We were halfway to the market when Carl slowed the car and said, "I'm going to pull over because there's something I want to talk to you about."

Here we go again! "You don't need to pull over," I said sharply, "just keep driving and say what you've got to say."

Taken aback by my response, Carl stammered for a few seconds then said, "This is of a very personal nature and I really do need to pull off the road to talk to you."

"Don't you dare!" I snapped, but by then he had slowed the car and edged onto the shoulder of the road. I had my hand wrapped around the handle of the door and was ready to bolt the second he leaned across the seat.

"Lani, I need you to understand something," he said slowly, "I'm very much in love with your Mother and I want to marry her, but I'd like to have your approval to do so."

The breath I'd been holding whooshed out and I burst into tears of relief.

"I'm sorry," Carl said apologetically, "Did I say something wrong?"

"No," I sobbed, "you said everything *right*."

That summer Mother and Carl got married and he moved in with us. I knew from the start that this relationship was special and I jokingly bestowed the name Pappy on him. It was a term of endearment, a name I had never given any of Mother's other boyfriends. Granted, we were still not a picture book family who gathered around the dinner table and discussed events of the day, but with Pappy there we took on some semblance of family.

After a year of modeling in New York, I had outgrown school, but I was still only seventeen—too young to settle into the seriousness of adulthood and too old to chase after the innocent pursuits of my youth. It seemed as though Duke was my only link with the life I left behind a year earlier. Everything else appeared strangely different—but the truth was that I was what was different. Although I was chronologically only one year older, I had grown a decade more sophisticated. I traded in the baby blue Chrysler that had been sitting in the driveway for a year and bought myself a Ford Fairlane, a jazzy pink and white convertible people recognized from a distance. "There goes Lani," they'd say, as I whizzed by and tossed a wave into the air. I was a cocktail waitress at Mac's Famous Bar, so nearly everyone in town knew me. They knew me, but ignored the fact that I was too young to be working as a cocktail waitress, so I stayed with it. It was a job I enjoyed and the money was good. When the town was filled with tourists, I could cover my car payment with what I earned in one night.

Although Dusty was long gone, my love of horses remained—so did my daredevil nature, which is how I ended up with an extra fifty dollars in my pocket and my arm in a cast. Now that I was back in Florida, I went to the Gymkhana races whenever there was an event. It was at one of those races that a cowboy tapped me on the shoulder and said, "Bert Faircloth is looking for you."

"Why?" I asked.

"He needs a rider."

"With all the cowboys around here," I laughed, "why me?"

"Nobody else wants to ride Big Red, he's fast but hard to handle." The guy shrugged, "Bert said you'd probably do it. He said he'd split the prize money with you if you win the quarter horse race. It's today's big event and first place pays a hundred bucks, but if you ain't interested..."

"I'm interested," I said and off we went.

Bert offered me a fifty-fifty split of the one-hundred dollar prize if I'd ride the horse to a win. "So I get fifty bucks," I questioned, "if Big Red wins the qualifying heat and the race?" I was thinking that fifty dollars would just about cover my car payment for the month.

"Yep," Bert nodded. "But bear in mind, he's a bit hard to handle."

"I've never met a horse I can't handle," I answered with Lani-style bravado. I took a look at the horse, and the stallion was just as described—big and red. His mane had been shaved, but he looked majestic nonetheless. I'd be racing against professional cowboys, so I would need any advantage I could muster up. I weighed almost one hundred pounds less than most of the cowboys and if I rode bareback I'd have an even greater weight advantage. I removed Big Red's saddle and climbed onto his back, ready for the first heat. When the starter's pistol sounded a shot, Big Red took off and crossed the finish line lengths ahead of the pack—but the problem was he didn't stop there. Instead, he took a ninety-degree turn to the right and kept going. With the horse's mane shaved and no saddle, it was all I could do to hold on until Big Red decided to stop.

When we cantered back to what would be the starting line for the final race, I said to Bert, "This crazy horse doesn't know when to stop! And do you know he does this weird right hand turn thing?"

"Yep," Bert nodded, "Them two things is sure enough his problem."

Obviously I had to find some way of hanging onto the horse in case he repeated his wild antics in the final race. I looked around for a fat, really fat, cowboy and asked to borrow his belt. I fastened the belt around Big Red's neck and got ready to ride again. When we lined up for the final race, Big Red was reasonably calm as he pranced beside the other horses and waited for the starter's pistol to pop. Once the gun sounded, he again took off to cross the finish line several lengths in front of the closest competitor. And once again, he kept right on going. Running full out, Big Red made another ninety-degree turn. Thank goodness for the fat cowboy and his belt! I managed to hold on and didn't fall off but no matter how hard I pulled on the reins, Big Red refused to slow down. He was a quarter horse headed for a six-foot high fence, a fence not even a jumper could clear, so I decided to bail out. Having experienced runaway horses before, I knew what to do. I swung my right leg over his neck with the intention of landing in a run and rolling my body into a ball to cushion the impact. The plan would have worked, had my legs not become entangled with Big Red's. Instead of landing on my feet, I hit the ground with my neck and shoulder, my arm crumpled beneath me.

As soon as I picked myself up, I knew my wrist was broken. Wrapping the kerchief I had worn on my neck around the broken wrist, I graciously accepted a cowboy's offer to boost me back onto Big Red, then rode to the Judges' stand to collect my prize money. I gave Bert his fifty dollars, helped him to load Big Red onto the trailer then drove back to the hospital in Daytona.

A young orthopedic surgeon eyed the dirt-caked clothes and Indian headband I was wearing then whipped out a pair of scissors and snipped off the arm of my plaid cowboy shirt. I was whisked off to the x-ray room to determine in how many places my wrist had been broken. After reading the x-rays, the doctor tossed my now useless sleeve into the wastebasket and teasingly raised an eyebrow. "Judging from the look of you," he said, "that was quite a fall. Your wrist is broken in two places; you're going to need a cast." He turned to wash his hands and continued talking, "You're pretty banged up so I think you'll be spending the night with us."

"Spending the night?" I'd planned on going to work when I left the hospital.

"At least one night," he said, "maybe more. I suspect there are a few other broken bones, but I won't be able to tell until we get some additional x-rays."

As it turned out, the doctor was right. I was in the hospital for two weeks with my neck in traction. In the fall I had fractured a vertebra in my neck, broken my shoulder, cracked a few ribs and as I already knew, broken my wrist in two places. During those days in the hospital, I received bouquet after bouquet of red roses—no name on the card, just the hand drawn outline of a bunny. Try as I might, I could not figure out who my admirer was, and left the hospital without knowing who sent the roses. Weeks later the handsome young doctor who treated me in the emergency room signed my cast with the same bunny caricature. *Mystery solved.*

A person with their arm in a cast doesn't make a very good cocktail waitress and, even though I was making a ton of money, I had to quit the job at Mac's. With my evenings now free, I began spending more time at the Daytona Beach Little Theatre, which is how Duke and I came to be sitting in the gallery watching a rehearsal of *My Sister Eileen*.

"A prostitute!" The director screamed, "I need a prostitute!" He turned and looked at me, "You," he said shaking a finger in my direction, "you can be my prostitute!"

"Excuse me!" I snapped indignantly.

"Get up here," he said still waggling his finger at me, "I need you to play the part of a prostitute."

"I can't play the part of anything, I've got a cast on my arm, in case you haven't noticed."

"Stuff, stuff, stuff!" he exclaimed swirling his hands in huge airborne gestures, "I don't need explanations of extraneous stuff, I need feet!" He went on to explain that all I had to do was walk across a raised platform so the audience saw legs and feet passing the basement window of Eileen's apartment.

"Okay," I answered, and I was hooked. Before the show opened, my legs and feet became those of a prostitute, a nun, an elderly man and a kid walking a dog. Duke was, of course, recruited for the canine role. I had fallen in love with the theatre when I was in New York and that winter the love affair continued. I appeared in every production the Daytona Beach Little Theatre did that season. Night after night, I'd party with the wonderful friends I had met at the Daytona Beach Little Theatre–Arlene the gorgeous leading lady who was destined to become my best friend and Lee Doyle the delightfully flamboyant director. Gay was what Lee proudly labeled himself, and it was easy to understand why. He was not only gay; he was a wild and happy heart who lived each day as if it were his last. What fun I had. I loved the pretense of being someone else on stage and going from there to the after theater parties and ultimately back into my life at home. After the show, I'd slip into my five-inch high heels and a black velvet sheath and then the group would load themselves into my pink and white convertible and off we'd go. I'd drive across town with the Little Theatre people bunched into the back seat, Lee Doyle's silver locks blowing in the wind, and a trail of laughter following in our wake. Once the dancing began, my glamorous high heels came off and remained tucked under the cocktail table until it was time to head for home. I may have been a sophisticate on the outside, but inside I was still a wild child, who loved nothing more than running through the days barefoot and carefree.

With Mother now settled down, the Tiers family considered me to be the most scandalous member of our clan. After Alice Paul stomped off with her suffragette attitude and all three daughters, Grandfather Tiers married "Aunt Polly" who was straight out of a convent and forever criticizing my activities at the Little Theatre. When I played the lead in Happy Birthday, a role where I supposedly drank alcohol and smoked cigarettes, Aunt Polly shook her head in distain and said, "Shameful, absolutely shameful." The issue enraged her to such a point, she telephoned the Little Theatre Board of Directors and complained that they were corrupting the morals of the community by allowing a seventeen year old girl to be drinking and smoking onstage.

The only result of Aunt Polly's phone call was that my friends teased me mercilessly. They thought such prudishness was hysterical, but I vacillated between thinking it funny and being mortified by it. The manner in which my theater friends teased me was good-natured—the way one teases an equal. Even though I was considerably younger than they were, they thought of me as one of them. *I was finally accepted for who I was.*

After the Florida Office of Vocational Rehabilitation ran out of money, I was forced to leave the Rusk Institute and there was nowhere to go but back to Daytona. This time it was a totally different experience. I was only two years older than I had been that fateful summer when I left New York for the first time, but now I was in a wheelchair. Instead of zipping through town in my flashy convertible, I labored to push my pegged chair from room to room and cope with the simplest necessities of everyday living. I had to be lifted from the wheelchair into bed and feed myself with a spoon fastened to my hand. Yes, this time it was different, but the most painful difference was that my best friend was no longer beside me. Mother and Pappy had given my precious Duke away.

I came home expecting my buddy to come running the minute I arrived, but there was nothing. No barking, no thumping of paws, no wet nose nuzzling its way into my lap. "Where's Duke?" I asked.

"We had to give him away," Mother answered.

"You can't do that," I exclaimed, "Duke's my dog!"

"We had no choice; with you gone he was just too much to handle. He became very aggressive, started growling and barking at people as they passed by, and—"

"Well I'm home now and I'll make certain he doesn't bark at anybody. You can call the people and tell them I want my dog back."

"I can't do that Lani...they've had Duke for too long."

"They haven't had him for that long, he was here last Christmas!"

Pappy, sensing a firestorm on the horizon, left the room and Mother gave one of those exasperated sighs indicating she would prefer not to discuss the issue. At my insistence, she began to speak. "When Hope Haven allowed you to come home for Christmas, we knew it was only for a few days. That was before you could sit up; you were still in a prone position and came home lying in the back of a station wagon. Pappy and I were afraid if you knew Duke was gone it could cause your condition to worsen, so we asked the new owners if we could borrow him for the few days you'd be at home."

"They're not Duke's owners," I said angrily, "I am!"

"No Lani, they are. We gave Duke away shortly after your accident. With us not knowing when, or if, you would ever leave the hospital we had enough to worry about."

I looked Mother defiantly in the eye, "So you decided a big fat lie would make me happy," I said. "Well, do I look happy?"

"I know you're angry because we gave the dog away, but what's done is done and that's the end of this discussion."

She was right. There was nothing more to be said. Regardless of how I felt, one truth remained—I was now a quadriplegic and dependent upon Mother and Pappy for virtually everything. *Another IS!*

I knew Pappy had no love of dogs and was probably pleased Duke was no longer around, but he did care about me and I believe he tried to make amends for my loss.

Just weeks after my return from the Rusk Institute I received two wonderful gifts from Hughes Supply, the plumbing and electrical supply house where Pappy had worked his way up to Manager of the Electric Department. One of the gifts was an electric typewriter; the other was a wheelchair with big fat inflatable tires in the front and bicycle tires in the back, a wheelchair designed for use in sand, a wheelchair that would enable me to go to the beach. *A wonderful IS!* That year, I gave Pappy a motion picture camera for Christmas and the first movie he shot was one of me rolling down the beach and waving happily at the camera until I suddenly popped out of the frame. "What the…" Pappy grumbled looking at the camera. Then he glanced up and saw that the inflatable front wheels of the chair had sunk into the soft sand and I'd been tossed head over heels onto the beach. Once Pappy saw how hard I was laughing, he began laughing and then Mother joined in—laughing at the two of us. The incident was hilarious when it happened, but it became even funnier as we watched the re-run of it Christmas after Christmas. That odd-looking wheelchair with its canvas seat and bloated tires gave me the freedom to go back to the beach I loved so much, but the typewriter gave me purpose.

I was determined to do something with my life, and now that I was back in Daytona, I was chomping at the bit to get started. With my physical limitations, I had to depend on my brain in order to have a meaningful career—being a high school dropout wasn't going to cut it. I needed a college degree; but to get into a college, I needed a GED, and wasn't old enough to take the test. In Florida at that time, you had to be at least twenty years old to take the GED and I was nineteen. I was home alone for most of the day and had a year to kill. It promised to be a very long year until Pappy walked through the door with that electric typewriter and a plan to set me up in a mail order business.

Day after day, I sat in my pegged wheelchair holding a rubber-tipped pencil in the gadget on my hand, plunging the typewriter keys down one by one by one—but I did it, and I did it happily. I typed labels and sent out novelty catalogs—first to my friends and relatives, then to everyone Mother and Pappy knew, then to friends of friends, and ultimately to names I pulled from the telephone book. Slowly the orders began to trickle in—a herringbone bath mat, two pumpkin scented candles, a blue plaid sewing basket...and so on. I pecked at the typewriter hour after hour, until every item was listed on an order form and sent to the company for fulfillment. That was back in 1960, there were no home computers or internet connections and when I hit the return key, my electric typewriter, one of the first ever produced, bounced along the desk the way a jackhammer bounces through a chunk of cement. Both Mother and Pappy started coming home for lunch, to no doubt check on me. So, after I'd pecked long enough to bounce the typewriter precariously close to the edge of the desk, I'd stop and wait until one of them got there to slide it back into place. Once the mail order business got going, it seemed my year of waiting to take the GED was not going to be all that bad—but the day I answered the telephone and discovered Dick Keegan's mother on the other end of the line, it got even better.

When I first met Dick Keegan, I had no idea what an important role he would play in my life. He was simply an admirer and I was a beauty queen. We met at the New Smyrna Beach Beauty Pageant, just days before the accident. I had seen and heard Dick as I strutted across the stage and knew he had to be one of my most ardent fans. Every time I stepped on stage, Dick elbowed the air horn strapped to his wheelchair and gave a toot—or two, or more. There was little else he could do. Dick was born with a horrific case of cerebral palsy, and his only physical ability was to shift his torso and move his right foot. Although unable to speak, he was able to communicate— spelling out words by pointing to letters with his right toe. The letters were stenciled onto a hinged board and when Dick wanted to say something the board was removed from the side of his wheelchair and placed on the floor in front of him. He employed that same toe to travel from one spot to another; and using the rearview mirror attached to his wheelchair, he pushed himself backward. That's how he moved through life...backward. But what Dick lacked in physical ability, he more than made up for in brain power. He was absolutely brilliant. His speech was limited to strange guttural sounds or grunts, but his mind overflowed with ideas and discoveries that most people would find inconceivable. In addition to all the systems and devices he created to make his restricted abilities functional, he played masters chess by mail. Dick also had an eye for pretty girls...an eye that occasionally got him into trouble. In one instance, he tumbled backward off a curb while eying a pretty girl and found himself sprawled in the street waiting to be rescued.

"Dick heard you were home," his mother said, "and he'd like to come for a visit."

Did he think I was still that stage-strutting beauty queen? I hesitated a moment, then asked, "Does he know about..."

Dick's mother laughed, "Of course he does. That's why he wants to visit; he plans to give you a few tips to make wheelchair living easier."

The following week, Dick's mother dropped him off in front of our house and he used his right toe to push himself up the walkway—backward of course.

That afternoon, Dick shared the dozens of ways he'd discovered to make life easier—simple strategies that enabled me to do things independently, things such as opening the refrigerator or closing a door behind me, quadriplegic tricks of the trade that I still use today. Working with Dick was an eye-opening experience; not only did he teach me so many ways to cope with the challenges of this new life, but he inspired me more than words can say. Despite the magnitude of his disabilities, he was happy and cheerful, living a full life and taking time to be everything a friend should be. In this new life, I was learning to be magnanimous. I was learning to like people and appreciate each individual for who and what they were—and Dick was a wonderful teacher.

It's amazing how people with disabilities learn from one another. These handicaps are so often called disabilities, yet the lack of one capability often gives birth to another as yet untapped ability. Dick taught me how to cope with numerous everyday living challenges; and Fred, a quadriplegic I met years earlier, taught me that being a quadriplegic doesn't prevent one from driving. Fred had suffered a service related injury that took away the use of his legs and to a lesser degree his arms, but it didn't prevent him from driving, nor did it stop him from creating things of beauty in his woodworking shop. It was his woodworking that first brought us together. A couple of years before my accident, when I still believed I could make my sister love me, I hired Fred to build shutters with dolphin shaped cutouts as a surprise for Dit and Joe's new house. We were now friends and Fred became another mentor.

One day, after Pappy had driven me over to his house for a visit, Fred said, "You know Lani, you can drive if you really want to."

"Want to?" I arched a brow and shot him this 'you've-got-to-be-kidding' look. "Of course I want to...but how..."

"By using your arms in place of your legs, like I do," he said. "Come on, let's take a ride down to the beach and you can give it a try. My wife can lift you into the driver's seat."

Even if I were to live another hundred years, I would still remember that day when Fred showed me how to drive the old car he'd jerry-rigged with hand controls. As we cruised up and down the long stretch of sand, I envisioned the wonders to come. I would be able to drive again; I could sit behind the wheel of a car and actually transport myself from one place to another! *Will wonders never cease!*

As I grew into my newfound abilities, the days rolled into weeks and the weeks into months. Old friends came to visit, I spent afternoons on the beach, and on weekends Pappy and Mother loaded my wheelchair into their Volkswagen and we headed for the Daytona Speedway. The races I'd gone to in years past took place at the familiar racetrack which ran along the old beach-road track, but while I was in the hospital, the new track was built. I loved the Speedway—loved the noise, the crush of people, the intensity—watching the cars circle the track with ever increasing speed pumped adrenaline through my system just as the Gymkhana races had done years ago. With each new adventure, my world was growing larger and even though I was plagued with ongoing kidney infections and high fevers, at times I found it difficult to think of myself as a quadriplegic. There was only one small spot of emptiness in my heart and that was the hole left there by the loss of Duke.

About six months after my return home, I received a telephone call from the family who had Duke. "How old is this dog?" the woman asked.

"Why?" I responded, curious as to why his age would make any difference since they'd had him for almost two years.

"Well, we can't really keep him any longer so we're planning to sell him."

"You can't do that! Duke is my dog! If you don't want him, bring him back. He belongs to me anyway!"

That afternoon the woman knocked on the door and Duke came running to my side as if he'd been waiting all that time for his rightful owner to come and get him. I nuzzled his face and he lapped his long tongue over my cheeks, nose and yes, even mouth. Germs? Who cared! This was the true joy of life—my best friend was back!

Unfortunately, my happiness was short lived. When Mother came in from work she took one look at Duke and said, "What is that dog doing here?"

"The people were going to sell him, so I told them to bring him back. Isn't it wonderful..."

"No Lani, it's not wonderful, and the dog is not staying—"

"But Mother, they gave him back. He's my dog, this was meant to be!"

"Meant to be or not, Pappy and I can't take care of both you and the dog. Be realistic, Lani. Pappy and I need every spare moment we've got to take care of your needs; we have neither enough time nor energy to care for a dog also."

Any argument I had got stuck in my throat, so I nodded and turned away. I loved Duke more than was imaginable, and if I couldn't keep him then I was determined to find him a good home. "Please don't make me return him to those people," I asked, "at least give me a day or two to find a good home where Duke will be loved and happy."

Mother nodded her agreement, and that was the end of our discussion. *Another IS!*

That night with Duke beside my bed, I remained awake for many hours and by morning I had made a decision. I called my friend Fred.

"Duke's a great dog," I said, "and very easy to train. He's incredibly smart and loves to be helpful. He's even won a number of obedience competitions. When you drop a piece of wood or a tool, he can get it and put it on your lap, that way you won't have to call Rosie to come and pick it up. Think what a help that would be!"

"You're right Lani it would be a help. Rosie is always complaining that she has to stop what she's doing to come and pick up something I've dropped, so I'm sure she'll love the idea." Fred chuckled, "Anyway, I've met Duke…and to tell the truth, he's a lot better company than Rosie."

I knew I had made the right choice. That evening Pappy and I delivered Duke to his new owner. I took one last look at Duke then wheeled myself away, happy because Duke would have a good home, but brokenhearted that his home wasn't with me.

Although I didn't say a word about the ache I felt inside I'm certain Pappy understood, because not long afterward he bought me a 1957 Plymouth Savoy. It was a beautiful turquoise green with bullet taillights and a pushbutton transmission mounted on a dashboard that looked like something from a spaceship. Pappy and Fred worked together to concoct hand controls that would work for me. Then, they had them properly installed. I can only imagine the mechanic's face when they handed him the bent screwdriver and said, "This is what she needs to regulate the gas." Funny-looking or not, I could slide the bent screwdriver over my hand and use my wrist to twist it. Twisting my bent screwdriver was like stepping on the gas pedal…vroom!

"Of course," Mother said, "before you take it out on the road you'll have to practice driving. This car is nothing like that Fairlane you drove."

So the two of us got into the Plymouth and headed for the old Tomoka Airport where the Friday night drag races were held back when I used to drag race. Mother helped me into the driver's seat and she sat in the passenger seat. "Go ahead," she said, "but don't expect this to be like…"

Before she finished her statement, I was whizzing along the asphalt. "Wow!" I exclaimed, "This is awesome!" Within an hour, I had driven all over what was once the airport and parallel parked between two overgrown bushes, several times.

"Well," Mother sighed, "I guess you're ready to venture out on your own."

Indeed I was. I remained behind the wheel of that Plymouth, twisted my bent screwdriver and drove home, knowing I had just turned a very important page in my new life. On the drive home, I thought back to three years earlier when I applied for my first driver's license.

I was sixteen years old and a know-it-all adolescent who had been driving for years with no license. Now that I was no longer driving Mother's car and had my own baby blue Chrysler, she insisted I also get an official driver's license. So one Saturday morning, we went down to the Motor Vehicle Bureau to apply for the license. I had no doubt I would pass the driving test. I had been driving for years and, on numerous occasions, even drove in the Friday Night drag races, although that was something Mother knew nothing about.

I expected to breeze through the test but something went wrong. Maybe I was trying to impress the officer who lowered himself into the passenger's seat and watched while I pulled out of the parking space, and drove down the road, making left and right turns upon his command. Maybe I simply wanted him to know what a really cool driver I was. Or, maybe after all those years of driving, I wondered why I even needed to have a driver's license. I no longer remember what I was thinking, but I do remember failing the test.

After I did a smooth-as-silk job of parallel parking, he handed me a card with a big black X in the square indicating "failed."

I looked at him shell-shocked, "You failed me?"

"I most certainly did," he replied curtly. "You were speeding, and did not have both hands on the wheel."

I could have argued the speeding part, but truthfully speaking, I know I had my left arm resting on the driver's side window. (That was the way cool drivers drove!) "But," I protested, "I did everything else perfectly."

"Yes you did," he answered, "but the law states that a driver must abide by the legal speed limit and have both hands on the wheel at all times!"

The second time I took the test, I watched the speedometer like a hawk, drove with both hands glued to the wheel, and spoke not a word. That time, I passed.

Adding insult to injury, after passing my re-test, I was then turned away because my birth certificate read *Barbara Lani Jones*. Ten years earlier Mother had legally changed my name to Lani Verner. Apparently Mother's word wasn't sufficient for the stone-faced woman behind the registration desk, in addition to my retaking the driving test, we had to obtain a letter from the attorney attesting to the legality of my name change, and have my birth certificate changed.

As a quadriplegic, having the ability to drive was an important step toward the independence I craved. But after thinking back on my first driving test, I decided to avoid any potential insurance problems by getting a new license based on driving a car with hand controls. Again, an officer climbed into the passenger seat and off we went. I was flawless, keeping both hands in position and sliding my bent screwdriver into a silky smooth acceleration. The officer sat there calmly making his checks in all the right places. Shortly before I pulled into the parallel parking spot, he asked, "Why are you driving a car with hand controls?"

"I'm a quadriplegic," I replied.

His eyebrows shot up and he did a double take. "You are?" he asked, with astonishment. He suddenly braced himself and grabbed the armrest with what could probably be described as a death-grip. Once the car was parked he quickly scrambled out of his seat, and handed me a ticket indicating I had passed the test. "I'm impressed," he said, "You handled the parallel parking better than about 90% of the people who take this test."

"Thank you," I replied smiling, and drove off happy.

In a few short months I would be twenty years old and would then qualify to take the GED. Once I passed it, I would move on to college. Still uncertain as to how I felt about returning to school, I had no doubt that it was a necessity. As I moved forward in life, I was going to have to earn enough to support both myself and a caregiver. Although my career was still undecided, I was determined to be totally independent and successful in whatever I elected to make my life's work.

Ten

After almost three years of depending upon other people to transport me from one place to another, having a car gave me the freedom of a magic carpet ride. I could go anywhere the road went. There was only one catch; someone had to lift me out of my wheelchair and sit me behind the wheel, then fold my wheelchair and put it in the trunk. After I had driven to where I was going, I also needed to have someone meet me and reverse the process, lifting me from the car into my wheelie. As the song says, I got by with a little help from my friends. Thank goodness for friends and family!

That summer I took the GED exam—whizzed through the verbal portion and struggled through the math, but came out a winner. I now had my high school equivalency diploma and I could register for college. I was ready for university study, but, unfortunately, they were not ready for me. I would first have to prove my learning ability by attending a Junior College. Since we lived in Daytona Beach, the natural choice was Daytona Beach Junior College.

Filled with excitement and determination, I wheeled myself into the Registrar's Office. "Hello," I smiled, "I need to register for the fall semester."

"Sorry," he said, "but most of our classes are taught on the second floor of two story buildings and there's no wheelchair access." He dismissively turned back to the papers he had been reading.

I could tell from his tone, he was someone who couldn't see the person beyond the disability. To him, I was not Lani Verner, the woman who had overcome substantial obstacles to get here, I was a quadriplegic and not worthy of his time. I moved past both his manner and comment and repeated myself, "I said I need to register for the fall semester."

He set the papers aside and looked squarely into my face, "Look, this isn't the right place for you. I think you might do better in the vocational school down the street."

I had been a bull grazing happily in my newfound pursuit of education, but this lummox was waving a red flag in my face. "A vocational school?" I replied angrily. "And given all this educational expertise of yours, do you think I'd make a better watchmaker or hairdresser?"

He looked at my obviously paralyzed hands and waited a moment before responding. When he finally did speak, his earlier intolerance was missing. "It's not because I doubt you're qualified to attend Daytona Beach Junior College," he said, "but we don't have elevators in the buildings and there's no way for you to get from the first floor classrooms to the second floor classrooms."

"That's no problem," I answered, "I can get myself to wherever I need to be."

"Oh really?" He arched his brow quizzically. "And just how do you plan to do it?"

"Levitation," I answered straight-faced.

"Levitation?" His mouth was left hanging open.

"Yes, I've mastered the art of levitating myself from one place to another." Although he rolled his eyes and shook his head in disbelief I remained straight-faced and serious. Before I left the building, I was registered for the fall semester. Now I had to figure out how I really was going to get up and down those stairs!

My first step was to find a caregiver willing to live with Mother, Pappy and me, someone who could lift me in and out of my car and help with my personal necessities. I found Ann. She wanted to attend college, but couldn't afford it, so we struck an agreement. She would serve as my caregiver and I would pay for her tuition and books. She moved into the third bedroom of my parents' house which also qualified as free room and board. When I say I paid for her tuition and books, that's precisely who it was— me. Mother and Pappy were in no position to take on those added expenses and while the Florida State Department of Vocational Rehabilitation covered the cost of my tuition and books, there was no allowance for a caregiver. The Vocational Rehabilitation Agency refused to pay for a caregiver; but, did agree to pay a dollar a day for Ken, a muscular male student, to carry me up and down the stairs to the classrooms—he became my levitation.

After all those years of hating school, there I was; not only working my way through college, but also working odd jobs to make enough money to cover my caregiver's college education. I found a dozen different ways to earn what I needed; and fortunately, I had always been a quick learner because now it was a necessity. I started reading to blind students, then moved on to tutoring other students, and eventually to writing term papers for less dedicated students. In later years, I realized that writing term papers for other students had not been an appropriate way of earning money, but at the time I was desperate. When I wasn't attending classes, I was studying. When I wasn't studying, I was working; and, when I wasn't working my brain was so over-stimulated I found it impossible to fall asleep. My days started early and ended late—and at times it seemed as if there were never quite enough hours for all the things I wanted to do, or needed to get done. Still, I pushed on. I had to. I was working toward a career that would one day provide the independence I wanted.

While I was at the Rusk Institute, I became familiar with the work of Speech Therapists and knew it was a career that would enable me to use my mental and verbal skills rather than my physical abilities. With that in mind, I began to soak up every bit of knowledge put before me and plunged into the educational challenge as never before. I signed up for as many classes as possible and, by some fortuitous quirk of fate, one of those classes happened to be Psychology. I elected to take the course, thinking it would be helpful in my career as a Speech Therapist, but, within a few short weeks, psychology became my career goal. I found that exploring the mind and helping people adjust their behavior patterns was a challenge greater and more interesting than anything I had ever known. Plus I'd be doing something that has always made me happy—helping others.

I can't say I loved college. I've never loved school, but I did love learning and couldn't get enough of it. After the accident, I had learned to love and appreciate people for who and what they were. I no longer wanted to be a loner. I wanted to make friends with my classmates and my professors. Unfortunately, in the early sixties, you didn't see people in wheelchairs attending college, working or socializing. Quadriplegics and others in wheelchairs were generally more reclusive. I was an oddity. When I first started attending classes, I noticed that being around a person in a wheelchair seemed to make my classmates uncomfortable, especially during the break time between classes, when they would gather in groups in the hallways and chat. So, whenever a group of my classmates glanced away to avoid an impolite stare, I rolled my wheelchair over and casually joined into their conversation. Before long I had more friends than I could count. It's funny how you don't always know where you belong, then one day you stumble on it and realize—the life you're living is precisely where you belong! During that first year, at Daytona Beach Junior College, my days were a whirlwind of activity. I was asked to join the Phi Sigma Sorority, made tons of new friends, and began taking on an ever-increasing number of jobs to pay for Ann's tuition and expenses.

In my second year of college, the Phi Sigma Sorority and their "Brother Fraternity" asked me to run for Student Body President. The only problem was they didn't get around to asking me until the day before the votes were to be cast. "You can do it Lani," they said, "You're the one person who can win this. You're popular and well-known."

"Impossible," I laughed. "Our opposition has already been campaigning for weeks; he has posters up all over the place."

"Say yes, and by tomorrow your posters will be all over the campus."

Naturally, I did say yes, and while I stayed up most of the night orchestrating what I would say in my campaign speech, my sorority sisters worked at printing posters and tacking them up along every wall. The next morning you could not walk through a hallway without seeing a dozen signs proclaiming "Vote Lani for President!"

That afternoon, the students assembled in the auditorium and the speeches began. I was the last to speak and a good majority of the students cheered as I shared my thoughts on things I believed to be in the best interest of our College. What happened next I can only excuse by saying I was carried away by my enthusiasm of the moment. Speaking into the microphone that broadcast my speech throughout the campus, I compared myself to FDR who also used a wheelchair. "If FDR could do it," I shouted, "why the hell can't I?"

My intent was earnest enough, but later in the afternoon I was called into the President's office. "Lani," he said, "that was a wonderful speech up until the last line. You should have known better. Profanity is inappropriate when speaking over the public address system."

I sat there feeling sheepishly ashamed. I had become good friends with both Doctor Roy Bergengren and his wife; on a number of occasions I'd even had dinner at their house. He had enough faith in my ability to ask if I would help start a charter junior college scholastic fraternity—Phi Theta Kappa. I was honored and privileged to do so. He trusted me and said I was one of his star students; yet I had nearly compromised our relationship with a foolish barrage of ill-chosen words. I learned a very important lesson that day, one that has lasted far beyond the uncomfortable moments of reprimand—once words escape your mouth, they can never be retracted so don't say anything that will bring sorrow or shame. It's a lesson I still try to hold onto—

although someone very dear to my heart, has said I sometimes fail to use the censor between my brain and my mouth.

Although I made a very good showing, I lost the election by thirteen votes.

During my second year at Daytona Beach Junior College, I focused on the possibility of becoming a psychologist and the intensity of my studies increased. I took Psychology 101 and 102, the only courses available at the Junior College. I used every waking minute working, attending class or studying. Verbal skills were my strongpoint, mathematics my weakness—which leads me to believe fate has a somewhat twisted sense of humor because in the last semester I was given the responsibility of teaching algebra to my classmates. As it happened, the teacher was in an automobile accident and the Dean needed a quick replacement for a brief period of time. "Find the person in each class with the highest grade point average," he said, "and ask them to teach the class until we can find a replacement." Ironically enough, that person was me. Even though I had the highest grade point average, I never attended high school and was not very good at math—especially algebra. I sought the help of another student, a real math whiz-kid, and talked him into tutoring me every night so the next day when a student was asked to put the problem and solution on the blackboard, I was able to explain it to the class. Not only did he help me survive my teaching stint with dignity, but working with him encouraged me to focus on mathematics to the point that I earned a B in the course.

Those were long and sometimes difficult days, I couldn't have done it without the many friends who helped me and Ken, the levitator who carried me up and down the stairs day after day. Even though I needed and appreciated their help, it felt strange for me to be so dependent upon other people. Up until my accident, I had always been a caregiver, a child who looked after the diabetic mother who refused to take responsibility for her own health. When Ken lifted me into his arms to carry me from one floor to the other it often brought back memories of my carrying Mother in much the same way...

I was fifteen years old and the Eighth Grade Sadie Hawkins Dance was coming up. I'd invited a boy from school to be my date, but Mother was having one of her days. Whenever things didn't go Mother's way, she used her diabetes as a weapon, threatening if I did one thing or failed to do another she might take too much insulin and go into shock. On the day of the dance, Mother happened to be in one of those moods, so she insisted I stay home and keep her company. "There will always be another dance," she said, "simply telephone this young man and tell him you have to stay home with your mother because she is a bit under the weather."

"You're not under the weather," I answered irritably, "You're just feeling lonely."

"Well perhaps I am being a bit grumpy and demanding, but if you leave me here alone, there's no telling what might happen. When I give myself a shot of insulin, there's no way of knowing how I'll react...you know I'm terribly prone to insulin shock."

"You're not prone to shock; you're just careless about how much insulin you take. You could do like other diabetics and test your blood every day—then you'd know how much insulin to take."

"I abhor the thought of pricking holes in my skin when it isn't necessary; besides, I can generally tell whether or not I need insulin. Once in a while I make a mistake, that's it, a once-in-a-while mistake."

"It's not once in a while, Mother. I can't begin to count the number of times I've had to carry you down the stairs, put you in the car and drive you to the hospital."

"On a few occasions, perhaps..."

"It hasn't been a few occasions," I snapped, "it's been going on ever since I was twelve years old. I was way too young to even be behind the wheel of a car. But time and again I carried your comatose body down the steps to the garage, put you into the car and drove from the beach, across the intercoastal waterway and over to the hospital on the west side of Daytona."

"Well it was just you and me Lani, who else was supposed to do it?"

"No one should have to do it. You should be more responsible about taking—"

Mother cut into my tirade with a sharp tongue, "I'm not going to discuss this anymore Lani; and you are not going out because I need you here in just case...insulin shock isn't something you can..."

There it was, the threat she used time and time again. It was her tool for manipulating me into doing exactly what she wanted. This was one time too many. I'd dealt with the problem often enough to know that insulin shock rendered Mother comatose for hours before it turned into a life-threatening issue. Even if she did willfully overdose on insulin, I could go to the dance and be home in plenty of time to get her to the hospital safely. "I'm sorry, Mother," I said, "but I am going to the dance. If you overdose on insulin, it will be because you wanted to punish me for not being here, so do as you will."

Ten minutes later I walked out the door. Although I projected an attitude of indifference, the truth was that I did worry about Mother. Yes, I went to the dance, but I left early and when I got home Mother was sitting on the sofa with a warm beer on the table and a book in her hand.

"Well, I hope you had a good time," she said coolly.

"Yes, I did," I answered and nothing more was said.

Later that summer Mother and I went on a month-long vacation to Key West. We were at the Naval Base Officer's Club when Charles sauntered over and asked if I'd like to dance. "Yes, I would," I answered and that was the start of it. I was fifteen years old, but looked like I was in my twenties. He was an Officer, handsome, debonair and adoring of me. We spent every free moment together, and before long I was in serious like.

"I don't think you should be spending so much time with that young man," Mother said.

"Why not?" I asked curiously.

"Because you're only fifteen years old, and that's too young to get involved in an affair."

"I know what I'm doing," I said sharply. "You just want me to stop seeing Charles so I'll be around when you feel grumpy and go tagging after you to do what *you* want to do."

"That's not why I want you to stop seeing Charles," Mother said, "The man is a sailor—alright, a naval officer—and although he's stationed here today, God only knows where he'll be tomorrow."

Of course I had some snappy comeback and one word led to another until what started as a relatively mild discussion became a shouting match that escalated into a poker-hot argument. I suppose I had one comeback too many, because Mother suddenly reached across and slapped my face. Whether you would call it a kneejerk reaction, a moment of rage, or a teenager's rebellion, I can't say—but without a blink of hesitation I slapped her back.

Mother just stood there looking at me and I could feel the shame closing in on me. "I'm so sorry..." I stammered. "I didn't mean to do that."

"Sit down, Lani," Mother said calmly. "There's something I think you need to know."

Without any further argument, I did as she asked.

"I know you don't understand my reason for making these demands," Mother began, "but the truth is, I'm only trying to prevent you from making the same mistakes I made. Just like you Lani, I was a wild child; I thought my parents had no right to tell me what I should or shouldn't do, so I let Morris Verner make love to me. The result was I got pregnant with Scott; so I was forced to drop out of high school in my senior year and marry a man I didn't love. I knew I didn't love Morris, but because of the shame I'd brought to our family, I had no other choice. When I moved into the Verner household, Morris's mother treated me like the biggest slut to ever cross her threshold. She warned Morris that if he ever

dared to get me pregnant again, they would disinherit him and he'd
be left without a cent of the family money. And the Verners had a
lot of money. They were one of the wealthiest families in
Oakmont, Pennsylvania. Yes, Mrs. Verner demanded that I live
there, but she made it perfectly clear Morris was to have nothing
further to do with me."

"Mrs. Verner made us sleep in separate rooms, but that didn't
stop Morris—night after night he'd come creeping into my
bedroom to make love. When I finally became pregnant with Dit,
Morris denied the baby was his and the Verners threw me out of
their house. I was nineteen years old and all I had to show for my
youth was a cloud of disgrace hanging over my head and an
unfinished high school education."

"You never finished high school?"

"I couldn't. Once I got pregnant I was considered a disgrace. It
was as if I wore a scarlet letter pinned to my chest."

"But Mother," I stammered, "If only you had gone to college,
you would have made a wonderful English Professor; your diction,
your grammar, your use of words; it's so perfect, how…"

"The Tiers family had money and they were aristocrats. We
lived in the second largest house in Oakmont and from the time I
was a baby, I was taught proper table manners and proper English.
I knew about the morality expected of me, but I thumbed my nose
at it, because I was young and foolish. Lani, I love you more than
life itself and I want you to have a rich full life, I don't want you to
make the same mistakes I did."

Mother was not someone who spoke about her past, she was
an extremely private person, so this was a side of her I had never
before seen.

She sat there for well over a minute saying nothing then gave
a sigh of regret. "By all rights, I should have given my children a
life of affluence and comfort; instead we've had to struggle just to
make ends meet. You're a beautiful young woman, Lani, and
you're capable of achieving all the things I never did; but heaven
help us, because you've got that same fire in your heart that I had."

Mother got up, went into the bedroom and closed the door, leaving me to think.

Ours was a loving but strange relationship with the role of mother and child often reversed. Although Mother was always responsible about providing food and shelter for her children, she was irresponsible in so many other ways, especially in ways relating to her health and lifestyle. As a young child, I took on the role of Mother's protector. I was her guardian, her caregiver. She in turn was my ruler and the balance of power was in her possession. I was permitted to drink and smoke when we were out together, but forbidden to do either when I was with my own friends. I could attract men to our table when we were together, but on my own I was expected to be the fifteen-year-old girl I should have been. To Mother, I was a readily available companion with whom she could party. Unfortunately, I was also her daughter.

The two years I spent at Daytona Junior College flew by in a frenzy of going to class, working and studying. I seldom took time for play, and if I did, it was the occasional weekend when I drove to Saint Petersburg to visit my friend, Crystal. This was the sixties. We were a generation of 'make love not war' flower children with long hair, soulful music, hippie clothes and psychedelic posters. I loved being part of this era. It was young, colorful, full of excitement and bursting with hope for the future. Many an afternoon Crystal and I would spend our time browsing through the 'Out of Sight' Shop; but sitting alongside the tie-dyed bandanas were shelves of drug paraphernalia. I ignored those things and moved on. Although I was part of the hippie culture and enjoyed every minute of it, I was working far too hard to take a chance on drugs that might interfere with my scholastic progress. As a child I turned my back on classroom studies; now I realized that every day of diligence brought me closer to my ultimate goal.

At the Daytona Beach Junior College graduation ceremony I was astonished when I received a number of scholarships, and was honored with a nomination to the Hall of Fame and being named the Outstanding Female Student. Somehow, I had metamorphosed into a successful student.

By the time I received my Associate of Arts Degree from Daytona Junior College, I had my career aspirations carved in stone. I was going to be a Clinical Psychologist. I was going to help people change their life for the better just as Smitty, Doctor Mead, Doctor Cooper and so many others had helped me to do. To do it I needed to obtain a Bachelor's Degree, so I began searching for a university that offered a Psychology Major and wheelchair access. The school turned out to be the University of South Florida. At that time, the University of Illinois was the only other university that was wheelchair accessible, and since my body couldn't tolerate the cold weather, Illinois was out of the question.

People sometimes wonder why I say I've led a charmed life, but consider this—USF was a brand new university and everything about it was perfect. Tampa offered a warm climate that I could easily tolerate; the University specialized in the arts and offered the psychology courses I needed; and the campus was totally wheelchair accessible. Vocational Rehabilitation purchased a new electric wheelchair for me, so I was able to roll my way from class to class, to the cafeteria, back to the dormitory and just about anywhere else I needed to go. I still needed a caregiver, to lift me in and out of the wheelchair and help with other necessities, but not needing another Ken was sheer paradise. Back then the University was a fairly small campus with only three dormitories and about six or seven other buildings. The unfortunate thing was that they didn't have the staff of career advisors one usually expects at a university. Of course to me that didn't matter; I already had my career goal fixed firmly in sight.

Florida Vocational Rehabilitation covered the cost of my tuition and books, but this time they also covered my board—a dormitory room. Once again, they refused to cover the cost of a caregiver, so I was forced to find a replacement for Ann and strike a similar financial arrangement. Only this time, we weren't living at my parent's house so I had the added expense of my caregiver's room and board. The added expense meant I had to find more work, earn more money, and study harder than I ever thought possible. At the Junior College, I'd been at the top of my class, but USF classes were different—chunks of information came at me fast and furiously, but unable to use my hands, I was slow taking notes. Thankfully, Mother had forced a well-trained memory upon me. When I was a child, she insisted on two very important things—the use of proper English and exercising an ability to remember what I had learned. She taught me silly ways of memorizing things such as the list of United States Presidents— from George Washington through LBJ, I had to name them in order. Back then, I considered it a waste of time, but later I realized how important those lessons were. As we'd sat and watched Jeopardy together, Mother had challenged me to learn, just as I was now challenging myself. I sat and listened to lectures in my various classes, mentally recording the important facts so later I could use my painfully slow writing skills to commit the information to paper. As a result, my brain went into overdrive and when I finally found time to sleep, I was unable to do so. With dark circles under my eyes and struggling to keep up with classes, I began to take prescription sleeping pills, a habit that remained with me throughout my years of university study.

The number of jobs I took on increased dramatically and my days of leisurely browsing through the 'Out of Sight' Shop disappeared. My sole recreation was an occasional visit to the local pub—our student hangout. In true college tradition, newcomers to the pub were challenged to chug-a-lug a gigantic mug of beer and the few who succeeded were rewarded with a personalized mug that hung on the wall behind the bar. Although my visits to the pub were few, my mug was proudly displayed there. As for me, I was generally in a classroom or study hall, or at the library tutoring someone, or in a dormitory reading to a blind student. At the end of those very long days, I wheeled myself back to my dormitory where Elise, my new caregiver, lifted me from the electric wheelchair into the small beach wheelchair that came with me. Having that funny-looking beach chair enabled me to wheel myself into the shower—a big step forward on my road to independence.

Our dormitory room was quite small and there was no outlet to recharge my electric wheelchair, so every evening Elise rolled my chair down the hall and connected it to the plug in the laundry room. Trust me, when I tell you that none of this was easy—worthwhile, definitely—but not easy. When my hair, which tends to be oily, needed to be washed and there was no time for a shower, I wheeled myself down to the laundry room, leaned over the big sink and washed it there. I did what I had to do and was ecstatic because I had the opportunity and ability to do it.

During the two years I spent at the University of South Florida, I worked harder than I'd ever worked in my life; but I told myself that once I had my Bachelor's Degree, I'd be ready for a career as a Clinical Psychologist. At least that's what I thought. I took every available psychology course along with anything else remotely linked to the field, but shortly before receiving my Bachelor of Arts in Psychology, I learned a PhD was required to become a therapist. *Oh no... more school!*

Attending the commencement service was not a mandate and since the graduation ceremony was to be held outdoors, with the graduates wearing black caps and gowns in what most likely would be a sweltering sun, I had decided not to go. Unfortunately quadriplegics are ill-equipped to tolerate extremes of either heat or cold, but when my psychology professors learned of my decision, they urged me to attend; and, thankfully I did. Anticipating the problem I might have, Mother and Pappy arrived with a bag of the newly invented blue freeze-packs and literally packed me in ice for the graduation ceremony. When I heard my name singled out for all those honors, I was overjoyed to be there. I was finally comfortable with myself as a college student.

I enjoyed being at USF, but the school was in its infancy and didn't offer graduate studies. Once again, I had to search for an institution of higher learning that had wheelchair access and would accept me. Oh yes...and, it had to be in a fairly warm climate since

I was so adversely affected by the cold. Regardless of how many layers of clothing I piled on, a few minutes in the cold air virtually re-paralyzed my muscles. I began writing letters and applying to southern universities. For weeks on end,   I received responses stating that my credentials were excellent but the school did not have wheelchair accessibility.

Then one afternoon, I received a call from Doctor Paul Segal, Head of the Graduate Studies Program in Psychology at the University of Alabama—a university I had not applied to and for good reason. George Wallace was the Governor of Alabama back then and he had not only vowed to maintain segregation, but he'd stood in the doorway of the University's Student Union Building with a shotgun to prevent one lone black girl from entering. I, on the other hand, was an ardent fan of Doctor Martin Luther King. He was bright, articulate and able to see a future far better than what currently existed. Alabama was definitely not a place I wanted to be. It was an environment into which I would never fit.

"The University of Alabama would like to have you complete your graduate studies with us," Doctor Segal said, "and I'm calling to offer you a fellowship."

"I didn't apply to Alabama," I replied with a rather rude intonation.

"I know you didn't, but…"

"Alabama must be a terrible university, if you're trying to recruit people who haven't even applied to the school."

"Actually it's a wonderful university. We have more applications than we can handle, but your professors at South Florida suggested I contact you—and they gave you such a glowing recommendation that it prompted our interest."

"Thank you, but I don't think Alabama is the right place for me."

"Don't jump to such a hasty conclusion. The University is not wheelchair accessible but we have a highly advanced psychology program."

"I don't believe in segregation," I blurted out.

He laughed, "Neither do I," he said, "the attitudes of Governor Wallace are not necessarily those of the University of Alabama."

We spoke for a while and after several minutes I realized that I actually liked Doctor Segal. "I thank you for the offer of a fellowship," I said, "but truthfully speaking, I need more than that. I have to support a full time caregiver; so I have to pay for her tuition, books, room and board."

He laughed again. He had an easy laugh, one that enabled you to imagine the smile on his face. "You drive a hard bargain," he said, "but I suppose I could throw in a teaching position."

At that point, I began to listen to his proposal in earnest.

"We've got a start-up psychology program that would be ideal for you. It's a specialized program of Clinical Psychology for Mentally Retarded Patients. It offers a chance—"

Interrupting him, I said, "I don't want to limit myself to mentally retarded patients."

"This is a unique opportunity."

"I appreciate that it's unique, but it's not what I want."

He sighed, "Well, I suppose I could arrange for you to go into our Clinical Psychology PhD program."

Shortly thereafter, I was enrolled in the Graduate Studies Program at the University of Alabama. But to me Alabama was still Alabama. I couldn't see myself living on a campus that discriminated against people because of the color of their skin. Using trust money Mother's sister left me, I bought a Dodge Dart and had it equipped with hand controls so I could drive to and from the university. I also bought a mobile home; although fairly inexpensive, it was configured to accommodate a wheelchair. Two bedrooms had been converted into a single large one, the hallway widened and the size of the bathroom increased. The trailer was twelve feet wide and close to fifty feet long—big enough to house both me and a caregiver. I made an exploratory trip to Alabama, rented space in a mobile home park as far from upscale as you can get, and parked my trailer.

Just as I had done at the University of South Florida, I recruited a student in need of financing and struck the same deal.

Now I had her tuition bills, an ever increasing number of books to buy and rent to pay. Even though my fellowship came with a paid teaching position, I needed a larger income to pay for those expenses. I began working multiple jobs. I was a full time graduate student and still I taught classes in Psychology 101 and 102; did counseling at the Student Health Center; worked with depressed patients at the VA Center; and, did counseling at the University's Psychology Clinic. In my few moments of spare time, I worked at the state mental hospital with psychotic patients and at the State School for the Retarded, giving specialized IQ tests to mentally retarded patients.

The week after I began studying at the university, I was driving my friend Charlene back to her dorm and we saw a huge bonfire in the middle of vacant lot.

"Oh look," I said, "it must be a pep rally for the football team."

She raised an eyebrow and looked at me as if I was crazy. "Are you kidding?" she asked.

I knew the University of Alabama was heavy into football, so I couldn't imagine why Charlene was acting so strange. "I'm not kidding," I answered, "there's a big game Saturday, so don't the students usually have a pep rally?"

"It's NOT a pep rally," Charlene groaned, "It's a Ku Klux Klan meeting!"

I slowed my car enough to see that she had been right. Hooded figures wearing white robes stood around the fire as they watched a wooden cross burn. They were celebrating their hatred of another race!

As soon as I got back to my mobile home, I telephoned Paul Segal. "I just drove past a Ku Klux Klan rally!" I shrieked. "What have you gotten me into?"

"Slow down, Lani," Paul replied in that soft spoken manner he so often used, "Tuscaloosa is the home of Robert Shelton, the Imperial Wizard of the Klan."

"What!"

"There's not much we can do about that Lani, so try to look past it."

"Good grief, Paul," I groaned. "What makes you think I can ignore it? I have a very difficult time accepting hate and intolerance. That's something I'll never get used to."

Unfortunately, people who felt as I did were a minority in Tuscaloosa. It was the Alabama of the sixties, a time when culture and education were outweighed by skin color; so when I began entertaining some of my black friends in my mobile home, I was evicted from the trailer park. I moved my mobile home to another trailer park; then two weeks later the situation repeated itself.

I gave up on trailer parks and leased some land from a peanut farmer outside of town, parking my mobile home on a high bluff overlooking Hurricane Creek. When the peanut farmer rummaged through my trash can and found evidence of the beer-drinking of some friends and classmates, I was asked to leave there as well. Obviously, the Alabamians of that day had established their own set of behavioral rules, ones which had nothing to do with human kindness, dignity or respect for others.

After leaving the peanut farm, I gave up on the trailer and rented it out. I then leased a large antebellum mansion in the center of Tuscaloosa. It was an area that had seen better days, but it had neighbors who went about their own business without much regard or notice of yours. The owner had plans to one day tear down the building and replace it with an office park, so when I explained my plan to open a boarding house, he had no objections. Once the lease was signed, I ran an ad in the newspaper and found Lucille, the perfect housekeeper. In those days, a domestic worker in Alabama received thirty-five cents an hour, but I paid Lucille the going wage for a white person—one dollar an hour. I now had a housekeeper and a house bare of furniture. Recalling Mother's negotiating skills, I approached The Salvation Army and struck a deal with them. They agreed to provide me with a bed and dresser for each bedroom and I agreed to donate back any and all excess furniture when people began to move in with their own belongings. Shortly thereafter, I opened what could easily be considered the town's most unique boarding house. The rooms came with dinner five nights a week, clean sheets every Friday and an available ear to listen to any and all problems—or as some referred to it, free counseling. Those who were unwelcome in other boarding houses were welcome here and my nonjudgmental approach to boarders eventually caused the house to be called Manic Manor. Although I was frequently in my room studying or preparing lectures, parties began to blossom—first, it was a few friends of the people who lived there, then friends of friends joined in, and before long the living room resembled the crowded coffee houses of Philadelphia and New York. Sometimes discussions about art, politics and the state-of-the-world lingered long into the night. Other evenings the music blared so loudly that it shook the plaster loose from the ceiling. Luckily, our closest neighbors were an antique shop on one side of the house and a school on the other, both of which were closed in the evening when the parties began.

Graffiti appeared in numerous places throughout the house, and it graced the bathroom walls with everything from poetry and profound thoughts to laughable limericks. It seemed that everyone had some bit of creativity to add to those bathroom walls. One resident, a commercial artist, painted the wall behind the toilet with a six-foot-high purple dragon, female of course, with long eyelashes, red lips and a polka dot bikini. Another resident contributed a path of red paint footprints that climbed the wall and crossed over the fifteen foot high ceiling. Before long, Manic Manor was known throughout town—it was a gathering place for all who cared to come. The door was always open and no one was judged by that monster called prejudice. My landlord, a young man gifted with a good sense of humor, would stop in every so often to read the new additions to the bathroom wall. One of my favorites was a laughable verse written by an ex-beau. It read—I once loved a beautiful girl named Lani, she drove me to drink. That's all I can be thankful to her for.

When the kitchen needed painting, we threw a beer party and the price of admission was a can of paint—any color. That night everyone took turns applying the paint they had brought and before morning we had a beautiful rainbow-colored kitchen. I often thought of that kitchen as the first 'Rainbow Collation.'

The Alabama of the sixties was shocking to me, not only because of the injustice of segregation, but because of the flagrant disregard for human life that seemed to be everywhere. Hatred hid in doorways and behind shuttered windows. Emotions bubbled up like boiling water. It didn't target just blacks, it was aimed at anyone who was different—with some of the worst treatment reserved for the mentally ill. Not long before my arrival, patients who had tendencies toward violence were caged like animals and left naked so they could be hosed down for bathing. Cruelty was the order of the day and the people who were part of the respectable establishment, turned their heads to the brutality rather than challenging it.

I had seen the ugliness of segregation in Florida, but never to the extent of what I witnessed in Alabama. For three years, I watched man's inhumanity to man. Finally, I informed the head of the Psychology Department that I had selected a subject for my dissertation. It was "The Modification of Racial Attitudes Using Hypnosis."

The coffee he'd been sipping spurted from his mouth as his jaw dropped open. "You can't do that," he gasped, "This is Alabama!"

"I realize that," I answered, "but it's high time somebody did something about—"

"George Wallace is our Governor! He controls the budget that funds our university!"

"So that's why we don't have one black student here at the university?"

"Well it's certainly a big part of why."

"Black people are human beings and they deserve an education as much as anyone else. You should feel embarrassed to—"

"I am embarrassed, but that doesn't change anything. The truth is, if Governor Wallace hears one of our students is writing a dissertation on the subject you've suggested, he'll cut off funding for the school—and, that's a guarantee."

At that point, the head of the graduate studies program was called in. He listened to my thoughts regarding the dissertation then said, "The first time I spoke with you Lani, I knew you were a woman ahead of your time but," he sighed, "a paper like this could cause serious ramifications for the university."

"But," I argued, "somebody has to do something—"

"I agree," he said, "I realize what's happening is wrong and I think Alabama is on the cusp of change, but the question is—do you want to take the university down to achieve it?"

"Well," I hesitated, feeling the weight of his concern.

"Why don't you take a week and think it over," he suggested. "Then, if you still want to use this as your dissertation topic, no one here is going to stop you."

I wanted desperately to write about the intolerance of segregation, about finding ways to overcome it and treat our fellow human beings as human beings. I'd seen the hooded Ku Klux Klan members dancing around bonfires, I knew the Grand Wizard of the organization lived right here in Tuscaloosa, and I knew that what they said was true. Because the hatred ran so deeply, Governor Wallace would most certainly cut off funding for the university. In trying to do right by one group of people, I would be destroying another. Decisions like this are never easy. I was certain my professors knew what my decision would have to be. Another IS!

The following week, I met with Paul Segal and the Psychology Department head for a second time. "I've decided to alter the subject of my dissertation," I said, "It will be *Modification of Attitudes Toward Mental Illness Using Hypnosis*."

Nothing more was said and, with a heavy heart, I began the research for my new dissertation topic. In time, my research was completed. But, little did I know, that it would never be written.

Eleven

It started with a terrible pain in my stomach, but between work, teaching assignments and the research necessary for my dissertation, I was putting in fifteen to twenty hours a day, so I ignored the pain and pushed through it until my stomach started to swell and I found myself on the verge of screaming. That's when I gave in and went to the Student Health Center, a six-bed facility that was slightly more than a clinic, but considerably less than a hospital. After a cursory examination, I was admitted and placed in a room with striped wallpaper and a hideous green divider curtain to supposedly provide the patient with privacy.

"Any chance you might be pregnant?" Doctor Vance asked, poking at my stomach.

"No chance whatsoever," I answered, "Unless it's another immaculate conception."

He gave me a doubtful-looking smile and suggested they run a pregnancy test anyway.

I reiterated there was no chance I might be pregnant, but what I said was immaterial, because they went ahead and did the pregnancy test. It came back negative. "I told you," I said.

"It could be a false negative," the doctor mused, "if you're no better by tomorrow, we'll give it another try."

"The results will be the same," I grumbled, "I'm not pregnant." I was dating, but without going into further explanation, I knew there was no possibility of pregnancy.

For the next three days both the pain and swelling continued to increase and, unable to come up with any other feasible diagnosis for my condition, the doctor performed yet another pregnancy test. Not only was the pain unbearable, but I found it impossible to sleep without the sleeping pills I had been taking for the past six years. On my third day at the Student Health Center, the striped wallpaper began to swirl and twist itself into spirals, the ghastly green curtain began to ripple and the ceiling hooks from which it hung rattled like some invisible thing was toying with them. Everything in the room seemed to be moving, everything was blurred, nothing clear. Suddenly, feeling that I had somehow become the subject of some strange experiment, I screamed.

Dashing through the door, the nurse asked, "What's wrong?"

"What's going on?" I shouted. "What are you doing to me?" My voice was so loud that Doctor Vance came running into my room.

"What's going on?" he asked.

"I don't know," the nurse replied, "she just started screaming."

"Something is going on!" I insisted. "The wallpaper is twisted; somebody is up there moving the curtain hooks…"

"Have you been doing drugs?" Doctor Vance asked angrily. Working at the Student Health Center, he had seen more than his share of college kids who had overdosed.

"I don't do drugs!" I shouted back. "I don't do drugs!"

"Get her chart," the doctor ordered and once it was handed to him he ran his finger down the list of medications I did take. "Ah-ha, sleeping pills. Did you take those every night?"

I nodded.

"For how long," he asked.

"Six, maybe seven years, but I have a prescription."

"It doesn't make any difference whether or not you have a prescription, those pills are addictive. And you've got all the symptoms of withdrawal."

"But, I was still taking the sleeping pills when this pain in my stomach first started."

"I doubt your withdrawal is related to the stomach pain," he said. "You've got something going on internally and it's too complex for us to handle here."

The next day, I was transferred to the city hospital in Tuscaloosa. After a few days the agony of my sleeping pill withdrawal ended, but the stomach pain remained. Like Doctor Vance, the hospital ran a pregnancy test and it came back negative. They explored countless possibilities, but after three weeks in the city hospital, they knew no more than they did when I was brought in. Acknowledging the seriousness of the situation, Mother and Pappy drove to Alabama and brought me home to be treated at the Daytona hospital. Dit worked as a nurse at the hospital and Mother at least had a modicum of trust in their patient care.

A week after I was admitted to the Daytona hospital, the surgeon in charge of my case confessed, "If it wasn't for the fact that you're a quadriplegic, we'd do exploratory surgery to find what's causing this, but since..." he let the rest of his words drift off.

"Do the surgery anyway," I said.

"I can't do that. Quadriplegics are not good candidates for exploratory surgery."

I was slender to start with, but after losing thirty pounds I was down to a bone-thin sixty-eight pounds and the pain was excruciating. "I don't care if the surgery is risky," I said, "You need to find out what's wrong! Look at me, I'm emaciated, whatever this is, it's killing me!"

"We're giving you something for the pain..."

"It's not enough, I need you to find out what's causing this and fix it."

"I'm not going to do exploratory surgery, there's too great a risk that..."

"I don't give a damn about the risk!" I snapped. "I'm the patient and if I'm willing to risk having the surgery, you have to do it!"

"No. There's a very realistic chance that you could die on the operating table—"

I interrupted before he launched into another tirade about how quadriplegics are not good candidates for exploratory surgery because of their breathing difficulty and a myriad of other problems—"I'm dying right now!" I exclaimed angrily, "So you either do the surgery and find out what is wrong with me, or you allow me to lie here and die—but if I die because you weren't willing to do the surgery I requested, my estate will sue you and the hospital for intentionally bringing about my death!"

"I'm not doing this intentionally, it's just that—"

"I don't want to hear another word about how risky this surgery is," I said breathing fire, "I'm going to turn this over to our lawyer! He'll address the ramifications of your refusal with the Hospital's Board of Directors."

That afternoon, Mother contacted our lawyer and set up a meeting with the hospital administrators, the doctor, the attorney and me. Once they were presented with the possibility of a long drawn-out lawsuit and disastrous publicity, the surgeon decided that since my gall bladder was no longer functional, they could list the surgery as a gall bladder removal. That enabled them to move ahead with what was probably ten-percent gall bladder removal and ninety-percent exploratory surgery. The day after our meeting, I underwent the surgery and although they did remove both my gall bladder and appendix—neither of which were the cause of my problem—the surgery revealed that my ovary had burst because it had contained numerous cysts and I had developed a severe case of peritonitis, a poisonous inflammation of the tissue that lines the abdomen and protects the organs. According to the surgeon, the inflammation was so extensive it required nearly a gallon of the antibacterial fluid used to treat peritonitis. Had I not had the surgery, I would have died. In the recovery room, my sister Dit came to me and in that whispery voice she used when she wanted to sound sincere, she said, "It's not cancer, isn't that wonderful!" *Cancer? Cancer was never a consideration in my mind.*

When I was released from the hospital, I went home with Mother and Pappy. I was overworked, overtired and dramatically underweight, so I decided to take a year off to rest and regain my health. After I had recuperated from the surgery and was feeling stronger, Pappy pulled out my old electric typewriter and placed it on the desk. I began to send out resumes, thinking I would work for a year, rest, get my strength back, and then return to the University of Alabama to complete my dissertation. I had gone to the university planning to bypass a Masters degree and work on obtaining my PhD in Psychology. Luckily, the research for my dissertation and the course work I did during those four years were more than enough to earn my earlier-ignored Masters, because I never returned to the University of Alabama.

Shortly thereafter, the job offers began to roll in—apparently, my credentials now outweighed the fact that I was in a wheelchair. The first to arrive was from Alabama, it offered me a position as Director of the Montgomery County Mental Health Center, with time off to teach Psychology at a local college. It was unquestionably an attractive offer, but it would mean returning to Alabama and the Alabama 1960's civil rights struggle. *No thank you!* Not only did I not want to live in a place where segregation was the law of the land, but I was afraid my outspoken opinions on the issue would get me arrested—possibly even lynched. The truth was I didn't belong in Alabama; it didn't like me any better than I liked it. Fortunately, several other offers arrived soon thereafter. None of which, thankfully, would require me to live in a place for which I had so little respect. Since I have always enjoyed teaching, I accepted the faculty position teaching Psychology at St. Petersburg Junior College. After the hectic four years I'd endured in Alabama, I felt teaching a class would be easy by comparison, and it was. Although I taught classes five days a week, with additional classes on two evenings, and performed psychotherapy on two other evenings, I was deliriously happy. I loved working. The work I did, the people I helped, the movement along a career path was an important part of who I was. Mine was a schedule some people might find daunting, but I was only working half as hard as I did in Alabama, and I was making more money. It felt as if I was on vacation! When I returned to work I fully intended it to be for only a year, enough time to fully recover and regain my strength, but I discovered that I enjoyed being a teacher much more than I had ever enjoyed being a student. I was no longer working just to pay for my living expenses and my caregiver's education. I had actually embarked on a career. Not once have I looked back and regretted that decision not to return to Alabama to finish my dissertation; nor has the lack of a PhD ever held me back from getting the job I wanted. *A very good IS.*

While I was teaching at the college, I challenged my students the same way I had so often challenged myself—to reach higher, to grow beyond their current capacity and to be all that they could be. To help them along, I conducted study sessions the week before a final exam—a large group met in the auditorium where I'd answer questions, explain concepts and reiterate much of the material relative to the forthcoming exam. During the break, I was with a group of students in the hallway when this very handsome, but rather strange young man wandered over wearing a wet-look purple paisley suit. He said nothing for a few moments, his glance traveling from face to face but stopping on no one in particular.

Finally, he spoke, "Who's the teacher here?" he asked with a rather cocky attitude.

Several students pointed a finger toward me.

He gave me a sexy up-and-down look then allowed his eyes to remain fixed on my face. "I've never seen a teacher who looks like you," he said with the intonation of a compliment, and he stood there, continuing to stare.

An uneasy feeling was beginning to settle into my chest when he finally spoke again.

"I'm supposed to meet Sue Grimes here," he said.

"There's no one by that name in any of my classes," I told him. "Perhaps you have the wrong night."

He shrugged, "Maybe."

The group drifted back to their earlier conversation, but mister paisley suit made no move to leave. He wandered along the hall, read some posters on the bulletin board and then rejoined our group, not making his way through the crowd but remaining on the fringe.

When the study session was over, the students left the auditorium and hurried off to join friends, study, or perhaps even sleep. I remained behind to organize my notes and papers. When I headed for the elevator, he was still there, leaning against the wall as if he were waiting for something or someone. My caregiver slid my key into the elevator panel and pushed the button. Then I turned to him and said, "At ten o'clock the janitor comes around to lock the building, you've got to leave or you'll be locked in for the night."

He looked at me and smiled, "Okay," he said. His voice seemed shy, but he had an arrogant swagger that would lead you to believe otherwise.

Looking back, I could claim it was the oddity of that purple paisley suit that prompted me to ask the next question, but I can't honestly swear it wasn't those piercing green eyes—they were as green as emeralds and deep as the ocean. "What DO you do for a living?" I asked.

"I'm a singer," he said and stopped there. It seemed as if he spoke only in short bursts of words and only when he had something that had to be said.

"Yeah, right," I replied laughingly. Okay, I knew by the suit, he wasn't a stockbroker, but a singer? I wheeled myself out of the elevator, across the lobby and out the front door. He followed along.

As I neared my car, he said, "Wait right here, don't go anywhere!" and then he tore off running across the parking lot. Uncharacteristically, I did as he asked. *Anyone with nerve enough to wear such a ridiculous paisley suit deserved my attention.* Moments later, he sprinted back with a guitar in his hands. He leaned against the front of my car and began to sing, *Leaving on a Jet Plane.* I was stunned by both the beauty of his voice and the emotion he projected into the words. I'd heard Peter, Paul, and Mary sing the song a thousand times before, but I had never heard it sung with the depth of feeling this man gave it. A single tear began to trickle down my cheek and I became so engrossed in the soulful sound of his voice that I forgot about the purple paisley suit and focused on the sincerity in his green eyes. When he finished the song, he sang another and I made no attempt to leave. Perhaps I would have sat there listening to him all night, but halfway through the second song someone opened a classroom window on the second floor and yelled down, "Shut up! We're trying to study in here!" The window slammed shut and we both laughed.

Given the latent attitude of arrogance and muscular build he had, I was somewhat surprised when he stepped back and allowed Kelsey, my caregiver, to lift me into the car—any number of men would have snatched that task to use as proof of manhood, but not this guy. He asked if he could see me again. I handed him my card, "Sure," I said, "If you need a good shrink, call me."

"Okay," he replied and walked away.

The weekend that followed was filled with a flurry of activity. On Saturday morning, I moved to my new house—the first house I ever owned—and spent two days settling in. On Monday, it was back to the fast-paced schedule I had grown accustomed to. That Saturday my girlfriend, a fellow graduate student in Alabama, arrived for a visit and together we headed for Miami to visit another of our classmates.

We partied into the wee hours of Saturday night and continued on Sunday, so I didn't arrive back at the house until almost ten o'clock Sunday evening. The minute Kelsey heard our car pull in, she dashed out the door to meet us. "You're never going to believe who came to see you," she said in a frantic whisper.

"Who?" I asked.

"That guy!" She must have noticed the puzzled look on my face, because she continued to explain. "The strange guy from the college...remember?"

She didn't have to finish, because by then I knew who it was. "The one with the purple paisley suit?" I asked.

She nodded. "Yes, he showed up early this afternoon."

"Did you explain I was away for the weekend?" I asked wearily.

"Of course I did, but he said he'd wait."

"Wait? He's still here?" What she said finally penetrated my exhaustion.

"Yes, he's sitting in the living room with a guitar on his lap."

"Good grief!" I was dead tired from a weekend of partying and in no mood for company, but it was impossible to get to the bedroom without passing through the living room—besides, I couldn't do that to the guy after he'd been waiting for me all day. *And then of course, there were those beautiful green eyes and that mesmerizing voice.*

Before I had a chance to say much of anything, he jumped up from the chair and began singing again. He sang *September Morn* and followed it with *Sweet Caroline,* but by then my eyelids were drooping, "I'm exhausted and have to get into bed," I said.

"Okay," he answered and left.

Once I got past the image of that ridiculous suit, I had to admit the guy was not only a singer, but a singer with the most beautiful voice I had ever heard. When I listened to him sing I was left wanting more...and more was precisely what I got.

On Monday afternoon when I returned home from teaching, there he was, sitting on the front step of my house with his guitar in his lap.

"Hi," he said sheepishly, then he began singing again—this time it was *Moon River.* You've got to admit when some good-looking guy shows up on your doorstep and starts to sing, it makes you wonder. "What are you doing here?" I asked.

"I wanted to see you again," he began thumbing his guitar and kind of sang, "I suppose you want to know my name...it's Jude...Jude Deauville."

I had to laugh, it was the strangest introduction I had ever experienced, but that was how Jude was; he could express himself in song much better than he could with the spoken word. And when he sang, it was moving to the point where it could draw tears from a dry eye.

Jude and I began a friendship that circled around the sound of his voice. He created words and melodies to express the things he wanted to say. These songs were unique, funny at times, touching at other times, but always clever. Six nights a week he sang at a lounge from nine o'clock in the evening until two, so his visits to my house were in the afternoon; day after day, I would come home from work and find him waiting for me with a broad smile and another beautiful song. Those afternoon visits continued for several weeks, then one night the doorbell rang at two-thirty in the morning. I was startled from sleep and lay there waiting and wondering what was happening. A sleepy-eyed Kelsey poked her head into my room, "He's back again," she said wearily.

"Jude?"

She gave a groggy nod. "He wants to see you," she said, "do you want to get up?"

"I don't think so," I answered, "but maybe it's something important, so why don't you bring him in here." It seemed only logical to me that a person who showed up in the middle of the night had some urgent need and I was after all, a psychologist. Moments later, Jude walked into my bedroom smiling. "Is something wrong?" I asked.

He shook his head side to side, "No," he said softly, "I just wanted to see you."

"It's two-thirty in the morning!"

"I know, but I just got off work." He seemed at a loss for words following that. He paused for a moment then began singing.

"I think Kelsey is trying to go back to sleep," I interrupted, "but any other time…"

He started to strum the guitar more softly and continued to sing. I don't remember the song he sang that night, but I recall it being soft and low with a gentle sound that would encourage sleep rather than disturb it.

Night after night, Jude came to see me in the wee hours of the morning and oddly enough, I began to look forward to those visits even though they were at two-thirty in the morning. When the doorbell chimed a few hours after we'd gone to bed, a bleary-eyed

Kelsey opened the door, escorted him into my bedroom, then went back to her own room and returned to sleep. Jude was extremely handsome, not excessively tall, but powerful in his appearance, and gentle at heart. Our conversations were never profound, thought-provoking or wordy—I was a listener and he sang.

After Jude had gone, I often thought back on the years before I knew him, years when I'd dated dozens and dozens of men, most of them considerably older than I was. They were men who were generally charming, debonair and handsome but the moment someone discussed the possibility of taking our relationship to the next level, I walked away. A psychologist would have labeled it 'fear of commitment' but I believe it was my memories of Mother and her long string of disastrous love affairs that left me with the feeling that I never wanted to get married. For many years I struggled to be an independent person and once I had that independence, it was not something I was willing to part with.

When the thought of loving someone crossed my mind, I'd flash back to the sight of Mother in her rocking chair, clinging to me when I was a four-year old child and weeping brokenheartedly because my father had left us. I'd remember her fights with other lovers, the angry words flying back and forth, the bitter resentment that simmered long after the shouting ended. I'd remember men who came and went, some without names, just a bunch of blurry faces bringing heartache after heartache. Yet Mother never gave up, she wrapped herself in fancy clothes and continued to search for the ever-elusive love she believed to be just around the next corner. After my father disappeared, the heavy weight of loneliness settled into Mother's heart and it was a burden that could only be eased by having a man in her life. So the string of lovers began…one after another, each one took what they wanted and eventually left her broken hearted. Those men took the love she offered so freely and then left her lonelier than she had been before they came into her life. Many years ago, I vowed never to let that happen to me. I had numerous boyfriends and some love affairs, but I had never given my heart away and I still was not ready to do so.

For a few months, Jude rang the doorbell every night at two-thirty. He was like clockwork—consistent and dependable. At first he seemed to be more comfortable singing than talking, but eventually we worked our way into conversations that sometimes lasted until the sun showed itself on the horizon. Although we appeared to have very few things in common, Jude fascinated me. Behind the golden voice there was a man of many mysteries, a man who had walked away from a New York recording contract simply because he didn't like the city. I was extremely committed to my pursuit of a career, but Jude wasn't. He just loved to sing and communicated best when he did it with a song.

I knew Jude was extremely fond of me, he made no secret of that, but I was not ready for any type of commitment and, as much as I enjoyed his company, the late night hours were taking a toll on me. I had early morning classes, and a schedule that often ran until eight or nine o'clock in the evening. More often than not, I had to start getting ready for work just moments after Jude left. Before long, I found myself totally exhausted and pushing through the days with only two or three hours of sleep. Eventually I told him, "This is not working."

"What's not working?" he asked innocently.

"This relationship. You're a night person and I'm a day person. I have to be up early for classes and I can't do it with only two or three hours of sleep. As much as I enjoy being with you, and I really do, this relationship is doomed because we're traveling on different roads.

An expression of sadness settled over his face, but he said almost nothing. As I mentioned earlier, Jude was a man of few words. When I watched him walk away that morning, my heart ached. I had grown as fond of him as he obviously was of me.

The following day was a Tuesday and when I arrived home that afternoon, I found Jude sitting on the front step of my house. "What are you doing here?" I asked.

"I quit my job," he answered, his tone as calm and level as if he had simply said hello.

"Quit your job?" I gasped, "You can't do that!"

"I already have."

"Why?"

"Because I love you and I want this relationship to work. I want to be with you forever."

A flutter rose in my throat—I was a woman who didn't do 'forever' and as much as I enjoyed being with Jude, I didn't want him to throw his career away for someone who was never going to get married. "You can't quit your job," I repeated. "You're a singer, a fabulous singer. Singers have to work at night."

"I'll get a different job."

"Doing what?"

He shrugged his shoulders, "I don't know yet, but I'll find something." He must have seen the look of concern on my face, because he stood, walked over and touched his hand to my face, "Don't worry Lani," he said, "this is good. It's all good."

True to his word, Jude, the man with the magical voice, found a job working for a construction company. Because he truly cared for me, he'd gone from being a sought-after lounge singer to being a day laborer who carried buckets of plaster up several levels of what would ultimately become a high rise building. He was definitely a man who knew what he wanted...and apparently what he wanted was me. In a few short months, our friendship evolved into that of lovers and eventually he came to live at my house.

Once Jude moved in, he suggested that he take over Kelsey's job as caregiver. "That's not a good idea," I answered, "You're my lover, not my caregiver."

"I can be both," he said, "I love you and want to take care of you."

"No," I repeated, "I feel strongly that a lover shouldn't be a caregiver; it's too much work, too big a responsibility, and sooner or later it will spoil the relationship."

"I don't consider taking care of you a responsibility," Jude answered, "I love you, Lani, when you love someone, it's what you want to do."

"In time, you'd get tired of doing it. I'd rather you remain my lover."

"I'll never get tired of taking care of you!" he said emphatically. "It's foolish to pay someone else to do what I want to be doing."

I argued the point for a long while but eventually had to admit he was right. It would be a financial relief not to have pay Kelsey's salary. Besides, the house was so small, it was almost impossible to move from one room to another without bumping into something or someone. In addition to Jude and the pet rooster that came with him, there was Tanya, who had been with me since graduate school. Tanya was a cat with an attitude. She was afraid of nothing and nobody. Dogs didn't chase Tanya, she chased them, and she did so with a vengeance! To say that our little group grew into a menagerie would be an understatement, for as time went by we added a pet pig, an Irish setter, a Yorkie, and an Afghan hound. The pig was an accidental acquisition, a rescue I suppose. The last stretch of highway on I-4 had opened just days earlier, so only a handful of cars were on the road. We were traveling home from Daytona and I was sailing along when I spotted a mother pig and her litter in the middle of the blacktop. Pointing them out to Jude, I said, "Those pigs will get run over if they don't move." I stopped and let him out so that he could shoo the pigs back to safety. The sand along the side of the road had been sprayed with grass seed and fertilizer, so it was still too soft for me to pull onto the shoulder. "I'll drive down to the next exit and turn the car around," I said, "wait for me over in the eastbound lane." When I circled back, the mother and most of the piglets were gone, but cradled in Jude's hands was one lone black piglet—a tiny baby, about the size of a toaster and almost as square.

"The others ran off and left this one," Jude said sheepishly. "We can't just leave it here."

Jude knew what I'd say before he asked. I grinned and said, "Okay," but by then he'd already put the piglet on the floor of the backseat. Moments later, a genuinely God-awful smell wafted past our noses—the scared piglet had pooped all over the white carpet in my new Dodge Charger.

Within days the piglet had been named Peggy, with a pronunciation that was somewhere between piggy and Peggy. At first, we fed her with a baby bottle, but before long the piglet was big enough and hungry enough to eat all she could get. Peggy remained with us for a number of months until a nosy neighbor peered through the knothole in our fence and saw her rooting around our backyard. When he complained about our having a pet pig, we had to let Peggy go. It took weeks for us to find the right home for her, a place where she would be loved and treated as a pet, and in the end it turned out to be a farm where school children learned about raising animals on a farm. Peggy would definitely get lots of love and attention there.

Although I originally had reservations about Jude being my caregiver, I soon came to realize it was an absolutely delightful arrangement. He was not the least bit intimidated with my being in a wheelchair. In fact, he virtually ignored my handicap, being neither sympathetic nor condescending. We talked, we laughed, we argued and we made love ignoring the shadowy wheelchair that occupied one corner of the bedroom. I marveled at how Jude was so at ease with the challenges of a quadriplegic. Then much later on, I learned that when he was five years old, his father was paralyzed in an automobile accident and had to spend the remainder of his life in a wheelchair. *Jude had lived with this nearly all his life, he understood.*

Before the accident, Jude's father, Ronnie Deauville, had been a well-known singer. He sang with bands like Tommy Dorsey, Benny Goodman, and Guy Lombardo. He also did the sound tracks for a number of movies. With a voice that carried the same mellowness as Jude's, Ronnie could have sung most anywhere he wanted but, after the accident, he was told that he would probably never sing again and was confined to an iron lung for almost a year. During that time, the family lived off of the residuals from Ronnie's records, but in time those royalties dried up and the family was forced to look for other options. The Deauvilles chose to live in the Canary Islands, where the cost of living was dirt cheap. After three years of being away, they longed for their homeland and returned to the United States. The Deauville family remained in the USA for a short while, but with circumstances no better than they had been previously, Ronnie, his wife, Patricia, and their youngest daughter, Elvira, returned to the Canary Islands. When his parents decided to return to the United States for a second time, they were uncertain where they wanted to live. When Jude and I drove to the Port of Fort Lauderdale to pick them up, we invited them to stay with us.

The Saint Petersburg house was small, but the guest room was absolutely tiny. The bed was a fold-out sofa and when opened up, it stretched from wall to wall without an inch of walkway around it. There was no way we could ask Jude's parents to take that room. The only alternative was for us to give his parents our bedroom and move into the guest room ourselves. I was tall, but slender, and Jude was accustomed to lifting me into bed. But when we moved into the guest room, he had to lift me out of my chair while it was still in the hallway and then crawl across the mattress on his knees to position me at the head of the bed. At times, this crazy process caused us to laugh so uproariously that his parents probably wondered what we were up to.

Eventually, I decided we needed to look for another house. It wasn't so much the size of the tiny house that pushed me into a decision, it was the size of the lot it sat on, the noise and congestion, and the feeling of being closed-in. Saint Petersburg was growing by leaps and bounds at that point and the traffic rumbled down our street at all hours of the day and night. If we dared to open the window, the honking horns and revved up motors prevented us from hearing each other.

Although I wanted to move, I had no immediate plans, nor did I have a house picked out. But Jude, knowing me for the person I am, realized that once I made up my mind to do something, it was going to get done. One night when I arrived home, I found our little one-car garage filled with a collection of used furniture he had purchased at the flea market.

"Where did all that stuff come from?" I asked

"I bought it," Jude answered proudly. "We're going to need more furniture when we get a bigger house. And, hopefully the house will have a bar, because I got a great deal on some whiskey barrel bar furniture and wrought iron patio stuff."

That was so typically Jude. He was a person who could imagine the sunrise on a day so thick with fog that anyone else would walk around blindly bumping into cement walls.

Twelve

After over two years of teaching at the college, I began to question whether I was wasting the training I'd had and the skill I'd developed as a psychotherapist. I was a good teacher, and to succeed in my class students had to want more than a passing grade. Like me, they had to have a genuine desire to learn about psychology, the study of behavior. It was rumored that students told one another my class was not an easy course, but in it they'd learn more than they thought possible. Unquestionably, teaching offered its own sense of satisfaction. But the realization that I could possibly make a vital difference in people's lives gnawed at my brain until I walked away and opened my own psychotherapy practice.

I am not the type of psychologist who allows a patient to simply ramble on about how much they hate whatever it is they happen to hate about their life—my role as a clinical psychologist is to aid the patient in understanding the nature of their problem and to guide them toward a solution to rebuild their life. I would most likely be referred to as a behaviorist. Unfortunately, I was the new kid in town and I was a psychotherapist without a PhD. I had to take whatever referrals I could get, and often they were people who did not seek psychotherapy of their own volition. My patients were often sent by an angry parent, a resentful spouse or in numerous instances, the court. Psychotherapy was offered as an alternative to prison or the juvenile detention center, so those patients often came with a heavy load of resentment and no motivation to change. They came because they had to. They were fulfilling a mandated obligation, but with no real desire to fix the parts of their life that were problematic.

On the all-too-infrequent occasions when I worked with patients who were self-referrals, it was a truly rewarding experience because I could help them better their life. But, trying to help people who want nothing more than to be left alone is like banging your head against a stone wall. People forced into psychotherapy are angry people who have fallen down and refuse to get up. Even psychologists with decades of experience have a difficult time helping people like that. Eventually the frustration of such work began to pick at me. A year later, when I received an offer to serve as the rehabilitation psychologist for the largest Goodwill Rehabilitation Facility in the country, I closed my office and accepted the offer, even though I had always avoided what I felt was the "stereotype" of working as a rehabilitation psychologist.

Shortly after I accepted the job at Goodwill, Jude asked me to marry him. My answer was no. It wasn't that I didn't care about Jude, I simply had too much baggage—too many memories of Mother and her failed marriage, too many memories of an abusive father and an unbelievably cruel husband. I could still picture Mother lying on the kitchen floor in a pool of her own blood as my father angrily stormed out the door. "He wasn't always this way," she would say apologetically, but still she stayed, allowing him to brutalize her and abuse her children. Mother was a strong woman, and during her lifetime she dealt with and overcame more challenges than most women could possibly withstand. But when it came to my father, she was helpless to do anything because she was so pathetically in love with him. I was determined that I would never allow myself to be in that position.

"Why won't you marry me?" Jude asked, "We're happy together."

"Yes we are, and let's leave it at that. I need to focus on my career and marriage sometimes ruins everything."

For the moment Jude accepted my answer and we continued on as before.

During my first few years with Goodwill, I worked with people who had all types and varying levels of disabilities; I helped them to discover untapped abilities and vocations that could eventually provide them with an independent lifestyle. Given the success of the program, Goodwill was awarded a contract for evaluating state prisoners in work release programs. The challenge was to determine their actual level of rehabilitation and reformation; then make a recommendation as to whether or not they were ready to be assimilated into society. The effectiveness of the state program ultimately garnered Goodwill a Federal Government contract for the evaluation of prisoners convicted of a federal crime and awaiting sentencing. Since I was known to be a keen observer of underlying characteristics, not always obvious in the standard psychological tests, I was given sole responsibility for this program. I found myself working with embezzlers, bank robbers, smugglers and the like. It was up to me to do a psychological case study of these prisoners and evaluate their prognosis for rehabilitation versus potential for a repeat performance. A person with genuine psychological problems needs treatment, those with larceny in their heart...well, that's another story.

I remember back in graduate school when I was given a little girl for personality testing—she was a beautiful six-year-old with blond ringlets and the sweetest smile imaginable. I put her through a considerable number of psychological tests, but was swayed by the child's angelic appearance and interpreted the results incorrectly. I concluded they had nothing to fear from the girl. Wrong! The child had been brought to me as a learning experience because I had an inclination to find something good in almost everyone. The girl had already been evaluated, so my assessment was simply a test, and I failed. She was virtually *The Bad Seed.* The experience taught me that sometimes an outward appearance and charming demeanor can momentarily trick the eye into seeing something beyond what exists, but as a psychologist, it was my job to look inside a person to discover the truth of who they were.

As part of Goodwill's Federal Program, I came across one prisoner, an attractive young woman who parked her Cadillac in front of the office and strolled in wearing an elegant fur coat. She had been convicted of robbing banks and was required to live in Goodwill's halfway house dormitory where she had constant supervision. The judge asked that I do a case study to evaluate her potential for rehabilitation. For several weeks she underwent the standardized psychological tests and hours of interviews. Her answers were well-honed, but something about her troubled me.

"I've reformed," she swore, "I'm going to get a job and walk the straight and narrow."

It's not easy to fool a well-trained psychologist, we've learned to see past lies and hover over the truth buried beneath. "Have you started looking for a job?" I asked.

"Yes," she answered, "I've got an interview this afternoon. It's in an office downtown."

When she sashayed out the door, I had a lump of suspicion that felt too large to swallow. I buzzed one of our counselors and asked that they follow her. As the woman claimed, she did have an interview that afternoon, but it was in the office of a bank. She wasn't looking for work, she was casing the bank for her next job! I immediately confined her to the dormitory and called the judge with the recommendation that she spend more time behind bars.

That woman was a singular instance in a long list of prisoners who were ripe with get-rich-quick schemes. There was the double-trouble jockey who bet against his own horse with counterfeit money; a smuggler who insisted he had no knowledge of how the bag of cocaine came to be in his suitcase; and, a banker who rewarded himself with a piece of the action when he made loans to underfinanced builders. Then, there were the prisoners with genuine psychological problems. It's possible to commit a crime in the semi-conscious state of fugue, a crime the person often has no recollection of having done—prisoners such as that were people who had slid off the edge of reality for a brief period of time and would benefit from psychotherapy rather than incarceration. Some prisoners showed a definite sense of remorse with the psychological testing and interviews indicating they would not be repeat offenders. In instances like that I was lenient, recommending treatment rather than prison, giving the person a chance to find a better IS on the road ahead.

My days were filled with the work I loved doing, and my nights were spent with Jude. I went from serious like to being in love. When it happened, I can't say. It was not a moment of epiphany, it happened gradually—day by day, intimacy by intimacy. He was there to comfort me on bad days, share my joy on good days, talk when I needed to talk and listen when I needed someone to listen. Jude always seemed to have a song that could make me forget everything else. We laughed together; we talked about things I had never discussed with anyone else; we touched the inside of each other's heart and shared almost everything— everything except our last name, which remained a bone of contention. At first the subject of marriage reared its ugly head only occasionally, but as the months and years rolled on Jude became increasingly insistent.

In the spring of 1974 Jude asked me to marry him for what may have been the millionth time, and I again answered no. "I love you," I said, "Isn't that enough?"

"No," he replied. "People who love and trust each other get married! I'm not your father and I'd never do the things he did. Now, if you don't believe me and trust me enough to marry me, then I'm leaving!"

"Leaving?" I was dumbfounded. This was something he'd never before threatened. "You can't leave," I said, "I love you and you know that."

"Then marry me."

I thought about a life without Jude, and somehow that was something I couldn't accept. Despite the ugly shadows that remain in the back of your mind, love can carry you to a place where there is faith and trust in another human being, although I was not yet at that place, I knew I did not want to lose Jude. After a few seconds,

I said, "Okay dammit," and accepted his proposal. *Hardly the storybook version of accepting a marriage proposal!*

As the weeks went by, my uncertainty about marriage brought an endless amount of agony. One moment I would think it was far better than losing the man I loved; then seconds later I'd remember the heartache of Mother's life and a lump of doubt would rise up from the pit of my stomach. Several times I suggested to Jude that we put the wedding off for a while longer, but he rejected the idea.

A week before the wedding, Jude and I got into an argument—over what, I can no longer remember—but in that moment of anger, I grabbed hold of the doubt inside of me and telephoned Mother and Pappy to say the wedding was off. "I wouldn't marry that SOB if he were the last man on earth," I raged.

Jude, in that overwhelmingly patient way he has, took the receiver and told Mother, "Pay no attention to what she says; Lani's just having a bout of temporary insanity. The wedding is still on; we love you and we'll see you in another week."

The weekend before the wedding, our friends, Dickie and his wife, took us out in their boat for a day of fun and sun on the water. "We'll cruise over and look at where the tugboat and barge ran into the Sunshine Skyway Bridge," Dickie said. As a construction worker, he considered a collapsing bridge to be of great interest. Dickie was one of Jude's Best Men—he had decided to have two. Nothing surprised me anymore. I had long ago come to understand the purple paisley suit wasn't the only unusual thing about Jude. There was no mold for the man, he simply did the things that made him and the others around him happy, which is why he had two best men. We spent the afternoon drinking wine, telling jokes and laughing until our sides ached. Then, because I had always been such an adventure-seeking individual, Dickie suggested we try jumping the waves. It meant aiming the boat at an oncoming wave and hitting it head-on so we'd sail through the air and land upright in the water. It sounded like fun; and it was, the first three times we did it. The fourth time, the wave was considerably higher, so we sailed through the air and landed hard—hard enough to throw me out of my seat and across the deck. We heard the snap, and I knew instantly the thighbone of my right leg was broken.

The following Sunday we were married; and what a wedding it was! It rained all morning, and as we watched the dark clouds hanging overhead, our vision of an outdoor wedding grew dimmer and dimmer. Shortly before lunch, the sky cleared, not enough for the sun to break through, but enough that our wedding guests would stay dry. We were married in a park down the street from where we lived. The service was performed by a friend of ours, who became a Notary so he could be the one to marry us. We recited vows that we had each written, vows that would forever be engraved on our hearts. With my right leg in a full-length plaster cast, and the footrest of my wheelchair stretched out in front of me, I was not your typical ballroom gown bride. I wore a white lace pantsuit with a crown of yellow roses and daisies circling my head. Jude was equally non-traditional in his yellow leisure suit and a silk shirt sprinkled with butterflies. As the song says, it was the dawning of the Age of Aquarius and we were truly the make love not war generation. As we stood before the Notary and spoke the words we had so carefully written, several guests began to snicker. Gradually the snicker grew into laughter, and I began to wonder what we were doing wrong. Our words were sincere, vows to honor and treasure one another for the rest of our life. *What was wrong?* Ten seconds after Jude was told he could now kiss the bride, several of our friends came rushing over to us. "Did you see that?" they asked laughingly.

"See what?" Jude and I replied simultaneously.

"Over there," Sara pointed to the edge of the lake behind our Notary—several pairs of ducks were fornicating!

"Looks like the ducks couldn't wait for your wedding night," Sammy chuckled. By then, almost all of our guests were laughing along.

Despite our insistence that they do nothing, Mother and Pappy had arranged for a wedding reception at the Holiday Inn and a friend of ours squired us to the reception in his limousine with the external loudspeaker blasting an introduction to the new Mr. and Mrs. Jude Deauville. The memorabilia of our wedding includes a collage of snapshots that easily could have been taken at a carnival—people laughing, drinking, hugging one another, dressed in everything from a long red satin gown to a muscle tee shirt. One colleague, known for her love of herpetology, came with a mild-mannered snake woven through her hair. At the end of the day, happy, exhausted and filled with the sense of being alive, Jude and I returned to our house.

We made love that night, just as we had done so many times before. Over the years, as my body became stronger and more active, I was able to both feel and enjoy intimacy. I took pleasure from every moment of our sexual encounters. *Definitely a good IS!*

It seemed each day of my life became better than the day before. I enjoyed working with Goodwill, I enjoyed the challenge of looking inside people who thought they could outsmart the system, and I enjoyed helping others who earnestly wanted to move on to a better life.

On weekends, Jude and I frequently went house-hunting. We wanted a bigger place, a house with room for all the furniture stored in the garage. I wanted a place with charm, atmosphere and doorways wide enough to accommodate my wheelchair. The problem was, we both had high hopes, but neither of us had very much money. Once he had given up his singing career, Jude went from job to job—sometimes working, sometimes not. And even though my work at Goodwill received accolades, I was paid a very modest salary. We also had to remain in Saint Petersburg, where I was close enough to drive back and forth to work.

Saint Petersburg was a city of contrasts— elegant mansions circled the bay, tiny houses were squeezed together in the old neighborhoods with cracked and buckling sidewalks, and the south side of town could probably be considered a slum. That slum area was what we drove through, the day we first saw Driftwood.

Frank, the Director of Rehabilitation Services at Goodwill had invited us to dinner at his home. But as we drove past buildings with broken windows and sprayed-on graffiti, I began to think I might have the wrong address. Four blocks past a house with a rusting tricycle in the yard and a sheet covering the window, we saw an arch carved with the letters D R I F T W O O D –we turned into the driveway and entered an unexpected oasis. We drove through the development before parking in front of Frank's house. It was one long street that wound around beautifully designed houses sitting on strangely shaped lots—some triangular, some square, and some that seemed almost oval. Most of the houses were designed with a Spanish flair, but each had a quality of uniqueness. Gigantic oaks stood guard over everything and the street seemed to swerve so as not to disturb the trees standing in its pathway. The road circled around a large park, past a countless number of century-old oaks, and then found its way back to front gate. At one edge of the community, the houses were larger and backed up to Tampa Bay; but Frank's house was situated fairly close to the entrance arch we had driven through. We parked the car in front of the house and went in. This was the type of place Jude and I dreamed of having, it was also the type of place we'd never be able to afford.

During the course of dinner, I mentioned that to Frank and his wife.

"If you're really interested in living here," he replied, "the house next door is for sale."

"That adorable little Tudor at the bend of the road?" I said.

"Yes," he nodded. "The house isn't as small as it looks but it needs some work, so you can probably get it at a decent price."

I felt my pulse quicken, and after that, I can't recall much about the evening. My mind was preoccupied with thoughts of living in this unique little paradise.

I called the realtor, Sue Ann Martin, early the next morning and that afternoon we went back to look at the house. As Frank had suggested, the one-hundred year old house was much larger than it appeared, but we could tell by bits of peeling paint and speckles of black mold, that it did indeed need work. Once inside the front door, I saw a magnificent stone fireplace to the right, and after making a ninety-degree turn, we found ourselves looking up into what seemed almost like the nave of a church. It was a room with a sixteen foot high cathedral ceiling and wood beams that stretched from one side of the room to the other.

"This is the living room," Sue Ann said, "and that's a working fireplace."

At the end of the room a loft was perched above a wall of bookshelves. The house reeked with charm but I tried to act nonchalant, fearing that an overabundance of love for it would drive the price up.

"Wait until you see the patio..." Sue Ann veered left and started down a narrow hallway leading to what had originally been the master bedroom and was now a small guest room.

"The hallway is too narrow for my chair," I said, but Jude was already halfway down the hall poking his head into the room. "It's just a little guest bedroom," he said hurrying back.

"Previous owners converted what was once the garage into a lovely master bedroom," Sue Ann headed toward the far end of the room. "It has an extremely large closet and... oh dear..." she sighed looking back, "This hallway is also too narrow for your chair."

"I'm afraid so," I nodded.

"No problem," she said brightly, "We'll go around and come through the back." She made a u-turn across the living room and motioned for us to follow. We went through the dining room into the kitchen and from there into a cement-walled all-purpose room with little use other than providing a closet for the washer and dryer and to serve as an exchange station for the doors leading to other parts of the house. One of those doors led to the master bedroom that was inaccessible for my wheelchair from the living room. Another one opened into a bar with built in seating along the wall and high windows that gave light without an invasion of privacy. I noticed the twinkle in Jude's eyes and knew he was imagining the room filled with his whiskey barrel bar furniture. Beyond the cement room was a walled in patio sprinkled with sunlight filtering through the trees. The wrought iron furniture stored in our garage would be a perfect fit.

I was in love with the house, with the wooded surroundings and the smell of Tampa Bay. It brought back long lost memories of the Tomoka Preserve. Jude was in love with the bar. Yes, the house was extremely inaccessible. It definitely needed repairs and it had neither heat nor air conditioning, but those things didn't matter because we both loved it. The price was a stretch and we knew we wouldn't be able to do any of the work right away, but this house was truly what we'd been searching for. Ignoring the slum we'd driven through to get there and the doorways too narrow for my wheelchair to pass through, we bought the house.

A few days after we moved in, a little lady with gray hair rapped on the back door. When Jude opened it, she was holding a silver tray with a bottle of bourbon and three glasses. She moved past Jude and set her tray on the table, "That thing gets heavy," she said, "but there's nothing like a glass of bourbon to help people get acquainted." She gave a grin, "I'm Maxine, your next door neighbor."

I couldn't help but laugh. She was like an elf delivering presents on Christmas morning. "Want one?" she asked motioning to the bottle.

Jude and I both answered no, but that didn't stop Maxine from enjoying hers. She pulled the top from the bottle and poured herself a drink.

Within minutes, she settled herself in a chair and began giving us the history of Driftwood. "The whole development was built by a Mexican artist," she explained, "and this was the first house he built. It was a honeymoon cottage for him and his wife. Every house in here is different, but they're all his designs. The man was a naturalist who favored aesthetics over practicality, that's why the lots are all different shapes. He designed around the trees instead of chopping them down." Maxine lifted her glass and took another sip, "Sure you don't want one?" she asked.

Maxine was in her 80s, she never confessed how far into her 80s she was, but she and her bottle of bourbon returned the next evening and before long it became a nightly ritual. On her second, or perhaps third, visit she placed her glass too close to the edge of the end table and it spilled onto the worn grayish-tan carpet in our living room; which prompted her to tell us about the floor beneath the carpet. "What you should do," she said swiping the spill with a hankie she pulled from her pocket, "is get rid of this grungy old carpet. There's some lovely magnolia planking beneath this stuff." She settled back into her chair. "I know, because I used to live in this house and I've seen that wood, it's a sight for sore eyes! This carpet... well, it's obviously seen better days."

Like many old houses, this one held souvenirs from a century of different owners. It was reminiscent of a seed sprouting branches in a number of different directions. The flat-roofed room that was once a garage was now the master bedroom. The Florida room had been added to one side; the bar was also an add-on, as was the all-purpose room with its seven doors leading to different parts of the house and the outside. Early on, there had been a breezeway separating the kitchen from the remainder of the house, but long ago it had been walled in and was now the dining room. It seemed as though every family who had lived in the house added something and left a piece of themselves behind. In time, I imagined we would do the same.

With the first heavy rain, we discovered the house had numerous leaks. By then, we had already come face to face with an army of palmetto bugs and oversized river rats. After a few downpours, Jude learned precisely where to set out pots to catch the water; and when we finally could afford to have a roofer repair those leaks, new ones sprang up. Some things came as a surprise, others we knew about when we bought the house. The too-narrow hallway meant that every night I had to take a circuitous route to get into the bedroom; and outside of the arched driveway stood the slum area with its ongoing string of reported break-ins and muggings. None of those things discouraged us, but with Jude working on weekends, we decided I should have some type of protection. So we found a home for our excessively good-natured afghan hound and replaced her with Patches, a harlequin Great Dane that no would-be attacker was willing to tangle with. When Patches was at my side, I was free to roam throughout the community, and I did. On a sunny Saturday afternoon, I would slide a collar on Patches and we'd head for the back of the development where I made friends with a gigantic blue heron and fished from a neighbor's dock.

As soon as we'd settled in, we began to invite friends to the house. They clustered around the bar drinking and talking for hours on end. Over time, those groups grew in number and evolved into parties that included business colleagues, neighbors and our eclectic mix of friends. It was not at all unusual to see a learned professor chatting with a snake charmer or a musician holding court with a group of doctors. Jude and I had equally unorthodox groups of buddies, and most times they mixed beautifully, but at one of our parties, a colleague called me aside and said he simply could not stay at the party. "Why?" I asked with astonishment.

"Why?" he repeated, as if he expected I already knew the answer. "Because the guy I've been talking to at the bar just told me that his business is importing marijuana, that's why. I'm with the State Attorney's office. I can't afford to hear what I heard." He left the party without hard feelings and apparently without any recollection of his earlier conversation.

Fortunately, that was the only time our mix of friends clashed.

About eight weeks after we moved in, Jude's brother came to visit. Together, the two of them broke through the wall to widen the too-narrow hallway and pulled up all of that ratty-looking carpet. With the grime and grit of years clinging to the wood, the planks looked worse than the carpeting they'd removed. We could hardly afford to replace all of the carpet and I was beginning to worry that removing it had been a mistake. After Jude and David ran a high-powered sander over the wood, it looked fractionally better—but nothing like I had expected.

"Don't worry," David assured me, "It will be fine once we're finished."

The process took almost three weeks to complete. Day after day they sanded, then scrubbed, then applied another layer of polyurethane coating, until at last the white magnolia wood came to life with clean, clear color and a rich black grain running through it.

Restoring the wood floor was one of the few things we did to the house. Unlike the numerous people who came before us, we did very little to change the place. We simply couldn't afford it, and besides, we loved the house even with its leaks, creaks, and wobbly bricks.

Thirteen

The year after we bought the house at Driftwood, I received notification that I had been named the Goodwill Disabled Employee of the Year. Although I was pleased to receive such an honor, I had no idea of the changes it would bring about. The award ceremony was simple enough, it basically consisted of a Public Relations Officer telling me what a wonderful job I had done and handing me a certificate of merit. But, it turned out to be the trigger for an avalanche of speaking engagements. With Jude as my caregiver, we travelled to places throughout Massachusetts, Texas, Colorado, Iowa, Ohio, California and innumerable other states. I went wherever Goodwill had an office and spoke about the limitless opportunities for people with disabilities. "The worst handicap you can have," I told the audience, "is a lack of belief in yourself." My visibility within the vocational rehabilitation industry grew along with the frequency of these trips, and I had the opportunity to meet many famous people. In Lowell, Massachusetts, I met Bob Hope and presented him with a Goodwill lapel pin. In doing so, I planted a kiss on his cheek. That picture appeared in newspapers across the country, which ultimately led to more speaking engagements, and an invitation to the White House.

Jude was always at my side, always supportive, always content to remain in the background. At the airports without a jetway, he lifted me from my wheelchair on the tarmac, carried me up the stairs leading to the plane and placed me in my seat.

Although we were what some might consider relatively poor, we were wined and dined like royalty on those trips, and on frequent occasions treated to sightseeing excursions.

In the fall I received an invitation to visit the White House, where President Gerald Ford would congratulate me on the work I was doing. I was awed—first at receiving such a prestigious invitation and then at the graciousness with which we were treated. Jude, of course, accompanied me. Before being taken to the Oval Office, we were given a private tour of the White House and I was able to see many of the places tourists never visit—the elevator that FDR used to get from floor to floor, the ballroom where Caroline Kennedy rode her pony, Macaroni, and banquet halls with chandeliers sparkling like a cascade of diamonds. After the tour we were taken to a small waiting area outside the President's office and ultimately into the Oval Office. President Ford was a big man but, looking up from a wheelchair, he appeared even bigger. We chatted about my work for a few minutes, then he presented me with a pin. It was in the shape of a gold bow with the Presidential Seal dangling from the center and President Ford's signature engraved on the back. I liked him immensely, and resisted the urge to tell him he had made a huge mistake in pardoning Richard Nixon. I wanted to say it, but knew it would be wrong to take advantage of this wonderful moment to express a political opinion. I have always felt that getting into politics is tantamount to selling one's soul to the devil, so why spoil the day by making a "pointless" point. From the Oval Office, we were taken to the White House Press Room, where President Ford spoke at a press conference and introduced me to a cadre of reporters. The moment he stopped speaking several hands shot up into the air and the President nodded to one of the reporters. "When," the reporter asked, "will the White House be issuing a statement as to whether or not you will run next November?"

President Ford scowled, "This press conference is not about me," he said, "It's about Lani Deauville and *her* achievements. As soon as we left the press room, I was swarmed by reporters shoving microphones in front of me. When asked what I thought of

President Ford, I again kept my opinion to myself and commented only on what a big man he was. Few people ever get to see Washington the way we did on that trip. It was one long whirlwind of excitement with sightseeing trips around the city in a chauffeured limousine and a countless number of memorable side trips, including one to Arlington Cemetery and another to a magnificent botanical garden.

Not long after the White House visit, Tom Herndon, the District Administrator for the Florida Department of Health and Rehabilitative Services, called and asked if he might come by my office to meet with me. I answered yes, of course, and he stopped in a few days later. It was a casual enough conversation during which he said he'd heard about the work I was doing and complimented me on a job well done. As I watched him leave, I sat there thinking how strange the visit had been—why, I wondered, did someone as important as Tom Herndon take time from his busy day to come by and visit a Goodwill staff psychologist.

About three weeks later my friend Angela called and said she was waiting for me in the parking lot. "I've got a van I want to show you," she said, "It's from Dad's shop."

Angela's father owned Speedy Wagon, a fairly small operation that converted an ordinary van into one that could be driven by someone in a wheelchair—without their ever leaving the wheelchair. For some time she had been urging me to consider a lift-equipped van, but my answer was always the same—"I'm happy with the car I have. It gets me wherever I want to go and that's all I need." I repeated it once again.

"All I'm asking you to do is give it a try," she argued.

I was in the middle of a hectic day with a million or more things calling for my attention, but I liked Angela and I knew she was well-intentioned, so I pushed the work aside and met her in the parking lot.

Angela was standing beside the van with my driving glove in her hand. "Here," she said, "you're going to need this."

I inched my electric wheelchair onto the lowered lift and pushed the power button. When the lift came to a stop, I maneuvered my chair into position behind the wheel and set the locking lever. Thirty seconds later, I was circling the parking lot, and then it was out onto the road. Suddenly I felt a freedom I thought I would never again know—with a van like this I could go anywhere and everywhere without needing someone to lift me in and out of the car. Within the first five minutes, I knew I had to find a way to make it happen. Now that I had tasted this type of independence, I was no longer willing to go without it. "I can't afford a new van," I said hesitantly, "but if I bought a used van, could I get a lift installed on it?"

She smiled. "That's exactly what I was thinking. My dad said he could do it, but you have to buy the lift."

By the time I returned to the office, my brain was ablaze with thoughts of how I might raise enough money to buy a used van. The lift was another issue altogether—they were expensive and although I had received a pin with the President's signature on it, I was still making the same small salary. The challenge of finding a way to fund a lift-equipped van brought to mind Vocational Rehabilitation Services. I dialed their number. "I would like to have you take me back as a client," I said, "I need additional vocational rehabilitation."

"You don't need any such thing," the counselor said sharply. The counselors at VR were well-known for their lack of both courtesy and diplomacy.

"Yes I do," I argued, "I can't get to and from work unless I have someone there to lift me in and out of my car."

"Well, you've got that…"

"I can't always count on someone being around and I would certainly be a lot more employable if I had an independent method of traveling to and from work without…"

A few years earlier, I had been named Vocational Rehabilitation Client of the Year. I was a shining example of their good work and, as such, had been the guest speaker at the Vocational Rehabilitation Program's Annual Meeting for over

1,500 Counselors and supervisors. I thought back on that afternoon—how I had been introduced with a long litany of achievements and then moved to the microphone. For better or worse, I am a woman who speaks her mind, and does so honestly. Still, I am certain that my speech was not what they expected. I began by expressing my gratitude for such an honor but quickly segued into an extremely blunt analysis of where the program fell short in serving the client. "All too often," I said, "the counselors provide little or no guidance. They neither help a client identify career opportunities, nor do they provide adequate information regarding the educational requirements necessary for the career." I went on to explain that I had entered college thinking that a Bachelor's Degree would prepare me to become a psychotherapist. I was not informed that, ultimately, either a Masters or preferably a Doctorate would be necessary. "And," I continued, "...the budgetary planning is terrible." I related the story of how at the Rusk Institute I suffered severe muscle spasms and underwent the surgery to stop them so I would be able to continue my therapy. "Two weeks after the surgery, I was told the program had run out of money and I was to be sent home, despite the fact that I had not completed the physical rehabilitation program! In such a situation, does this agency not have a moral and fiscal responsibility?" A portion of the audience stood and cheered. As I looked around the room, I realized those standing were the newer and younger counselors, the ones who favored change and agreed it was long overdue. The older counselors who had been with the agency for a long time and grown complacent, remained in their seat, with scowls stretched across their faces.

That was just a few short years ago, and I still had a certain level of visibility, so the Vocational Rehabilitation Program could hardly ignore my request and ultimately agreed to take me back as a client. They would pay for both the installation and the lift; but they refused to pay for a van, even a used one. I was halfway to the goal line and one obstacle was not going to stop me. I sold a few pieces of jewelry inherited from my wealthier relatives and raised enough money to buy a used van. When I found one that was affordable, it had white bumpers and spots of peeling paint. There were two small windows in the back doors and none on the sides; there was no question it had once been a delivery van, but it was operational and that was all I needed.

Once the van was delivered, I was a free woman.

About a month after the District Administrator visited my office, I received a letter stating there was a Client Relations Coordinator position open at HRS—the position reported to the District Administrator who had spoken with me. For me this would be a sizable step up the ladder of success, so I jumped at the opportunity and applied for the job. After nearly a month of fact-finding, they narrowed the prospective candidates down to three finalists; the first was the Administrative Assistant to the HRS District Administrator, next the District Personnel Manager for HRS, and lastly there was me. We were all asked to submit a paper outlining what we would do in our first week as the Client Relations Coordinator for HRS. This was a newly created position statewide. There would ultimately be eleven Client Relations Coordinators, one for each of Florida's eleven districts. But since the position had not heretofore existed, there was no definite job description. If you were astute enough to read between the lines you could tell that it was HRS's intention for this person to field client complaints and bring about satisfactory resolutions. Fortunately, I have always taken an analytical approach to problem solving and I did the same here. My white paper stated that, before doing anything, I would first meet with each department head to identify the problems and stumbling blocks. It went on to add I would also elicit their input in determining the best approach to bring about a favorable resolution of the problem. I knew I was the dark horse, since the other two candidates were already employees of HRS, and I was an outsider.

A few weeks later, I was in Boston speaking at an event that would be my last appearance as the Goodwill Disabled Employee of the Year. Jude was working and unable to make it, so I had a friend come along as my caregiver. She knew I had applied for the job at HRS and also knew I was anxiously awaiting their decision.

Halfway through my speech a young man walked over and whispered in my friend's ear. She got up from her seat and followed him to a telephone in the back of the auditorium. A few minutes later she replaced the receiver and returned to her seat. I glanced over and she gave me the thumbs-up. Supposedly I had gotten the job on the basis of the paper I'd written, but I have always had a sneaky suspicion the HRS District Administrator had me in mind for that job the day he visited my office.

Just as I suspected, the position of Client Relations Coordinator meant I was the complaint department for every disgruntled client in our HRS district—and there were quite a few of them. Most were justified in their complaints, their requests for assistance had been turned down, their telephone calls went unanswered, and, they were bounced from one counselor to another without anyone answering their plea for help. True to the strategy I had outlined in my white paper, I called the three Network Managers together to discuss what we might do to rectify the overwhelming caseload of problems.

I had already spoken to a number of clients, so I knew precisely what the problem was—unfortunately, they didn't. "Who do you work for?" I asked the group.

Answers came flying back at me—the Governor, the District Manager of HRS—a few even said they worked for me. "Wrong!" I replied emphatically. "You work for the residents of this District, the taxpayers. You work for the people you've been pushing aside and treating terribly. They're the ones who pay your salary! I've heard that our counselors often treat these people as if they are looking for a handout; well, they are not! These people have paid their taxes and they're entitled to whatever help we can give them. They're not beggars, they're clients, and without them you would have no job!"

One of the Network Managers, a somewhat arrogant man from Pinellas County stood up to speak; "Maybe so," he began defensively, "but at times *those people* can be so..."

"You should be ashamed of yourself!" I said cutting him short. "The moment *those* people approach us asking for assistance they

194

become a client, and moving forward I expect you to treat them as clients, without exception! We may not be able to solve every problem for every person, but we can do a lot better than we are."

After that meeting, the situation began to improve albeit slowly and sometimes begrudgingly. HRS provided a huge diversity of services to the community, but they were an out-of-control agency, with a proliferation of sub-agencies under one gigantic umbrella and hardly anyone had a handle on all that was happening. There were eleven districts in Florida and all of the District Administrators reported to the Governor. The District Administrator was the person in charge of our district, and I was his voice in the field. On any given day, I might work with a citizen who had been turned down for food stamps, a child who had to be removed from a volatile home, or an elderly patient who was questioning the quality of care in a specific nursing home. Every issue was critical, both to the client and to me.

With the HRS office located near Clearwater, my drive time to and from home had tripled, and I spent a good part of each day traveling from one county to the other to meet with clients and HRS staff. HRS held their statewide meetings in Tallahassee, so I also had to attend those. As my level of responsibility increased, so did the demands for my time and the length of my workday. I went from day to day resolving one chaotic situation after another. It was both exhilarating and exhausting.

With my recently acquired lift-equipped van, I was free to come and go without assistance, so I arrived at the office early and left late which afforded me precious little time for cooking. On those evenings when we could squeeze out a few minutes, Jude and I chopped and mixed dishes that could be cooked quickly or tossed in a crock pot the following morning. The Driftwood house came with a stove that had probably been there since the house was built, but for me, it was a treasure. Most stovetops are too high for me to reach, but this wonderful old-timer had burners that slid out like a drawer. I didn't have to reach for them, they came to me. Jude chopped, sliced and diced, while I mixed, stirred and cooked. I had come a long way since the first day at the Rusk Institute, when managing a spoon attached to a holding glove was an astounding achievement. Over the years I had taught myself how to use my arms in place of my hands; I could thread the handle of a utensil between my fingers and use the strength in my arm to maneuver it. *Where there is a will, there is a way but sometimes you have to look hard to find it.*

From Monday through Friday, I belonged to HRS, but when weekends rolled around, there was always Jude and our wonderful house at Driftwood. Often, we spent our Saturdays sitting on a neighbor's dock, sipping icy cold lemonade and fishing. I seldom drank alcohol now. I had lost the inclination, which was probably because of my increased happiness. Definitely a good IS.

About once a month, we'd get into my van and drive across the state for a visit with Mother and Pappy in Daytona. I looked forward to those visits because now it was so much easier for me to talk to Mother. Once she married Pappy, she'd let go of the chain that bound me to her side, now we spoke openly and without reservation. I had also grown. I had come to understand that Mother's fear of letting go was because of loneliness. I had been the one constant in her life, the one person who was always there. She needed me, my father, the love of her life, had left her and I was the singular link to him. Mother was strong in a million and one ways, but when it came to emotions of the heart, she was extremely needy. Now, Pappy, wonderful Pappy, had at last fulfilled her need.

The year I turned fourteen, Mother and I planned to spend Christmas Eve together as we always did. With Scott living in Philadelphia and Dit now married it was going to be just Mother and me, but that was okay. We would spend Christmas Eve ogling the pile of presents beneath the tree and offering our guesses as to what they might contain.

"The red one looks like a box of candy…" Mother would say, and I'd laugh knowingly.

Although we were still living close to the bone, there were always countless presents beneath the tree—part of them for Mother, even more for me. None of them were extravagant. There might be a Hershey bar, some new socks, note paper or a fancy ball point pen. But the value of the gift didn't matter. It was the sharing of Christmas joy that filled me with such delight. I was speculating what might be in the large box Scott had sent from Philadelphia, when the telephone rang. It was Mother calling from work, "I just wanted to let you know that I will be home late," she said.

Anxious to start our Christmas Eve together, I asked, "How late?"

"I can't say exactly," she answered, not giving any further explanation.

"But, we always spend Christmas Eve together..."

"Don't worry, I'll be there, I'll just be a little late."

I heard someone in the background call her name, then Mother said goodbye and hung up the telephone. Duke and I were left sitting in the living room, with no knowledge of who she was with or what she was doing. I turned on the television and tried to watch a rerun of *It's a Wonderful Life*, but it wasn't a wonderful life. I was all alone on Christmas Eve. I cuddled against Duke and tried to tell myself Mother would be back in plenty of time for us to celebrate Christmas. When the movie was over at eight o'clock, I turned the television off and began cooking dinner. I prepared a meatloaf and put it into the oven to cook; then I made mashed potatoes and string beans. When the oven timer buzzed, I took the meatloaf out, fixed two plates and set them on the counter. By then it was almost nine o'clock. Mother would surely be home any minute. Nine-thirty rolled around, and the food was getting colder. I ate my dinner and put Mother's plate in the oven to stay warm.

I could feel the anger swelling inside of me as I waited hour after hour. It was close to midnight when I took Mother's plate from the oven, broke the dried-up piece of meatloaf into pieces and fed it to Duke. I threw the remainder in the garbage can. It was Christmas Eve—a time when most people were at home with their family, so where was Mother? I began to worry she'd gotten into an accident and was lying dead somewhere along a deserted roadside. I paced back and forth across the living room and waited. One o'clock came, then two, and finally about forty-five minutes after I'd watched the hour hand pass three, I heard a car in the driveway. Frantic, I rushed outside to find Mother in a car with a man I had never before seen. She had passed out. The driver of the car was quite obviously drunk. To say I was enraged would be the understatement of the decade! I jerked open his door, pulled the man from the car and punched my fist into his face. "It's Christmas Eve!" I screamed. "Christmas Eve!" The man fell to the ground; his nose bleeding. I left him lying there and crossed over to the passenger side, with Mother seemingly unconscious, I lifted her from the car and carried her up the stairs to our house. I then removed her clothes, pulled a nightgown over her head, and deposited her carefully in bed.

Mother had always worked hard to provide me with a wonderful Christmas and she'd reveled in every expression of delight as we opened our presents. It was a fun time for both of us, but that night I was in no mood to celebrate anything with her, so all alone I trudged into the living room, pulled the presents marked with my name from beneath the tree and opened every last one of them. The box from Scott contained a fluffy teddy bear coat I loved. But despite that wonderful coat and the substantial number of presents Mother bought for me, it was the worst Christmas ever.

The next morning, Mother made no mention of the night before, she simply went about the day as if nothing had ever happened, and silently opened her gifts. At one point, she questioned why I hadn't waited to open my presents with her, but after I responded with an angry glare, nothing more was said. It was sometimes difficult to know which version of Mother I was dealing with—the one who absolutely adored me and considered my welfare above all else, or the one who was so hungry for love that she constantly reached out to the wrong men.

In late 1979, Mother told me she was going into the hospital to find out why she was having breathing problems. Since I had virtually been her caregiver for a good part of my life, I automatically answered, "Okay, Jude and I will drive over Friday evening."

On Saturday morning we were in the room with Mother when the doctor walked in.

"Well," he said hesitantly, "I'm afraid I don't have very good news for you." He clipped an x-ray to the lightbox hanging on the wall and flipped the switch to on. "See this dark area," he said pointing his finger to the spot in question, "it's a cancerous growth in your lungs."

Mother already had two strikes—the first was that she had been a heavy smoker all her life; the second was that for as long as I could remember she had predicted she would one day die of cancer. Never mind that she that she allowed my father to beat her senseless, that she drove while she was having insulin shocks or that she ignored all of the cautions set forth for diabetics, she had carved her ultimate destiny in stone and now we were face to face with the enemy. The third strike was hanging on the wall.

Jude moved closer and wrapped his arm around my shoulder. After having made a comeback from the grave myself, I believed a strong will could overcome even the most impossible odds, so I asked, "What's the best way to treat it?"

"Unfortunately, there is no treatment," the doctor answered. "The cancer is too large and too advanced, at this point, it's untreatable."

"How long do I have?" Mother asked matter-of-factly.

"A year, a year and a half maybe…"

"But…" I stammered, "There must be something…"

"Lani," Mother sighed, "It is what it is, and there's nothing anyone can do about it."

That was an IS I found very hard to accept. In so many ways, I had always been Mother's caregiver. I sat beside her when she was lonely, I was the convenient friend she could take along when she needed a drinking companion, I was the one who made sure dinner was on the table and I was also the one who whisked her off to the hospital when she overdosed on insulin and slipped into shock—now, when she needed me most, I was helpless to do anything.

There was no question, Mother and my life together had been tumultuous, but perhaps that was because we were more alike than I had ever realized. Mother didn't share my love of animals—she tolerated them, maybe even "liked" them—but we both had the same iron-willed determination and the same instinct for survival. Mother overcame abandonment, poverty and poor health but she survived and, she took care of her three children—although at times her methods of doing so were a bit haphazard, she did it.

Once I knew my time with Mother would come to an end in the foreseeable future, I was determined to make the most of every moment. Every Friday evening I rushed home from work, then Jude and I drove from Saint Petersburg to Daytona to spend the weekend with Mother and Pappy. Each Sunday evening we returned home.

Fourteen

The year and a half that followed was, in some ways, the best Mother and I ever shared. Long after Pappy had gone to bed, we would sit together talking about days gone by—about the mishaps, misunderstandings and arguments that now seemed laughable. We talked about the good times we had shared.

One evening Mother said, "Remember the Christmas we bought Lee a BB gun?"

"Of course I do." I laughed, thinking back on that year. I was living in Alabama and attending Graduate School, and while I was home for the holidays, Mother showed me the BB gun she and Pappy had gotten for my nephew. I'd suggested we try it out, and we did. Pappy filled a cardboard box with wads of newspaper, drew a bulls eye target on paper, taped it to the box and placed it at the far end of the hallway. After numerous rounds of competition and laughter raucous enough to wake the dead, Mother and Pappy both conceded that I was by far the best shot. "I still have the BB gun you gave me," I said.

Mother laughed. "I suppose there are very few people who would give their grown quadriplegic daughter a BB gun, but you had such a good time with the one we bought for Lee, I couldn't resist."

"I really did have fun with it. When my trailer was parked up from the creek on the peanut farm, my friends and I used to go out back and shoot at empty beer cans." I thought back on how I would slide my rigid finger in front of the trigger and use the strength of my arms to pull back. In those days I wore a stiff Polio Sitting Corset that braced my torso so my back was strong enough to handle the weight of the BB gun. And it's a well known fact, that I have always enjoyed the sports most girls shun. Our rebellion against conformity was one of the things Mother and I had in common. As a child, I thought Mother was ridiculously proper, but when I learned the truth of her marriage to Morris Verner, I realized she was only trying to give me some semblance of the aristocratic heritage she had lost with her youthful antics.

Mother and I talked of many things that year, things which we had never before spoken of, emotions that had been pushed back to make room for the everyday task of staying alive.

"I'm not afraid of dying," Mother said, "because whatever heaven or hell there is, can be found right here on earth." She hesitated a moment, and I could detect a tinge of fear in her eyes. "But..." she sighed, "I am concerned about that moment when I draw my last breath. I wonder if I'll panic the way I did when my friend, Harold, held me under the water at the Oakmont Club swimming pool."

I knew she was thinking back to an event that happened when she was a child. It was something I could ease her mind about because I had stood at death's door myself. "When I went through that near-death experience at Baptist Memorial Hospital, it wasn't at all frightening," I said. "It was warm and welcoming, almost like a lamp in the window begging you to come on in." What I said was true, I was sitting beside Mother at that moment, not because I was afraid of death, but because I fought to live. If I had allowed myself to follow that inviting beacon of light, I would have left this world with too much living left undone.

With Mother it was a different story. She was tired of life's struggle. Her life had not been an easy one. It had been one of working multiple jobs to provide for her children, one of lost loves and abusive husbands, one of searching for love and not finding it until Pappy came along. With Pappy, Mother found the happiness and contentment she had so long sought. She was, for perhaps the first time in her life, happy. It was an ordinary life; one where she and Pappy had dinner then sat together and watched television, or playfully raced one another on the slot car track they'd set up. It was a life I'd consider rather boring, but to Mother, it was perfect.

Always a heavy smoker, Mother enjoyed her cigarettes the same way she enjoyed her lukewarm flat Schlitz beer. Once cancer showed its ugly head, I hoped she'd abandon the habit; of course she didn't. Her cigarettes were stashed in the nightstand of the guestroom where Jude and I spent our weekends and every so often she popped in for a smoke.

"Does Pappy know you're still smoking?" I asked.

The only response I received was a mischievous grin. The likelihood was that he did know, but chose to say nothing because he was torn between wanting Mother's time to be as long as possible and wanting her days to be as pleasurable as possible.

Mother had gone through a bout of ovarian cancer and survived. Maybe Pappy was hoping against hope that she could do it again. I was in graduate school when Mother underwent that surgery and I remember my trip home all too well. I left Alabama the day before her surgery, but arrived at the hospital after visiting hours because of a flat tire. I was met by a nurse who told me it was too late for a visit and I should come back tomorrow. I explained my reason for being late and told her Mother was scheduled for surgery the next morning. Not giving an inch, she stood there shaking her head side to side. Although Mother and I have had our differences over the years, one thing has always been true. Through good times and bad, we'd loved one another fiercely. When my patience was worn thin from explaining, I told the nurse that I came to see Mother, and I was going to, which, despite her protests, was exactly what I did.

Mother made it through the surgery just fine—physically; but mentally she'd already decided she was destined to die of cancer so she figured she'd just stop eating and get it over with as soon as possible. Fortunately, Mrs. Eubanks, the Mayor's wife, was Mother's roommate. On the second day of her refusal to eat I told her if she didn't start eating, I would be forced to feed her.

"Don't be preposterous," Mother said, "You can't force me to eat. You're physically incapable of feeding me."

"I can and I will," I answered.

The plate in front of Mother contained a piece of meat, mashed potatoes and peas. I maneuvered the fork into my hand and stabbed the meat. "Eat," I demanded, "because if I have to feed you, I'll start with those peas; and, since I'm not so good with a spoon, some of the peas just might go flying across the room and land in Mrs. Eubank's lap."

Mother's aristocratic bearing rose to the surface and with an appropriate amount of indignation, she said, "You wouldn't..."

"Oh yes I would," I answered and Mother, fearing I might, began to eat.

At the time, I pooh-poohed Mother's claim that she would die of cancer, but now a new breed of the beast had take up residence inside of her and this one was meaner and uglier.

That year, I again learned to live with less sleep than needed and grew accustomed to eating less-than-perfect meals. Although my responsibilities at Goodwill had grown by leaps and bounds, thoughts of Mother were never far from mind. I had enough on my plate and had no interest in changing jobs, so when the Staff Director for the Governor in Tallahassee, called and asked me to become the State Director of Vocational Rehabilitation Services, I turned him down.

"I wish you'd take time and think about this Lani," he replied, "You'd have free rein to run the agency as you see fit, and it's an opportunity for you to help others like yourself."

I liked working at HRS and wanted to stay close to Mother so there were a dozen reasons for me not to take the job, but I agreed to think it over. That night I discussed it with Jude, but intentionally avoided any mention of the increase in salary I would get. "We'd have to live in Tallahassee, which means leaving this house," I said.

"Lani, whatever you decide to do is okay with me," Jude replied.

"...And, we'd be so far away from Mother..."

"Whatever, you decide," he repeated.

"...Plus, I love this house, it's so perfect...it's got charm..."

"It's also got leaks, but Lani, whatever you decide is okay with me."

I thought about the job for almost a month; I talked to Jude, I talked to Mother, and I considered every pro and con imaginable. The Governor's Staff Director called five times asking if I'd made a decision and every time I said that the logistics weren't right for me. He insisted I think it over a bit more and upped the ante.

In addition to the fact that Tallahassee was over one hundred miles further away from Mother, one of my many reasons for being reluctant to take the job was VR's reputation. I felt they were a poorly-managed agency, with too little concern for their clients. Working at HRS, I had built a stellar reputation. I was respected by the District Administrator, co-workers and clients equally. I didn't want to sully the reputation I now had by being associated with such a disreputable agency as VR. When I finally told Jude they were offering me three times as much as I was now earning, he felt I should give the job serious consideration.

That weekend we discussed the offer with Mother and Pappy and they agreed with Jude.

"Don't worry about me," Mother said, "Pappy's here and he takes very good care of me."

They gave each other a knowing smile and I could see the depth of Mother's happiness. Even though his resignation meant losing his pension, Pappy loved Mother so much that he quit his job at Hughes Supply to stay at home and take care of her.

"Besides," Mother said, "Dit comes by every morning on her way to work."

Dit was a nurse and I knew she had been checking on Mother, but somehow I had always pictured myself as the child who would be Mother's caregiver. Neither Dit nor Scott ever had the relationship with Mother that I had. But in later years, I think Mother came to see Dit as not just the child that added disgrace to disgrace, but a real daughter. We had a pecking order in our family—I was Mother's favorite child, perhaps because we were alike in so many ways, perhaps because she loved my father with such ardency, but assuredly it wasn't because I was the best-behaved. As children, Scott outranked Dit, but in later years the order was reversed.

Although Mother had her favorites, she took great pride in all of her children's successes and she earnestly urged me to accept the position at VR. The following week I accepted the offer and we began making plans to move.

I started my job as Director of Vocational Rehabilitative Services on December 22nd, just three days before Christmas, so that year Jude and I didn't make it back to Daytona for the holidays. With the exception of the Christmas Eve Mother went partying, this was the only Christmas we had not celebrated together—it was also her last Christmas.

On January 6th, Dit called early in the morning to report Mother did not want to get out of bed that day. A heavy weight of sorrow settled in my chest and I realized she was dying. Mother always got out of bed in the morning. She made herself do it even when she was in pain and even after surgeries that would have most people bedridden for a week, Mother would be up and walking the next day. I telephoned VR and said I would not be in; then Jude and I got into my van and began driving.

We arrived in Daytona late that afternoon, and when I entered Mother's room she gave me a weakened smile, "I'm glad you made it," she said softly.

I maneuvered my chair closer to Mother's bed and held her hand throughout the afternoon. She was so weak, that we did little talking. Somehow, we both sensed we had already said all the things that needed to be said. Occasionally, Mother would expel a gurgling belch and mumble "Swahili," but before I could ask the meaning, her eyes were closed again. *Swahili?* Ladylike behavior was something Mother had always insisted on, belching was only fractionally better than running through town naked. If a belch escaped your lips, you were to bow your head with an appropriate show of embarrassment and excuse yourself. *Excuse me—sure, but Swahili?* Although I was not willing to leave Mother's side to ask

206

why she kept repeating such an odd word at this time, I made a mental note to ask Pappy about it.

It was probably late in the evening when Mother opened her eyes and said, "Don't forget your promise, Lani."

"I haven't forgotten," I answered giving her hand a squeeze.

"Do you remember the words?"

I nodded, "How could I possibly forget them." That poem, *The Cremation of Sam McGee* was one of the thousands of things Mother made me commit to memory. I expect you to recite it at my funeral, she would say laughingly.

I knew Mother was nearing the end of her life and I was not going to allow her to die alone, so I remained beside her until four o'clock in the morning. When exhaustion finally overtook me, I called Jude and asked if he would sit with Mother while I took a thirty-minute rest. Jude lifted me into our bed and I fell asleep the moment my head touched the pillow. My intention was simply to close my eyes and rest my body for thirty minutes, but physical and mental exhaustion pushed me into a frenzied sleep and Jude, concerned about my well-being, refused to wake me.

Dit arrived at six AM and after one look at Mother, she told Jude to get me immediately, which he did. Mother died less than one minute after I arrived and took hold of her hand—I have always believed she was waiting for me to be beside her in death as I had always been in life.

There was a small family service at the house and, in keeping with Mother's wish, I cleared my throat and began to speak.

> *There are strange things done in the midnight sun*
> *By the men who moil for gold;*
> *The Arctic trails have their secret tales*
> *That would make your blood run cold;*
> *The Northern Lights have seen queer sights,*
> *But the queerest they ever did see*
> *Was that night on the marge of Lake Lebarge*
> *I cremated Sam McGee.*

Now Sam McGee was from Tennessee,
where the cotton blooms and blows.
Why he left his home in the South to roam 'round the Pole,
God only knows.
He was always cold, but the land of gold
seemed to hold him like a spell;
Though he'd often say in his homely way
that "he'd sooner live in hell."
On a Christmas Day
we were mushing our way over the Dawson trail.
Talk of your cold! through the parka's fold
it stabbed like a driven nail.
If our eyes we'd close, then the lashes froze
till sometimes we couldn't see;
It wasn't much fun, but the only one
to whimper was Sam McGee.
And that very night, as we lay packed tight
in our robes beneath the snow,
And the dogs were fed, and the stars o'erhead
were dancing heel and toe,
He turned to me, and "Cap," says he,
"I'll cash in this trip, I guess;
And if I do, I'm asking that you
won't refuse my last request."

Well, he seemed so low that I couldn't say no;
then he says with a sort of moan:
"It's the cursèd cold, and it's got right hold,
till I'm chilled clean through to the bone.
Yet 'tain't being dead — it's my awful dread
of the icy grave that pains;
So I want you to swear that, foul or fair,
you'll cremate my last remains."
A pal's last need is a thing to heed,
so I swore I would not fail;
And we started on at the streak of dawn;

but God! he looked ghastly pale.
He crouched on the sleigh, and he raved all day
of his home in Tennessee;
And before nightfall
a corpse was all
that was left of Sam McGee.

There wasn't a breath in that land of death,
and I hurried, horror-driven,
With a corpse half hid that I couldn't get rid,
because of a promise given;
It was lashed to the sleigh, and it seemed to say:
"You may tax your brawn and brains,
But you promised true, and it's up to you,
to cremate those last remains."

Now a promise made is a debt unpaid,
and the trail has its own stern code.
In the days to come, though my lips were dumb
in my heart how I cursed that load.
In the long, long night, by the lone firelight,
while the huskies, round in a ring,
howled out their woes to the homeless snows —
Oh God! how I loathed the thing.
And every day that quiet clay
seemed to heavy and heavier grow;
And on I went, though the dogs were spent
and the grub was getting low;
The trail was bad, and I felt half mad,
but I swore I would not give in;
And I'd often sing to the hateful thing,
and it hearkened with a grin.

Till I came to the marge of Lake Lebarge,
and a derelict there lay;

*It was jammed in the ice, but I saw in a trice
it was called the "Alice May."
And I looked at it, and I thought a bit,
and I looked at my frozen chum;
Then "Here," said I, with a sudden cry,
"is my cre-ma-tor-eum."
Some planks I tore from the cabin floor,
and I lit the boiler fire;
Some coal I found that was lying around,
and I heaped the fuel higher;
The flames just soared, and the furnace roared —
such a blaze you seldom see;
And I burrowed a hole in the glowing coal,
and I stuffed in
Sam McGee.
Then I made a hike, for I didn't like to hear him sizzle so;
And the heavens scowled, and the huskies howled,
and the wind began to blow.
It was icy cold, but the hot sweat rolled down my cheeks,
and I don't know why;
And the greasy smoke in an inky cloak
went streaking down the sky.*

*I do not know how long in the snow
I wrestled with grisly fear;
But the stars came out and they danced about
ere again I ventured near;
I was sick with dread, but I bravely said:
"I'll just take a peep inside.
I guess he's cooked, and it's time I looked";
... then the door I opened wide.*

*And there sat Sam, looking cool and calm,
in the heart of the furnace roar;
And he wore a smile you could see a mile,*

and said: "Please close that door.

It's fine in here, but I greatly fear,
you'll let in the cold and storm —
Since I left Plumtree, down in Tennessee,
it's the first time I've been warm."

There are strange things done in the midnight sun
By the men who moil for gold;
The Arctic trails have their secret tales
That would make your blood run cold;
The Northern Lights have seen queer sights,
But the queerest they ever did see

Was that night on the marge of Lake Lebarge
I cremated Sam McGee.

Written by Robert Service

Throughout her life Mother had a dislike for the cold, and she felt it more severely than most. When I bounced across the yard in a bathing suit, Mother wore a shrug. When I wore a strapless sundress, she wore a long sleeve sweater, and thus developed her love for this poem and the request that I recite it at her funeral. "There have been enough tears in my life," Mother would say, "I don't want any more at my funeral." Yet, looking around I could see a number of eyes filled with water. "Mother said, no tears," I reminded them. That's when Scott, now in his fifties and back in town for the funeral, bounded into the center of the group and did a summersault. The sight of a grown man rolling across the floor, caused a ripple of laughter to echo through the room and I know Mother, who truly enjoyed having a good time, was laughing with us.

That night, thoughts of Mother brought memories of her repeating the word Swahili after every gurgling belch and I asked Pappy why she would be saying such a thing.

He gave me a soft smile of remembrance, "Your mother's cancer had spread throughout her body and the sickness caused her to belch quite often," he said, "so she was constantly excusing herself and feeling embarrassed. I explained there was nothing to be embarrassed about. She was simply being a good Swahili."

"What's being Swahili got to do belching?" I asked.

"I told her Swahilis consider it rude not to belch after a meal; they believe if a guest doesn't let out a good long belch, they haven't enjoyed the meal."

I eyed Pappy suspiciously, "Is that true?" I asked.

He shrugged. "Can't say it is; can't say it isn't. But, it certainly made your mother feel less embarrassed about belching."

I pulled my chair closer to Pappy and held his hand. We had both lost someone who would forever remain in our hearts.

Fifteen

Once back in Tallahassee, we began to live in a house we had settled for because time was short, and we wanted to spend every last minute of it with Mother. This house was no Driftwood. That had been a home, this was simply a house; and it was one that offered literally no wheelchair access. Before moving in we had a ramp built, but it was a clumsy thing that took up over half of our garage space and was still difficult to navigate. With a million memories vying for space in my mind, I began my new job.

I was the first woman and the first disabled person to ever hold the position of Director of a State Vocational Rehabilitation Program anywhere in the United States, so I was facing a huge challenge. The problems that constituted my reason for not wanting to accept the job initially were now *my* problems, and, it was up to me to see that they were fixed. Suddenly I became an unpaid lobbyist, traveling back and forth to Washington, soliciting funds to support the internal structure that the VR agencies nationwide needed to function appropriately. I knew exactly how it felt to hear the words—*sorry, you can't continue your rehabilitation because the program is out of money*—and I made up my mind that no Florida client would ever hear that statement under my watch. It was going to be an uphill battle because of the numerous roadblocks standing in my way, but I was determined to turn the agency around and create a client-friendly environment. The fact that VR was not viewed favorably by other agencies in the

HRS family didn't help. We were the odd man out, the only agency that received Federal funding and was not an entitlement program. A number of people thought VR was out of place in HRS group and belonged under the Department of Labor or the Health Department, but we were where we were and I had to deal with it.

Any change I hoped to bring to VR got off to a slow start because too many counselors remembered my brashly critical Client of the Year speech, and I was perceived as the enemy. It took months to convince most counselors that I hadn't come to fire them, but to help them to run a more efficient client-oriented program. And, a few were never convinced. Attitude was one problem, but far larger and far more ominous, was the issue of financial reporting. VR had gone through years when they stopped programs because they were out of money; and other years when they under spent and left money on the table, money that was eventually allocated to Sheltered Workshops throughout the state as grants. I began to stress the importance of record-keeping and following the standardized accounting procedures. It helped but we were a long way from where we needed to be. One of my first moves was to hire Joe Pankowski, an HRS Management Fellow, as my assistant director – an excellent choice since he was smart, loyal, and well-liked by both VR and HRS.

1981 was my first full year at VR. It was also the International Year of Disabled People and the convention dinner was held in Orlando. As the Florida State Representative I attended, along with people from other states, and countries stretching across the globe. Bob Graham, the Governor of Florida, was there with his wife. Both of them spent the entire evening going from table to table, talking to people, lifting tiny children with gigantic disabilities into their arms, and cuddling them as if they were their own grandchildren. They had so much love to give and they gave it freely.

Later that year I began to take an interest in a Children's Home located a short distance from our house. Every day, I drove past it on my way to work, and every day I found myself wondering about the children inside. One weekend, I suggested we go over for a visit and ask if we could do anything to help out. Jude loves children, so of course he said yes and we spent the entire afternoon at the Children's Home.

Within a few months, we had formed a bond with two boys, an eight-year old and a twelve-year old. They were two of three brothers who had been dropped at the home by a well-intentioned minister. Their mother had been incapable of caring for them. She kissed them goodbye and left without a word about coming back. The older boys lived in the same house. Their younger brother, a six-year old, was housed in a separate residence. Since the two older boys were living together, we considered taking both of them in as foster children, but before we could do so, the eight-year old was adopted by another family. The six-year old had physical and behavioral disabilities—problems which would have been difficult to handle under any situation, and would be even more so given my disability—so Jude and I decided to foster just the eldest boy, Thomas. For the first forty-four years of my life I had focused on taking care of Mother and readying myself for a career. Suddenly, I found myself caring for a twelve year old child. When we first decided to do this, Jude and I were uncertain as to how we would deal with having a child in our lives. But within a few short months of serving as foster parents, we knew we wanted to eventually have a child of our own. Thomas was a warm and affectionate child who responded with delight when we did things with him. At times I would watch Thomas and Jude working on a project together and it was such a heartwarming sight that I wondered why we had never before thought of having children.

Thomas remained with us for almost a year, and then he returned to the Children's Home to watch over his baby brother. He was convinced that his mother would someday come back for them. Once he was gone, there was a certain emptiness in our life. It was an emptiness that the long days of work and traveling from coast to coast for speaking engagements, could not fill. I missed the sound of blaring music, I missed seeing the joy that came with each new adventure, and I began to realize I wanted a child of my own. That thought remained in my head as the weeks and months rolled by,

Jude was not quite as convinced as I was and tried to distract me by suggesting we buy one of the Arabian horses we visited at the ranch. He was probably hoping the horse would take precedence over my desire for a child of our own. I have never been one to turn my back on the offer of a horse, so I took Jude up on his offer and selected Sparky, a dark Arabian Bay Gelding with a white blaze on his forehead. Sparky was boarded at the ranch, and when I wasn't traveling we would go there several times a week to visit and ride him. Jude would lift me from my wheelchair onto the gentle horse's back, and then climb on in front of me. With my arms hooked around his waist, we'd ride off, leaving my wheelchair parked in the dust. Apparently, such an event was worthy of newspaper coverage, because one day a reporter from the Miami Herald called me at the office.

"I understand that there's a crazy quadriplegic woman who rides horseback," he said. "Would that be you?"

"Guilty as charged," I laughed. "My husband Jude and I ride together."

He asked a dozen more questions, and then said, "I'd like to do a feature story on this. Would you mind if a photographer and I come up for an interview and to shoot some pictures?"

"That would be fine," I laughed. I found it rather amusing that something so natural to me was a feat of amazement to others. Of course, it was thirty years ago, and at that time most quadriplegics simply accepted their fate and sat at home in a wheelchair.

Within a few days, the Miami Herald reporter showed up with a photographer. Getting the information he needed for his story was a breeze; but, when the photographer began taking pictures, the camera click and whirring of the film as it moved forward startled Sparky and caused him to bolt. Luckily Jude was right there and able to catch me before I hit the ground. This scenario repeated itself numerous times before the photographer settled for a shot of Jude lifting me onto the horse. The reporter thought it was such a daredevil thing for a quadriplegic to ride, but at that point in my life, some of my happiest moments had been those spent with animals, especially horses. Sitting in my wheelchair in the center of a training paddock, I used voice commands to successfully train Sparky to walk, trot and canter on a long lead line. Although I loved doing it, it did not take away the desire for motherhood that had blossomed inside of me.

That spring, Jude and I began to talk about adopting a baby, and we started our search for a new house. Still trying to get over the loss of Mother, I focused my efforts on work, which wasn't all that hard to do since there were a million and one things calling for my attention. By then, I had come to the realization that as the Director of the VR program, there was no way I could get the budgetary issues under control without having a computerized accounting system; so I invested in one and that proved to be a turning point. We became the first HRS agency to have computerized accounting and once it became operational, we had a complete picture of our budget requirements and efficient tracking of agency expenses. All of a sudden HRS took notice and began to acknowledge the work we were doing. As a quadriplegic woman and the Director of Vocational Rehabilitative Services, I was a paradox to the industry. And, on top of that, I had created a successful turnaround for VR. I was the *can do* example, and, as such, found myself in great demand as a guest speaker for VR meetings throughout the country. I explained to audiences that by giving our clients a vocation, we moved them from the tax liability column to the asset column of the taxpayer's ledger. These were people who wanted to work, and vocational training enabled them to do it. Instead of receiving a government subsidiary, they were now paying taxes.

I lobbied for increased funding and the State stepped up to the plate with a twenty-percent match for all of the Federal funding I obtained. My goal was to make VR proactive by not simply training people after they had disabilities, but by also educating the public on the prevention of accidents such as mine. VR created a *'Feet First, First Time!'* awareness campaign to prevent spinal cord injuries caused by diving accidents. It was utilized throughout the State, and reduced the number of diving injuries in Florida by half in the first year.

Although Jude and I enjoyed traveling from place to place, that schedule slowed our progress in house hunting. We seized the weekends as a time for relaxation, a time to cook together and enjoy each other. Jude was truly a sweetheart, in every sense of the word. He took time off from work and traveled with me as my caregiver, he helped with the cooking and every Friday he came home with three long stemmed roses. I had at one time been reluctant to marry him, but now I couldn't imagine my life without him.

One Saturday, while he was at work, I decided to show my appreciation by making him a very special dinner, which for me was no easy task. When we cooked, Jude was my hands, I cooked, stirred and mixed, but Jude did all the paring, slicing and chopping. I worked all day, but I finally put together a dish of eggplant parmesan fit for a king. All I had to do now was bake it. I set the eggplant on the table and switched the oven on. While I was waiting for it to heat, the telephone rang. I became engrossed in the conversation, and when I turned back, the baking dish was empty. Patches, our Great Dane was standing there with a smile on her face and a ring of tomato sauce around her mouth. Before I could say a word, she took off running. Furious, I gave chase, but with her darting from room to room, it took several tries before I cornered her in the bedroom. "Patches," I yelled, "You are in big trouble!" I'm not certain what I was going to do to a Great Dane who outweighed me, but as it turned out I didn't have to do anything. Patches hung her head and looked up at me with soulful eyes and a truly penitent expression. Some people claim dogs are incapable of having such an expression, but after seeing the look on Patches face, I knew better. When Jude arrived home that evening, I told him about the wonderful eggplant parmesan I'd made for him, but there was nothing to show for all my effort. Jude couldn't stop laughing.

On Sunday morning, we had our traditional breakfast of a Mimosa and a Mexican Omelet. Then we once again went house hunting. That was the day we found the house at Shannon Lakes. It was a three-bedroom ranch surrounded by trees and flowers. I was then, am now, and will be until the day I die, an outdoor person, and this was the house of my dreams. Not only did it have a garden ablaze with color, but the lots on both sides of the house were wooded and vacant. Beyond one wooded lot, a paved path ran down a hill to the edge of the lake. That paved path would enable me to get to the lake in my wheelchair. *Euphoria!* We circled the walkway to get a glimpse of the back yard and I saw the swimming pool. It may seem strange for a quadriplegic to say this, but swimming was always my favorite form of exercise. Although I no longer had the use of my legs or hands, my arms were so strong that I could swim laps for over an hour, with a single five- minute rest stop. By doing a modified butterfly stroke on my back, I didn't have to turn my head to breathe, and I used a fiberglass pole with a harness hooked around my waist to eliminate the need for turning to reverse direction.

"I love it," I whispered to Jude and he whispered back, "Me too," then we rang the doorbell. The inside of the house was as wonderful as the outside. For me, Paradise was a place where I could put my van in the garage, wheel my chair through almost every room of the house, have a lake to fish in and a pool to swim in. The beautiful stone fireplace in the family room was a huge bonus—we loved having a fireplace and were lucky enough to find at least one in every house we had owned, with the singular exception of that first house in Saint Petersburg. The only doorway my chair did not breeze through comfortably, was the bathroom; but Jude was so strong, he simply lifted me from my chair and carried me in. With the purchase of that house, we were halfway to our goal of having a house that was truly a home, and a child to call our own. The house that had taken us almost a year to find was the easy part.

There was never any question about the fact that we met the qualifications necessary to be adoptive parents, but we learned the wait for a white Anglo-Saxon child was over five years and there was no assurance that it might not be longer. I was already forty-six and couldn't afford to wait five years, so Jude and I began to think about adopting a racially-mixed baby. We had just about finalized our decision to go that route, when he called me from work one day.

The excitement in his voice was obvious, "I think I've found the baby we're looking for!"

Aware that he was calling from work, I exclaimed, "At the Halfway House?"

"Yes and no," Jude answered. "The baby's not here, but Mike told me his niece just found out she's pregnant; and she's in no position to keep the baby."

I could feel my heart beating faster with every word Jude spoke. Mike, an English Teacher at the school, was not just a co-worker, he was Jude's best friend and I was friends with his wife Sara. They knew how much we wanted a child of our own.

"Her baby is due in February and Mike thinks with circumstances being as they are, there's a good chance she'll let us adopt the baby."

"Really?" I asked, almost afraid to believe in such a miracle.

"Of course, Mike has to talk to his niece about it. She just found out yesterday, so she probably hasn't made any other plans."

Five minutes after Jude hung up, I was on the telephone looking for an adoption lawyer. Although we didn't have a lot of money, we hired an adoption lawyer who was reported to be the best in all of Tallahassee.

Mike and his sister had both been adopted into a loving family, so they were familiar with the process and had no trouble convincing the frightened young girl that as adoptive parents, we could give her baby the love and the life it deserved. Our lawyer handled the negotiations.

Once the decision was made, I asked the adoption lawyer, "How does this work? What do we do now?"

"I would suggest," she said, "that you and Jude pay for all of the girl's prenatal care and hospitalization expenses, and allow me to act as the liaison between you and the birth mother."

Worried this might be too good to be true, I asked, "Is there any chance that the mother would change her mind and keep the baby?"

"There's always a chance of that happening," she answered, "even after the baby is given up for adoption, the natural mother has three months to change her mind before the adoption becomes final. In this case, I think it's highly unlikely. This young girl can't keep the baby because she has no way to care for it or provide the things a child needs."

I felt a huge sigh escape my chest, "Oh my gosh," I gasped, "...for a mother to give up her baby so it can have a better life is the most generous thing I have ever heard of."

"It is," the lawyer nodded. "With so many families wanting to adopt a child, I wish more unwed mothers would do it rather than turning to abortion."

We signed the papers, and a sigh floated up from my chest. "I am thrilled beyond words," I said, "and please promise this young girl we will give her child a lifetime of love and care."

My heart was racing as we left the lawyer's office. *This was really happening!* In a little over seven months Jude and I would be parents. *Halleluiah*! My heart was filled to the brim with amazement and a rapidly swelling love for the baby yet to be born. The following week we began decorating a nursery. My favorite pastime became browsing through the baby store located a short distance from our house. After careful consideration, we chose a canopied crib made of natural wood with side spindles close enough that he-or-she could not get their precious little head stuck in between the bars. At that point, I had no knowledge of whether the baby was a girl or boy so I opted for a crib set of yellow and white checked gingham and a bumper pad with a rainbow stretched along the side and puffy white clouds at both ends. The following week, we went back and bought a musical mobile to hang beneath the crib's gingham canopy. As it tinkled out the melodic notes of *Somewhere Over the Rainbow,* little rainbows circled overhead and our baby would have something to amuse him-or-her in quiet moments. No one had yet mentioned the fact that there might not be many quiet moments. We went back week after week. Months before the baby was due we had already acquired a nursery full of things to keep the child warm, dry, amused, rocked and fed along with a wall hanging to match the rainbow motif. I took the infant swing we purchased and set it in the family room where we spent most of our time; then I sat the Teddy bear in the seat of the swing and waited for our new arrival. I could sit there for hours watching that swing whooshing back and forth, imagining our baby giggling and laughing. I even took pictures of Ted, the bear, in the swing and sent them off to friends and family. A mother with her child blossoming inside of her could not have been happier, prouder, and more thrilled than I was waiting for my adopted child to arrive.

Jude and I began discussing baby names. My mother had given me an exotic and unusual name and I wanted to do the same for our child. We first addressed the issue of a boy's name and reached a decision quickly, in one evening actually. I said, "What do you think of the name Brian?"

Jude hesitated, "Not bad," he said, "but I like Ryan better."

"Me too," I replied, and our decision was made. If the baby was a boy, he would be called Ryan Anthony Deauville. At that time the only Ryan I had ever heard of was the actor Ryan O'Neil, but over time, it proved itself a popular name for his generation.

We struggled with a girl's name and bounced our thoughts off of one another for weeks before we finally decided on Danielle. "Danielle Deauville," I said, "that's a mouthful." Although a hundred or more times we laughed about what an odd sound such a name had, we stuck with it simply because there was nothing we liked better.

About two months before the scheduled birth, Sara, the English Teacher's wife, called and said that the baby's mother needed to have an ultrasound. "She's huge," Sara said, "and the doctor thinks she might even be carrying twins."

Jude was already my caregiver and with the new baby he'd have more responsibilities, so I wasn't sure how he would react to the idea of two babies. "Maybe you'd better not mention this to Jude," I said, "at least, not before we're sure she's having twins."

"Well, the doctor said it was either twins or an extremely large baby."

"When is the ultrasound?"

"Next week. When I find out if it is or isn't twins I'll call and let you know."

I was anxious to know even the minutest detail about our new baby, so of course I asked her to inquire whether it was a boy or girl when they did the ultrasound.

"I'll let you know whether to expect one baby or two," she said, "but I'm not going to tell you what the sex is."

"Why not?"

"It will ruin the surprise. Just wait; you'll find out the way most mothers' do."

"I'm not most mothers, and if I were carrying a child at my age, I'd require an ultrasound—ergo, I would then know the sex of the baby. So you can just go ahead and tell me."

"Sorry," she laughed, "but the answer is still no." She then claimed she had a pot about to boil over and hung up the telephone.

After the ultrasound, Sara called and told me not to expect twins. "The doctor said it's just a very large baby."

"And…" I said inquisitively.

"And, it's healthy," she laughed.

"And…" I repeated.

"I know the sex of the baby," Sara said, "but as I've said before, I'm not telling you."

After several minutes of going back and forth on the issue, I said, "You've got to tell me, because a friend of mine who has all boys has sent me three cartons of baby clothes but they're all boy clothes, so if it's a girl I need to go out and buy her something to wear. If I dress a little girl in boy clothes, she could grow up with gender identity confusion."

Sara laughed so hard she could barely speak, then she finally said, "Lani, I don't know how you do it, but somehow you swing people around to your way of thinking."

She then told me our baby was a boy. *A boy*. I would have loved the baby regardless of its sex, but truthfully speaking I was hoping fervently for a boy. I'd been a tomboy all my life and didn't know anything about girlie interests such as dolls, tea sets, hairdos and lacy pinafores. I knew how to throw a football, break a horse or start a fire with a few sticks of wood, but if the baby had been a girl I would have had an awful lot to learn. *A boy—wow! Ryan Anthony Deauville.*

Knowing that Ryan was a boy slowed the passing of each day to a crawl; and only after what seemed like endless days of waiting, the phone call came on a Wednesday morning while I was in a meeting with the Governor. The adoption attorney told me our baby had arrived, but because of his size, had to be delivered by Cesarean section. I asked the questions all mothers ask—Was he healthy? Did he have the right number of finger and toes? Of course, at that point, I was already in love with Ryan and I couldn't wait to hold him regardless of how many fingers and toes he had. Then I asked when I could bring him home.

"Friday," she answered. "Until then you are not to go near the hospital."

"What if I just—" Apparently she knew I was going to say peek into the baby room, because she interrupted with a resounding no. She warned that were I to visit the baby room, there was a risk of running into the mother and there could be no mistaking the deliriously happy woman in a wheelchair.

After that call, the only thing I could think about or talk about was Ryan—the baby who in just two days time would be *our son*. I reentered the meeting in a very celebratory mood.

The Governor smiled and said, "Lani, you've done enough today. Go home and get ready for your baby."

"I don't need to go home now," I answered, "I want to spend every minute of my six-week maternity leave with Ryan once he comes home."

The Governor chuckled, "This isn't part of your maternity leave, it's just a little well-earned time off. Now go on, get out of here; get ready to be a mother."

Little did he know…I had been ready for months.

When I told Pappy about Ryan's birth, he insisted that he and his new wife come up to drive Jude and me to and from the Fort Walton Beach Hospital.

"I know how excited you are," he said, "and I also know you'll be looking at that baby in the rearview mirror; so rather than have you kill yourself and everybody else, I'll drive. That way you and Jude can sit in the back seat with the baby."

I could hardly argue with his way of thinking, and besides, Pappy was the closest thing I'd ever had to a father, so I wanted him to share this happy moment.

On Friday morning I couldn't wait to get going, and insisted that we leave long before we had to. As a result, we arrived in Fort Walton Beach long before we were to meet the adoption attorney. I wanted to wait at the hospital, but Jude and Pappy insisted on having lunch.

"Sitting in the lobby is not going to get you that baby one minute sooner," Pappy said, "and besides, we're hungry."

I was shocked to think that they could actually eat at a time like this and argued that I wanted to wait at the hospital.

"It's senseless to just sit here," Jude said. "We can't do anything until the adoption attorney arrives."

"Maybe I could just go up and take a quick peek…"

"She told you not to, and if we stay here, you'll badger everyone to take you up there, so let's just go have lunch and come back when it's time."

"I won't badger everyone—" I started to say, but was interrupted.

"Yes, you will!" they said in unison.

So off we went to the Sizzler Steak House, where I refused to eat, or even place an order. As the three of them devoured a hardy lunch, I eyed them with a glare, making obvious my plea for expediency. I couldn't understand how they could gobble down food, when all I could think of was, that in moments, minutes, or perhaps an hour, I would finally be holding our son. It seemed the wait had been endless, but now it was almost over and the excitement of at last seeing Ryan made my heart pound with joy. After two long hours at the Sizzler Steak House, we returned to the hospital, and were still too early. The adoption attorney breezed by forty-five minutes late, gave us a wave and told us to wait in the lobby, she would be right back. We waited…but it wasn't a short while, it wasn't even a moderately long while, it was an eternity and I began to worry that something had gone wrong. *What if the birth-mother had changed her mind?* That was over twenty-five years ago, and yet my mind still pictures the moment when our adoption attorney stepped out of the elevator carrying a blue bundle, walked across the lobby and placed Ryan in my arms.

Sixteen

I was the first to hold Ryan, and while he was still in my arms, Jude looked down at the newborn keeper of my heart and exclaimed; "Oh my God...he looks like a lizard!" Before I even had time to take another glance, Jude followed that gut-wrenching statement by asking, "Can we give him back?" and I burst out crying. I don't cry easily, but when Jude said that about the precious baby I had been carrying in my heart for over eight months, a floodgate couldn't stop the tears from coming.

"I'm sorry..." Jude stammered, "it's just that..."

He didn't need to say it, one glance told the story. Ryan was such a big baby that he never dropped and had to be delivered by cesarean section. Even then, the doctor had a difficult time lifting him out. The bundle of joy lying in my arms had two black eyes, forceps bruises, and swollen cheeks that looked like they were stuffed with cotton. He was about as unsightly as a newborn baby can possibly be. At that moment, I'm not certain if I cried because our baby's appearance was so disappointing, or because Jude had jokingly suggested we give him back. I can now look back and laugh, because within weeks Ryan turned into one of the sweetest and most beautiful babies I've ever seen.

Happiness is the trump card that outplays everything else and holding our new baby was the happiest moment of my life, so my tears quickly subsided and Ryan was proudly passed to Pappy who, although never actually a father, was a fabulous grandfather.

On the ride home Jude and I sat in the back seat of Pappy's car with Ryan securely fastened into the car seat between us. I felt as if I could scarcely contain the excitement and joy surging through my heart. As I watched the rise and fall of Ryan's tiny breaths I had to keep telling myself—this is real, he's here, and he's our son!

Once we arrived home, Jude changed the baby's diaper and placed him in my lap, giving me the pleasure of feeding our son his first bottle. After Ryan was fed and burped, Jude laid him on his tummy in the hand-carved cradle we were going to use until our newborn was big enough for a crib. I sat beside the cradle and watched. I think I expected him to fall asleep now that his tummy was full, but Ryan was big, inquisitive and strong. So, as I sat watching, he lifted his head and his shoulders began to rise as if he were doing a push-up.

"Jude," I screamed, "come quick, Ryan's going to crawl out of the cradle." My voice carried a sense of urgency, so both Jude and Pappy were there in a heartbeat.

"He's only two days old," Jude said, "he can't possibly crawl yet."

With my being someone who lived by defying the odds, I knew that doing the impossible was sometimes possible and I wasn't willing to risk the life of my son to find out. "Ryan's too big for that cradle," I said, "please put him in the crib, before he crawls out!" Ryan spent ten minutes in the infant cradle and then moved up to a crib. He was a baby over-achiever and I sensed that as he grew this would be the pattern of his life.

The first night Ryan cried all night long and, feeling my baby's agony, I found it hard to close my eyes. Jude found it hard to close his ears; so when he heard Pappy, who was an early riser, stirring about, he lifted Ryan from the crib in our bedroom and carried him into the living room. Jude handed the baby to Pappy and said, "Here, do something," then he returned to bed.

"Pappy doesn't know anything about babies," I warned nervously. "You can't just give him the baby and come back to bed!"

"Yes, I can," Jude answered then he rolled over and closed his eyes.

A short while later, the crying stopped—apparently, Pappy knew more about babies than I thought. After a few hours sleep we got up and found Pappy was pacing back and forth across the living room with Ryan against his shoulder. That was the only time Ryan cried when he was put to bed; the second night and most of those that followed, I sat beside the crib, stretched my arm through the spindles and gently rubbed my baby's back until he fell asleep.

For the first six weeks I was home on maternity leave, and I can honestly say those were the most awe-inspiring weeks of my life. Anticipating my need, I had hired a delightful young lady to help me physically care for Ryan during that time. Day by day, our son grew stronger and more aware of his surroundings. He ate well, slept soundly and cried only when he had a stinky diaper or was hungry. Motherhood was a joy way beyond anything I had ever dreamed of. All the awards and accolades I had received over the years couldn't hold a candle to the thrill of holding Ryan in my arms. When he was just a few days old I began to share my love of the earth with him. After I fed him his bottle, fumbled my way through dressing him, and cuddled him into my lap, we went for an excursion—rain or shine. When it drizzled rain, I tucked him inside my yellow poncho and the two of us headed down to the lake in my motorized wheelchair. On our very first trip, I plucked a leaf from a ligustrum bush, cleaned it and placed it in his tiny hand. "This is a ligustrum leaf," I explained, "it came from a bush planted in the earth, plants produce oxygen for the air we breathe—they're living things, just like you and Daddy and me..." There I was explaining the wonders of nature to my infant son as he looked up at me with big blue eyes and chubby cheeks. I delighted in him and he took delight in the words I used to name the long-legged water birds, small animals, flowers, fruits and berries. I held onto each magical minute with our new baby and watched the calendar with days passing by like rapid heartbeats. On the last day of my maternity leave, my heart grew so heavy it felt like a lead weight pressing against my soul. I wanted desperately to remain at home with Ryan, but the awful truth was we needed my salary to make ends meet.

Fortunately, the school at the halfway house for delinquent boys where Jude worked closed down for summer vacation in May, so when I returned to work, he remained at home to care for the baby. I knew Ryan was in good hands and didn't worry about his well-being, but it didn't stop me from being envious that I wasn't the one at home with our son.

The hours of my workday seemed to crawl by at a snail's pace, and although I managed to move ahead at full throttle, I couldn't wait for evenings and weekends. I felt that every moment I spent at work was one that I had missed spending with Ryan—a moment that could be the one to treasure...the first time he sat alone, the first time he held a spoon, the first time he reached for the activity pad hanging on the side of his crib. There would be so many firsts and I was petrified of missing a single one.

Going back to work was an IS I had to deal with, so I made every moment away from Ryan count. To avoid the morning and evening rush hour traffic, I got to the office an hour earlier and left an hour later. There was always more to be done and too little time in which to do it, so I never stopped. Jude and I no longer had time to leisurely cook together, so on a good day we threw something into the crock pot and had a hot dinner waiting. On all too many days, we settled for fast food or junk food. Little by little, the hectic pace and poor diet caught up with me and I was hospitalized with pneumonia. After that, I found it increasingly difficult to bounce back. But after over five years of working to rectify decades of mismanagement at VR, my efforts were finally paying off. We were on budget, our Federal grants had nearly doubled and the office morale was beginning to show promise. Although our agency had never before participated in the annual intra-agency HRS volleyball tournament, that year we won it. I saw a light at the end of the tunnel. Then I heard the train whistle coming up behind me.

The Florida State Appropriations Committee and I were on a collision course. At issue was VR's compliance with the Federal Law mandating guidelines for the prioritization of vocational rehabilitation services. Prior to my tenure, the Federal Government had repeatedly warned Florida's VR that they were not in compliance with the established guidelines and threatened to cut off funding if that didn't change. Under my administration it did change, and for the first time in years VR was in full compliance with the national guidelines. The Federal guideline in question specified that more severely disabled clients were to receive primary consideration in the distribution of vocational rehabilitation services funding, and the clients with less severe disabilities be considered a lower level priority. I had been there— I was one of those with severe disabilities that the system had failed to provide for, and yet, I had gone on to prove that even in the most challenging situations, vocational rehabilitation was possible. It was important to me, both as a person with a disability, and as the Director of VR, to make certain our agency complied with the Federal guideline that was fair and just.

The head of the State Appropriations Committee felt differently. He was a former VR client who had lost the use of his arm to Polio. He had then been rehabilitated by the agency and sent for a college degree. Afterward, they set him up in his own public relations firm and he eventually became a State Legislator. Since he had fared so well, he convinced other Committee Members that the most profitable pecking order for VR clients would be to rehabilitate those with less severe disabilities first, and then address the needs of those with severe disabilities, if there was funding left over. Of course, I took exception to any such policy. Not only was it outrageously unfair, but it flagrantly flew in the face of the Federal Government Guidelines. Our discussion on this raged back and forth for some time.

"VR could lose its Federal funding if we follow your guidelines," I told him.

"You can get the less-disabled clients back to work faster," he said.

He failed to respond to my argument about losing our Federal support, so I tried arguing against the point he had made. I stated what to him should have been obvious, that people with minor disabilities can often return to work in their own field without requiring rehabilitation.

He came back saying, "The faster you get any type of client off of VR's client list, the better your group is going to look."

"Looking good is not what we're about," I argued, "VR is here to help people who genuinely need help. The core purpose of vocational rehabilitation is to enable our clients, especially those with severe disabilities, to lead a more productive life."

We never did reach an agreement on the issue. I flatly refused to go against Federal Guidelines and he refused to give in. Not long after our discussion I received a call from the Chief of Staff to the Governor.

"Lani," he said, "you've got reconsider this hard line stance you've taken against the Head of the Appropriations Committee. The guy you're tangling with has influential connections and he's got the Governor's ear on this issue. I can't help you out on this one. The bottom line is— you've got to go along with the Appropriations Committee's mandate."

"It's prejudicial," I said. "And, it goes against the Federal Guidelines!"

"I understand and I'm sorry," he said, "but you're just going to have to live with it."

"I can't live with it," I snapped back. "Using their guidelines, the Federal Government will cut off all the funding I've obtained and fewer clients with severe disabilities will get the rehabilitation they need. Do you really expect me to accept that?"

Again he gave a sigh of resolution, "Listen Lani, I know what a great job you've done at VR, and I know you've done it all on your own, but when it comes to this issue, I don't think you have much of a choice."

"Yes I do," I answered sharply, "I'll resign before I go along with something like this!"

"I understand your position on this," he said, "but I won't accept your resignation."

"Then just let me do my job."

"If doing your job means letting you continue to prioritize the most severely disabled clients, then I can't do it. My hands are tied."

"Well, mine are not!" I answered. I knew I had to work, but I also knew that based on what I had done with the VR turnaround, another job would be easy enough to come by.

"Look Lani," he said, "You're much too important to the HRS family for me to let you walk out. I know you're not willing to stay with VR under these conditions, but the State has a new program we're trying to get up and running and I'd really appreciate it if you would take over the project."

I had no alternative but to listen. The job offered to me was a lateral move in which I would direct the development and start up of a transportation program to provide lift-equipped bus service for people with disabilities and elderly persons. The Program for Transportation Disadvantaged was a joint effort between HRS and the Department of Transportation and it was a cause I could feel good about, so I accepted the position. When I hung up the receiver, I pictured myself as part of the unfortunate group of severely disabled clients who would now be turned away, and felt a wave of disgust surge through my body. Truthfully speaking, although I had enjoyed seeing VR blossom into a true client-service agency, the long hours and hard work had taken its toll on me and my health was declining. With an ongoing string of illnesses, constant exhaustion and a pallor that at times appeared almost grey, I welcomed the opportunity for change—and hopefully more time to spend with our rapidly growing son.

In the fall Jude had to return to work, and I was forced to find a day care center for Ryan. By then he was four and a half months old, but he was curious, strong and self-confident. He wasn't a baby who would be content lying in a crib for hours on end. He needed a place where he could play, explore and grow. Unfortunately, many of the day care centers I looked at were little more than jail for babies. They were dropped into a crib in the morning and seldom taken out. I went from place to place investigating facilities and with each viewing my heart seemed to grow heavier. Finally I came across an awesome facility run by Florida State University—it was perfect. A round-faced black woman sat in the rocking chair, the only piece of furniture in the big room, and she creaked back and forth as she fed a baby his bottle. It was a carpeted play room that was shampooed every night so babies could be put down to crawl and explore when they weren't sleeping. The only problem was that, the day care center had a limited capacity and a long waiting list. As I said earlier, I am not a crier, nor am I a beggar. I grew up in a family that operated on survival mode, everyone had to be independent, and I was independent to a fault. But my child's happiness was at stake, so I reached inside of myself, gathered the most pitiful voice I could find and begged. "I'm forty-six years old," I said tearfully, "and Ryan will be the only child I'll ever have…please…you've got to take him."

"We're full-up," the receptionist replied sympathetically. "And, besides, there's a long waiting list of people who are ahead of you."

The urgency of my pleas increased. "Ryan is special, he's strong, athletic and curious; I can't possibly put him in some jail-house day care center…please…"

After a considerable amount of begging, pleading and cajoling, the receptionist called for her boss to come out and I repeated all the tearful arguments I had made earlier. Finally they agreed to accept Ryan, adding with a smile, "There is always a crib available, because all of the babies don't sleep at the same time. But," the boss warned, "don't you dare tell another soul that we've bumped you to the head of the line, or there will be the devil to pay."

"Not a word," I replied joyfully as I gave her a hug, "not a word!"

Just as I expected, Ryan loved the day center. He crawled all over the playroom, played with toys on the floor and usually ended up in front of the mirrored wall, where he'd spend a few minutes poking his tummy with his finger and then laughing at the baby in the mirror doing the same thing.

I lived for the evenings and weekends we spent together as a family. Happiness was a sun-dappled day when we'd go to the lake or spend the afternoon splashing around the pool. Loving the water as I do, I'd taken Ryan into the pool when he was only six days old and he loved it—hated his bath, but loved the pool. So on a lazy afternoon, Jude would lift me onto our chair float and place Ryan in my lap; paradise couldn't be any better than that.

Ryan was strong, happy and healthy and it was a good thing, because I lifted him the way a mama gorilla lifts her babies—wrapping my arm around his body and swinging him into my lap. I had grown up a tough little survivor and it appeared that Ryan was doing the same. When I traveled for business, he and Jude came along. We were, in every sense of the word, a family, not a patchwork family such as I had grown up in, but a real family like those I had envied as a child.

That October, Ryan began to use the furniture to pull himself upright and by the time he was seven months old he was walking. When he was nine months old, he could toddle over to my wheelchair, climb up the sidebars and lift himself into my lap for a diaper change. Because I don't have the use of my hands, diaper changing was not one of my better skills, but Ryan and I did it together—clumsily and with the closure tabs far looser than they should be. Ryan was quick to catch on to the fact that Mommy's diapers were a lot looser than Daddy's. So, after I'd struggled to close the tabs using two hands instead of fingers that could pull it tight around his belly, that little rascal would stand in front of me raise his arms over his head and yell "Ta-dah!" It was the expression I used when we finished changing his diaper, but with Ryan holding his arms up, his tummy was stretched taut, so the new diaper inevitably dropped to the floor and the laughter began. Once that happened, he'd run around naked until Daddy got home.

Other than the recurring health problems, my life was about as perfect as it could be. Yes, I would have preferred to stay at home with Ryan, to never have missed a single milestone in his life, but now we needed my income more than ever before. I wanted our son to have everything he wanted and I remembered only too well how as a child we so often had to make-do with what we had. Making-do wasn't good enough for Ryan.

Heading up the Program for Transportation Disadvantaged enabled me to work without the political pressures that had been so prevalent at VR and it was a less stressful environment. But it also had a limited lifespan, because once the program was up and rolling, I would have nothing more to do. I had received assurances that once the project was completed, I would move to a comparable position within the HRS family of services. I wasn't thinking that far ahead, my thoughts were focused on my family and the job at hand when I received the news that my wonderful Aunt Eleanor, Mother's sister, was terminally ill. Aunt Eleanor was living with her daughter, Sue, in Richmond, Virginia, so we packed a bag and headed for the airport to begin the trip that would ultimately change our lives.

Seventeen

Aunt Eleanor was the middle sister in Mother's family. She had married well, so she and her two daughters lived a comfortable life that Mother might have envied. Contented in her role as housewife, Eleanor frowned on Mother's more flamboyant lifestyle and more than once suggested she adopt me so I could enjoy the lifestyle I deserved. Mother, of course, would not even consider such a thing.

"Eleanor," she said indignantly, "Just because Judd happens to be a good husband, it does not make you a better mother! Lani and I manage just fine and we need neither your pity nor financial assistance!"

On the flight to Virginia, Ryan sat in my lap and chattered happily while Jude and I spoke about my childhood in Daytona and my fond reminiscences of Aunt Eleanor. "I've always been close with Aunt Eleanor," I told him, "I was four years old when I fractured my skull for the second time in three months and Aunt Eleanor used to show up at the hospital every day..."

"Twice in three months?" Jude gasped, "How'd you do that?"

"The first time, my father and mother were driving our housekeeper home after work. The housekeeper and I were sitting in the back seat and when she got out of the car, she didn't close the door all the way. In the 1940s, the back doors of a sedan opened from the front to the back; and being an independent four year old, I decided to close the door myself. Unfortunately, my father had already pulled away from the curb and picked up speed so the wind caught the door and I flew out onto the pavement."

"You're kidding..." Jude stammered.

"No, that's exactly how it happened. The doctor told Mother I had to stay flat on my back for six weeks, and I had traces of the asphalt burn on my face for a very long time."

"Then what," Jude asked, "it happened again?"

"No, the second accident occurred about six weeks after I was home from the hospital. Dit's horse kicked me in the head. She had him tied to a post in the back yard and I was walking behind the horse when Scott's dog started barking and nipping his hooves. When the horse kicked at Skipper, he got me instead. I was flat on my back for another six weeks. That was when Aunt Eleanor visited me in the hospital every day and brought bowls of Junket."

"What's Junket?" Jude asked.

"Sort of a thin pudding," I said, thinking back fondly, "Aunt Eleanor used food coloring and made it in bright colors. Those bowls of Junket looked so festive, I felt happy before the spoon even touched my lips." *A memorable IS.*

When Jude eventually leaned back in the seat and closed his eyes, I thought back on the days of my childhood and our visits to Ormond Beach. Mother was the youngest of three girls; Eleanor, the middle child was such a frail newborn, she reportedly had to be carried on a satin pillow; Alice, the eldest, was the bossiest and most regimented in her ways, but she more than made up for it by marrying Laurie, a man we children adored. When I was about eight years old, Aunt Eleanor and her brood left Daytona, and moved to Ormond Beach where they lived in a huge house with a sprawling lawn. They transformed the garage of that house into a stable, allowing Sue's horse to graze the grass in the fenced yard.

Little wonder the short trip to Ormond Beach was my favorite getaway. Not only did Sue have her own horse, but so did Ann, Aunt Alice and Uncle Laurie's older daughter. Ann was an excellent rider, but her horse was high-spirited and temperamental, so her younger sister Carol and I were not allowed to ride it—which made the thought of climbing on the horse's back all the more appealing. When the others were occupied elsewhere, Carol and I would often slip into the stable, climb up, sit on the horse's back and pretend we were riding into the wind, even though we would not dare take the horse from her stall. For us, that forbidden challenge provided a thrilling adventure we chuckled about for hours afterward. Since Carol was closer to me in age, she was my mischief-making partner, but it was Ann who I secretly wished was my big sister. Ann, the older version of the tomboy in me, could lasso a calf and pull it to the ground—that was something that made her stand extremely tall in my mind's eye.

When the plane touched down in Virginia, Sue, Aunt Eleanor's older daughter was waiting for us. "Mother's not doing very well," she told us sadly, "in fact Jennie has come down from Pennsylvania to be with us." Once Jude settled Ryan in my lap, Sue picked up the diaper bag and led the way through the airport to the parking garage. "Jennie is staying at the Regency," she said, "and they've also made arrangements for you to stay there." Jennie's husband Dan was the heir to a candy company fortune, and Jennie wanted for nothing.

"The Regency," I said, "isn't that kind of expensive?"

Sue laughed, "You know Jennie, she's got more money than she knows what to do with and she loves showing it off."

When we checked in at the Regency, we were escorted to a very spacious suite equipped with a crib for Ryan, a bottle of chilled champagne, a basket of fresh fruit and a gigantic vase overflowing with flowers. We settled in quickly and then continued on to Sue's house. I knew at times I was pushing myself, beyond what should have been my limit, but we only had three days to spend with Aunt Eleanor and I didn't want to waste a moment.

One look at Ryan was enough for Aunt Eleanor to fall in love with him. "So this is the amazing little boy I've heard so much about," she said smiling.

As we sat there talking, Jennie motioned for Jude to follow her into the kitchen. Never one to mince words, or hold back something she wanted to say, Jennie blurted out, "Lani doesn't look so good, what's the matter with her?"

Like me, Jude was someone who minimized problems rather than allowing them to balloon out of proportion. "She's got a pretty hectic work schedule," he said, "so she's probably overtired."

"Lani had pneumonia a few months ago, didn't she take time off?"

"She was home for a while, but not long. Lani likes to work and with the office calling her every few hours, she decided she might as well go back to work."

"Well," Jennie huffed, "Obviously it wasn't enough time, because she looks terrible. She's so thin, and her color is ghastly..." Jennie went on for several minutes with her detailed analysis of what my supposed problems were. Finally she said, "In my opinion, Lani shouldn't even be working!"

Jude patiently answered, "Maybe not, but she loves her work and truthfully speaking, we need the income."

"And what about Ryan," Jennie snapped back, "Don't you think he needs his mother?"

"When Lani's not working, she spends every minute with him and he adores her," Jude said defensively. "During the day, Ryan's well-taken care of at the daycare center."

"Daycare center!" she exclaimed, "Ryan in a daycare center!" With a loud huff and a look of determination spreading across her face, Jennie said, "This has got to change. I want Lani to quit working! I want her to stay home, take care of her health and take care of that sweet little boy."

Losing patience with the conversation, Jude said, "Well it's not going to happen because first of all we can't afford it, and secondly, Lani enjoys working."

"You will be able to afford it," Jennie replied with an air of superiority, "I can see to that! As you well know, Dan and I are quite wealthy and if Lani will quit working, I'll provide enough money for you to build a house wherever you want to retire and I'll fund your living expenses for the remainder of Lani's life."

"Wow," Jude sighed, "That's an extremely generous offer, but in all honesty, I know she won't even consider taking you up on it. She's too independent and she's never been one to accept a handout. Lani takes a lot of pride in her work and what she's accomplished."

Jennie continued going on about how unhealthy I looked until she at last convinced Jude to talk to me about her proposition. I of course answered just as he had expected, with a resounding no. "That's very nice of her, but I've never depended on anyone to pay my way," I said, "and I'm not going to start now."

Throughout the full three days of our visit, Jennie seized every opportunity to pull Jude aside and harangue him about how sickly I looked and how much Ryan needed to have his mother at home to take care of him. I thought our return to Tallahassee would put an end to the discussion, but Jennie continued to call until finally she persuaded Jude that her plan was in the best interest of all. I steadfastly refused the offer, not because I felt it ill-intentioned, but simply because I did not want someone to take care of me financially. My independence was something I had fought hard to win and I guarded it zealously. Jennie, who was herself a diabetic, understood the risks and challenges of dealing with disabilities, so in a last ditch effort to change my mind, she bonded with Jude and they played the trump card. "If you continue this pace," they warned, "you'll be dead within a few years; and Ryan will be without a mother!"

Ryan was something my heart held far more precious than my independence, and the thought of not being there as he grew into a boy and ultimately a man was something I simply could not bear. Deep down in my heart, I knew from the moment I first held Ryan in my arms that I wanted to be a stay-at-home Mom. Now I was being given the opportunity to do so. Yes, it meant leaving what I had worked so hard to achieve, but it also meant that I would always be there for our son and nothing in the world was more important him. The following week, I spoke with the Director of HRS and told him that when the Disabled Transit project was finalized, I would be leaving the agency. Despite his protests, three months later, when the last of my project responsibilities was complete, I walked out of HRS for the very last time. I had been with the agency for ten years, just barely long enough to qualify for a meager pension, but long enough to build a storehouse of memories – both positive and negative.

I had spent the better part of my life working, but now I was moving on to what would be the most important job of my career—that of being a mother. Although we had been living in Tallahassee for almost seven years, the truth was that I had no real love of the city—mainly because it was a city, a big impersonal city. I missed the small town friendliness of the Daytona I knew as a child, the wooded preserves, the unhurried pace of people who had time for a smile and a hello. So, before we began this new life of ours, we had to decide where we really wanted to live. There would be no more trudging off to where a job or education took you, we were now free to choose a place where we truly wanted to live—a place where our family would spend the rest of our life.

The Speedway now drew throngs of visitors and Daytona was no longer the sleepy little town I had known, so we moved on to thoughts of other places and narrowed it down to two of my favorites. Key West, an island three miles wide and five miles long, was impossible not to love for someone who enjoys nature as much as I do and it was a place where the chaos of city life was non-existent. Our other choice was Vero Beach. We had spent several days in the Vero area back in 1984 when I gave the Commencement Address to the graduating class of the Indian River Community College in nearby Fort Pierce. In our explorations we discovered that Vero was a charming town with graceful old homes and a scattering of new developments on the ocean and yet it was a place undiscovered by tourists—it was the Daytona of thirty years ago. Jude and I both loved Key West, but the reality was Vero Beach had better schools. Ryan was still a toddler but it was easy to envision him attending the prestigious Saint Edwards School, where graduates were virtually assured of being admitted to an Ivy League University.

With Ryan strapped into his car seat and a certain lightness rising in our hearts, we drove down to spend the weekend in Vero. We lunched at a waterfront café, drove along the beach and searched the quiet residential streets. We looked at one lot after the other, but in comparison to the two-acre plot our Shannon Lake house sat on, these were tiny in size and many of them were sequestered inside gated communities, which Jude and I both considered a bit too snooty. After driving past dozens of properties, Jude bought a local newspaper and we went to dinner. While he was scanning the real estate listings, I read a single column article called "the Police and Sheriff's Department." During the preceding week there had been only two crimes worthy of a listing. The first was a stolen bicycle, the second was a naked drunk behind the parking lot of the Kentucky Fried Chicken Restaurant. Practically no crime—this was definitely the town where I wanted our son to grow up. The following morning we began a more serious search of properties and when we came across a gigantic oak tree in the front yard of a home-site at Castaway Cove, our decision was made. The lot was very small, but it was in a beautiful family neighborhood and close to a school that Ryan could attend once he was older. We telephoned Jennie and told her of our decision.

"You're doing the right thing," Jennie said, "it sounds like a charming community." Despite her generosity and the openness of her attitude, the thought of allowing another person to control my fate was still strangely troubling. Whatever doubts I had were squashed beneath the joyous thoughts of ultimately spending every hour of every day with Ryan. I could now watch him grow, see him learn to ride a two-wheeler, bandage skinned knees, escort him to his first day of school, I could be a full-time Mom. I knew then, I would never allow myself to be called Mother. I was going to be Mom, or Mommy, or whatever name settled onto his tongue. I had already bestowed a nickname on Ryan, to me he was Booger Butt. It was a term of endearment drawn from the endless string of dirty diapers. Hopefully, in time, he would discover his name for me—it could be anything except MOTHER. "Mother" was too reminiscent of my Mother, and I was determined that Ryan would have a far healthier relationship with me than I had with my Mother.

In the weeks that followed, we decided on a builder to construct what would be our dream house—a house with full accessibility, down to and including a drive-in shower. I was giving up my financial independence but I would now be able to move throughout the entire house with no restrictions. There would be no narrow doorways, or step down ledges. For the first time in my life, I would live in a house that adapted itself to me instead of it being the other way around. By the time the plan was finished and the foundation poured, I was looking forward to the move more than I dreamed possible.

One afternoon shortly after I had officially retired from HRS, Jennie called, "Guess what?" she asked excitedly.

"What?" I answered, waiting for the other shoe to drop.

"Dan and I bought a house in Vero Beach too, so we'll practically be neighbors. Of course, our house," she boasted, "is right on the beach."

Once she described the house, I knew precisely which one they had purchased. It wasn't just a house, it was a beachfront mansion.

"We'll keep our place in Pennsylvania," she told me, "this will just be a vacation house; a winter getaway for when the weather turns cold—and so I can be close to you and that darling boy Ryan."

Jennie and Dan closed on their Vero Beach house long before the walls of our house were framed, so when we traveled back and forth to watch the progression of building, we stayed at their beachfront mansion—in the downstairs maid's quarters, naturally.

Once I accepted the thought that I was losing my financial independence, the only sad thing about leaving Tallahassee was that we had to find a home for Patches, the Great Dane we'd had for almost eight years. Not only did we love her, but so did Ryan. Patches was Ryan's guardian, and the closest thing he'd ever had to a Nanny. On the day before we were to leave Shannon Lakes for the very last time, we took Patches over to Henry and Maggie's house and returned without her. They had known Patches for years and loved her as we did, so they were happy to have her. But for weeks afterward, Ryan would ask, "Mommy, where Patches?" I would again explain that Patches was now living with our friends because she was used to running free on a big two-acre lot and wouldn't be happy in a back yard that had barely room for a swing set. "Okay," he'd say, but then a day or two later he'd ask if it was time to go get Patches yet. Although I was pleased to see our child with the same love of animals that Jude and I shared, it had a bittersweet quality of sadness, knowing such a love can sometimes bring great sadness.

Eighteen

Once we were settled into our new home at Castaway Cove, my transition from Harried-Executive to Stay-at-Home-Mom became a lifestyle that I had never envisioned. Ryan was at the age where every day brought another change, another step forward into life, another new achievement... and the most beautiful part was that I could be there to share these things with him. Shortly before his second birthday, I began to introduce Ryan to the concept of toilet training. After decades of being a Clinical Psychologist, I saw the challenge as little more than operant conditioning, a term coined by the famous psychologist B.F. Skinner to describe the consequences of rewarding a particular behavior to promote that behavior in the future; and that's exactly what happened. About a week before his birthday I explained to Ryan that he was becoming a big boy and since he was going to be two years old, we were going to get rid of those soggy old diapers and let him start wearing big boy underwear, "And, to celebrate your big boy birthday," I said, "you can choose whatever you want to drink and all day long you can drink as much as you want of it."

"Anything?" he asked wide-eyed.

I nodded, "Yes, anything. What would you like?"

"Coca-Cola," he said grinning

After years of treating too many children that were hyperactive because of sugary treats, I had never made Coca-Cola part of Ryan's diet, so I had no idea where he'd learned about it.

But anything meant anything, and it was only for one day. "Yes," I answered, "you can have Coca-Cola. And..." I said teasingly, "you can even choose a special treat to go with it. Then every time you tinkle in your potty chair on the toilet, I'll pop one of those treats into your mouth." After the Coca-Cola response I half-expected he would ask for M & M's which are generally the kid-favorite, but he surprised me again.

"Black olives," Ryan answered enthusiastically.

"Are you sure?"

He grinned excitedly, "Yes, please."

"Okay, black olives it will be. But remember, you only get the treat after you tinkle in your potty chair."

Ryan nodded, but there was already a gleam of expectation in his eyes. Every day that week he asked if it was the day yet. "No," I'd answer, "your birthday is on Thursday, this is only Tuesday."

On Thursday morning, he woke me bright and early, "Now? Can I have my Coca-Cola?"

"Breakfast first, then Coca-Cola," I answered.

When the last spoonful of Cheerios disappeared, Ryan asked, "Now?"

"Yes, now," I laughed and handed him a full glass of Coca-Cola. When he finished, we opened a new can of black olives, took them into the bathroom and set them on the counter."

"May I have my olive now?" Ryan asked brightly.

"Not yet," I answered shaking my head, "Olives are the treat you get when you tinkle in the toilet on your potty chair."

"Oh." Ryan gave me a rather pensive look then suggested, "I tinkle now." He pulled down his new big boy underwear and climbed onto the potty chair. After a minute or two with no action he asked, "Olive now?"

Again I shook my head, "You have to tinkle in the potty first."

We waited.

After what was probably only a few minutes but seemed an eternity I heard a stream splash into the potty. "Great job," I said beaming; and popped an olive into his mouth. "Now," I asked, "are you ready for more Coca-Cola?"

"Yes, please," he responded with a big grin.

We continued the process throughout the morning, with me always nearby to pour him another glass of soda or ask if he thought it might be time to tinkle again. Several hours and numerous olives later, Ryan was completely potty-trained and never needed another diaper.

The years of his childhood seemed to fly by in a handful of heartbeats. Two quickly turned into three, and Ryan was baptized at the Episcopal Church with Jennie and Dan as his Godparents. Ryan was always smart and inquisitive, so when I told him that he was going to be baptized, I had to explain the details of everything that would happen. In the middle of the Baptism service, the Priest hesitated long enough to catch his breath and I can only suppose Ryan thought he had forgotten what to do, because in his sweet child's voice he turned to me and said, "Mommy, isn't this the part where he's supposed to pour water over my head?" Ryan's attempt at assistance struck the priest funny and he laughed out loud. The remainder of the baptism ceremony was executed with broad smiles from everyone except Ryan, who took the whole thing very seriously and wanted to be certain it was done correctly.

Ryan was blessed with Jude's people skills—he loved everyone and everyone loved him. You simply couldn't help yourself. I was a tough little kid who danced to the drummer I heard and didn't much care what anyone else thought about it. I didn't go around looking for fights, but if a fight came looking for me I was ready for it. People either loved me or didn't, sometimes it was a little of both. Ryan on the other hand, was impossible not to love. He tried to be friends with everyone and he'd go out of his way to do something he thought would please. After the Baptism, we took pictures outside the church and when Uncle Dan squatted down for a shot alongside Ryan. In an effort to be equally accommodating, Ryan squatted also. That snapshot has remained one of my favorite pictures of Ryan.

The year that Ryan was three was a magical one—it was the year he went from being a toddler to a little boy. It was also the year he made his first lifelong friend.

It was early afternoon when the doorbell rang. I opened the door, looked out and saw no one. I started to close the door, but before I could turn away, the bell chimed again. I reopened the door and as I again looked for where an adult would be standing, I heard a voice say, "Hey, I'm down here!"

A knee-high person dressed in kid's clothes was standing there. When he began to speak it was with the most adult-sounding statement I'd ever heard from a child.

"I understand that you have a son approximately my age," he said.

For a moment I was unsure if he was the person talking; "Are you a midget dressed in kid's clothes?" I asked suspiciously.

He gave me a look of indignation, "No," he said, "I'm four years old!"

"Four years old," I repeated, "Well, we have a son who is three…"

"That will do nicely," he said, then circled past me and strolled into the house.

That was my introduction to Dane, Ryan's first real friend. From that point on, they were inseparable. It seemed they both enjoyed the same things; things such as swimming in our pool, riding their bikes, challenging each other on Ryan's swing set or playing in the outdoor fort. On rainy days, they'd be inside playing with a wooden train set that we'd bought for Ryan on Christmas. It had endless possibilities for adding pieces to the set so Ryan received stretches of track and railroad cars as gifts for any number of occasions. With all the pieces that had been added, they could construct a lengthy maze of railroad routes that ran from one room to another and crossed under tunnels made from sofa cushions. Once removed, the cushions from the sectional in the living room took on a magical quality as they were piled one on top of another constructing a fort that was used for endless hours of play and numerous sleepovers. As the boys became older, they were sometimes allowed to sleep in the outdoor fort, which wasn't all that dangerous since our yard was surrounded by a privacy fence and they were always under the watchful eye of Mom and Dad.

Ryan and Dane got along famously and rarely disagreed. In their friendship for one another, they both found the brother they wished they had.

Before long, our house became the neighborhood hub for kids to play. But to play at our house, a child had to know the rule and agree to abide by it. *By now I'm sure lots of mothers are thinking...good luck with that!* It was a simple enough rule and not used excessively. When a child did something that was bad, or potentially harmful to the others, I would say "SIT!" and they had to drop and sit in the precise spot where the infraction occurred. The other kids had to ignore the sitter and move on with whatever they were doing. To end what I considered a figure-it-out session, a child had to first tell me what they had done wrong; then they had to explain what they should have done in that situation; and lastly, they had to tell me what they would do next time they encountered the same circumstances. If they got all three parts right, I would smile and say, "WONDERFUL!" The child could then get up, give me a hug, a kiss on the cheek, and go back to playing. If they refused to admit what they'd done, or state how they'd change their behavior, they had to sit there and be ignored until they were ready to do so. It was remarkable how the kids were able to zero-in on their errors and come up with a better solution.

Dane caught on right away and before his little bottom hit the floor he was already confessing his crime. Minutes later, he'd go back to playing. But Ryan, although he had more than his share of Jude's lovable people skills, had a stubborn streak that, in a way, resembled my own. So when he had to sit—he sat, and sat, and sat for the longest time before he would finally give in and acknowledge what he'd done. Ryan named it "The Inevitable Sit" and the name stuck.

As a child I had been beaten so often and so furiously by my brother and sister for every perceived wrongdoing that I was vehemently against using corporal punishment on any child. This was especially true for Ryan, so the inevitable sit became my method of discipline. In all his years of childhood, Ryan only received one spanking, and that was absolutely laughable. I remember the spanking only too well, but I can no longer remember what Ryan did to provoke me to that end. Whatever it was, it pushed me way beyond the inevitable sit so I gave Ryan a stern look of determination and said, "Okay, that's it! Ryan, you're going to get a spanking! Drop your drawers, climb up here and get across my lap."

Ryan had never before been spanked, but he'd heard tales of the dreaded punishment from Dane, a mischief-maker extraordinaire who apparently had received numerous spankings. Ryan's lip began to quiver, but he did as he was told.

Now to the funny part—I had to use my triceps to stretch my arm out to even reach his behind and the triceps is one of my weakest muscles—so in spanking Ryan's behind, I could just about raise my arm and then allow it to drop down on his butt. I smacked him once with that ridiculously weak arm then said, "Okay, that's it! Now, let that be a lesson to you!"

"That's it?" Ryan repeated, looking astonished as he scrambled down from my lap.

I could no longer control my laughter. "Yes, that's it," I said trying to push back a grin, "and I hope you've learned your lesson!"

"That was the whole spanking?" Ryan laughed.

"Yes," I sighed, "that was the whole spanking."

At that point, we both began laughing at the ridiculousness of the entire procedure, but Ryan, forever wanting to please did say, "I learned my lesson, Mommy, you won't ever have to spank me again." And I didn't.

I don't believe violence is the answer to anything, so as a child Ryan was taught fighting was not the way to settle disagreements. The only exception to my no-fighting rule was self-defense in the event a much larger or older boy started the fight. That happened once when Ryan was about nine or ten and two older boys jumped on him after they'd gotten into an argument about the kickball rules. But it was his one and only fight, and for the remainder of his boyhood years he relied on reason and friendliness to overcome future challenges.

It turned out that my cousin Jennie had been right in insisting I stop work, not only because I had the joy of spending time with Ryan and watching him grow, but because of my health. Decades of long work days, an enormous amount of travel, and poor eating habits had taken a toll on my health so with each passing year I was experiencing a greater number of illness, bladder infections and digestive problems. Obviously I was spending too much time in the hospital because Ryan knew how to scramble through the wires and tubes so he could climb into the hospital bed to cuddle with me. My answer had always been to push through the discomfort and focus on the enjoyment of being with Jude and Ryan—but providence has a way of stepping in and taking care of the things you try to ignore.

It started with a visit from Jude's younger sister Elvira. Elvira was married to Sam, a biochemist and psychologist she met when she and her parents lived in the Canary Islands. Elvira and Sam now lived in Canada, where Sam had formed a cooperative to produce a nutritional superfood he created. The second day of their stay, Sam who is a walking synthesis of *you are what you eat*, pulled me aside and said, "Lani, your color doesn't look good, and I've noticed you tire more quickly than you used to. Are you feeling okay?"

"Well-enough, given my circumstances," I answered, but Sam's question hit home. Constantly on the go, I didn't allow myself the luxury of stopping long enough to think about my health; he was right, I did tire easily and over the past few years it had been one illness after the other. He saw something I had chosen to ignore. "But, I do find my energy level is a lot lower than it used to be," I admitted.

"The problem," Sam said, "is that you're not getting the vitamins and minerals your body needs for good health. I'm going to send you a bottle of a dietary supplement I created to help the kids that I work with. I want you to start taking it."

"I'm already taking a multi-vitamin," I said dismissively.

"That's not enough!" Sam replied. He then launched into his story about how people don't eat the alkaline-rich fruits and vegetables they need to maintain their body's pH balance. "This new powder I've formulated," he explained, "provides the nutrition you'd get from a plate full of fruits and vegetables," he gave me a sly grin and added, "...the fruits and vegetables you're obviously not eating!"

He went on to explain how vitamin pills are synthetic substitutes, whereas his miracle powder consisted of twenty-nine healthy fruits and vegetables compressed into an enzymatically alive powder that could be mixed with water or fruit juice.

"And..." I said, waiting to hear about the small print additives.

"And nothing," Sam replied, "it's simply a concentrated form of nutrition—superfood nutrition!"

Sam is a walking encyclopedia of information on health and nutrition, and once he has a listener, he can expound on the subject for hours. After he'd assured me that this new powder would help to stimulate my immune system, he had my ear. "It's not just another vitamin pill?" I repeated skeptically.

"It's totally different," he answered. "Over-the-counter vitamins are processed with preservatives so they'll stay fresh for a long time, the healthy enzymes are gone. The supplement I'm sending you is processed, but it's not cooked; all we remove is the moisture; the food enzymes are still alive. You get the nutritional benefit of those fresh fruits and vegetables you're not eating, and, you get dietary fiber without all that bulk."

"It's worth a try," I said rather unenthusiastically, then tactfully moved on to another topic of conversation.

Two weeks after their return to Canada, a package arrived. Inside the box were two bottles of nasty-looking green powder and Sam's hand-written mixing instructions. Following directions I stirred it into a glass of cranberry juice rather than the water Sam had suggested and forced it down.

That afternoon I telephoned Sam. "This stuff tastes terrible," I grumbled. I was going to say it was grainy, gritty and altogether unpleasant but before I could do so, Sam began laughing.

"I know," he said, "I'm working on improving the taste. It may take some getting used to, but stay with it Lani—you'll be amazed at how much better you're going to feel."

I had my doubts but agreed to stay with it for a month. Every morning I mixed the green powder into a glass of fruit juice and drank it down. On the fourth day my tummy began acting like Mount Vesuvius preparing for an eruption. I telephoned Sam. "I don't think I can keep taking this stuff," I said, "it's upsetting my stomach."

Sam listened to my explanation of the problem I was having then said, "Good."

"Good?" I questioned.

"Yes, good. It's doing just what we want it to do—it's detoxifying your system, getting rid of all the unhealthy food that's been accumulating in your stomach and intestines." Once again, he convinced me to stay the course.

A few days later my tummy was fine, but my sinuses were so clogged that I could barely breathe—then they started to drain. Aha! I had been right. I was having an allergic reaction to the stuff. Once again I called Sam, and once again he convinced me that his yucky green powder was doing exactly what it was supposed to do—it had now moved on to detoxifying my sinuses. Admittedly, I kept drinking the concoction in part to humor Sam, but more so because as illogical as it seemed, I hoped that it would indeed improve my health.

About a week later, I awoke one morning and found my face covered with tiny little whiteheads. Now I knew for certain I was allergic to something in that mix, so I called Sam before I even brushed my teeth. "I'm sorry for waking you so early," I said, "but I think I'd had some sort of severe allergic reaction—my face is covered with pimples!" The desperation in my voice had to be obvious, but Sam simply laughed.

"Have you washed your face yet?" he asked.

"Well, no…I thought I should call you right away…"

"Go and gently wash your face, then pat it dry with a soft towel," Sam said. "I'll hold on and wait while you do."

I did as he'd instructed, not scrubbing abrasively but gently running a soapy terry cloth over my skin and then blotting it dry. I looked in the mirror and the pimples were all gone. Hurrying back to the phone, I told Sam what had happened.

"That's what I thought," he said, "It's still detoxifying you; the supplement is making your skin healthy and getting rid of the bad cells that were in your skin."

"Are you sure…"

"I'm positive, and, I've got good news; I've adjusted the formula and I think you might like the taste of this better. I sent you a bottle; let me know what you think."

A few afternoons later I received the second package—this one containing a single bottle of green powder along with a note from Sam reiterating what he'd said earlier.

This batch had a smoother texture but the taste was still yucky. Bear in mind, I was used to milkshakes, hamburgers, fried chicken—all the things that tasted good but were bad for me—I hardly knew what healthy food was supposed to taste like.

Sam continued to formulate and reformulate the powder and I continued to drink it offering my comments and suggestions on each new mixture. I was his guinea pig, and as a quadriplegic I made a terrific guinea pig, because if this miracle powder could address the issues inherent with quadriplegics, it was capable of anything. As Sam and I worked toward finding a way to improve the powder's taste and texture, better health slipped through the back door and settled in.

Jude and I were outside playing ball with Ryan when Marie, a neighbor from the next block, happened by on her bicycle. She took a look at me and screeched to a stop. "What have you been doing!" she exclaimed.

A bit puzzled by her reaction, I answered, "Playing ball with Ryan."

"No, I mean what have you been doing to *yourself*...you look fabulous!"

"Really?" Her statement astonished me and I had to pause a moment to think about it. I knew I was feeling better...but looking better? That came as a surprise. "For the past three weeks I've been taking this nutritional supplement I got from my brother-in-law," I finally said.

"What is it and where can I get it?" Marie questioned.

I laughed, "It's called GreensPlus but he only sells it in Canada. If you want, I'll order a bottle for you."

"If it's doing this for you, I certainly do want a bottle," Marie said. Then she climbed back onto her bike and pedaled off. "Call me when you get it," she shouted as she rounded the corner.

Two weeks after Marie picked up her bottle of GreensPlus, she was back again. "I need to order four more bottles of this green stuff," she said.

"Four?" I echoed with surprise, I knew one bottle should have lasted her for about a month. "How many times a day are you taking it?" I inquired incredulously.

"It's not just me taking it," Marie beamed, "I've been giving it to my husband, George, and you can't imagine the change that's come over him!"

"Change?"

"I'll say! After his father died five years ago, George got so depressed that all he did was sit on the couch and stare at the television; he wouldn't even come to the table for dinner. I had to bring him dinner on a tray. Nearly drove me crazy. Anyway, once I got him drinking that green juice, he started to perk up."

"Did he..." I was going to say more but Marie was on a roll so I just listened.

"Those hall light bulbs have been burnt out for over a year and after six months of asking him to change them and him doing nothing, I gave up trying. Then three days ago without a word from me, he hauls out the ladder and starts replacing them!" She paused long enough to catch her breath then carried on. "Not only that, but yesterday when he got home from work instead of plopping down on the couch, he said he was going for a bicycle ride and asked if the girls and I wanted to join him. You can't imagine how happy I am to see George getting back to himself."

"Oh Marie," I sighed, "that's so wonderful."

"It's better than wonderful, it's an absolute miracle! That's why I need four more bottles and if you could ask them to rush the order, I'd appreciate it."

I had to laugh, Marie was one of those delightful people who flitted and flew around the neighborhood spreading good news the way a bee spreads pollen. She was ordering another bottle of the green drink for her and George, but the three additional bottles were for neighbors who had heard the word.

Within a few months, I was calling Sam almost every day to place another order. Finally I decided to just go ahead and order a few cases of GreensPlus, so I'd have it on hand to sell. That worked quite well, but before I knew it, the guest room was filled with cartons—it seemed that the more I ordered, the more people wanted to buy, and I was forever being asked where else GreensPlus could be purchased.

"I've got a friend in Ohio," Lulu Barnes said, "and she could really use some of this!"

Jude and I would volunteer to ship a bottle to the friend in Ohio then the following month we'd get a second order from the friend along with two more for their friends. Pretty soon, I had to create a pathway for my wheelchair just so I could get through the boxes of GreensPlus we had stored in the house.

As the number of orders increased, Jude and I began to think we should establish our own business since we were already sending bottles of GreensPlus all over the country.

When the incorporation papers were drawn up, we named Jude CEO, knowing that he would stack stock, do deliveries and take care of anything else that needed doing. I would continue to handle the paperwork, billing, and customer calls.

Before we got much more than one toe in the water, Jennie heard that I was working and immediately withdrew the annual stipend she'd been giving me. So there we were, no income and struggling to operate a fledgling business out of our guest room. For a while, it was tough making ends meet but even on the roughest days we were encouraged by what GreensPlus was doing—not only for our customers—but for me personally. I had energy to burn and felt better than I had felt in many, many years.

Nineteen

Suddenly our life changed faster than I imagined possible. I went from being comfortably retired to selling bottles of GreensPlus out of cartons stacked head-high in our guest room and throughout much of the house. Jude and I quickly came to the realization that our sideline had somehow blossomed into a full-fledged business. We decided to make what was a monumental move for us; nervously scraping together the last of our savings, we launched Orange Peel Enterprises, doing business as GREENS+.

When I say the last of our savings, I truly mean the last of our savings. We were now bottomed out—there was no money for advertising, publicity or sales promotion—all we had were the pass-along recommendations we received from the handful of customers we had. Jude ordered one-hundred bottles and began giving them away just to get people to try the product. It worked, and slowly new orders began to dribble in. Word of mouth was spreading our name around, but we needed to get business cards; a friend recommended Faber Press.

Faber Press was in a warehouse behind an old wooden "cracker house" that looked abandoned. It sat facing the street and as Jude walked by, he eyed the building and thought of my frustration with trying to maneuver my wheelchair through the stacks of cartons. When he entered the warehouse, Dot Faber looked up from behind an oversize desk and said, "Need something printed?"

Dot Faber was a tiny woman who, standing on tiptoes, wouldn't make it to five feet; but her voice was loud enough to splinter glass. She was the consummate New Yorker, no fluff and folderol on the outside, but inside a heart of gold. Jude smiled, explained what he needed, and gave her a down payment on the order for our first business cards. Once that was done, he asked if she owned the building out front.

"That old wooden house?" she said, "Yeah, I own it."

"Would you ever consider renting it?" Jude asked.

"Sure. You wanna rent it?"

"Maybe someday," Jude said, "Right now we're just getting our business started and we can barely afford the business cards."

Dot shrugged, "The place is just sittin' there empty," she said, "so take it."

"Really," Jude reiterated, "we can't afford it right now."

With a scowl, Dot thumped her hands onto her hips, "Did I ask for money?"

"That's a very generous gesture, but with our business just getting started I don't know how long it would take for us to catch up on the back rent and that wouldn't be..."

"Hold on!" Dot said in a voice that thundered across Jude's, "Seems you got a hearing problem—I didn't say nothing about money!"

"But..." Jude stammered, "I don't know when..."

"OiVey!" she shouted using the pretense of frustration, "You don't gotta pay me nothing! You move in, when you make money you pay; you don't make money, you don't pay."

But...the arrears..."

"No arrears," she said with her arms in the air and palms facing Jude, "No arrears!"

Jude stood there looking dumbfounded.

Dot fumbled through her desk drawer then pulled out a key and handed it to him, "So, what're you waiting for?" she said, "Get your stuff and move in!"

Jude mumbled a thank you and turned to leave, but as he neared the door she called out, "Just be careful where you stack stuff 'cause there's termites in that back room."

Later that afternoon, Jude and I went down and looked through what was to be our new office. No question, it needed work—lots of work. We would have to hire someone to help with painting and repairs; so I called Loretta. Loretta was a woman with a million answers in her apron pocket and she knew where to find whatever you needed—whether it was a hug or needle in a haystack.

I had become friends with Loretta about six or seven months earlier, but we'd been waving hello to each other for almost a year. Every Tuesday afternoon Loretta arrived at Reynold Smith's house shortly after lunch and spent the afternoon tidying up messes and watching over the children while Reynold and his wife were at work. A last minute emergency brought Loretta and me together and from that moment on she became a treasured friend; the sort of sister I had always wanted.

Ryan was practically never left with a babysitter—he wasn't whiney or disruptive, so we took him along everywhere we went. We realized that sooner or later there were bound to be occasions when Ryan couldn't come, so we prepared for that eventuality by trying out a babysitter who came highly recommended. One evening we engaged the sitter and went to dinner without Ryan. Needless to say, he was the topic of conversation throughout most of the dinner and before dessert was served, I was anxious to start home. When we arrived home, the babysitter was watching television.

"Where's Ryan?" I asked.

"In bed, fast asleep," she answered smiling, "I didn't even have to mention bedtime, he just went into his room, got undressed, put his pajamas on and came out carrying his blanket and teddy bear."

I had to smile knowing how very Ryan that was.

"At seven o'clock on the button, he told me it was time to go night-night!" With an expression of amazement, she shook her head and sighed, "Most kids fight tooth and nail to stay up later than they're supposed to; but that's the first time I've ever had a child tell me it's time for them to go to bed!"

It surprised the sitter, but it didn't surprise me—because that's the way Ryan was.

The emergency that brought Loretta into our life occurred a few weeks later. The babysitting test had gone off without a hitch, so this time we felt considerably more comfortable leaving Ryan at home while we were out for dinner. The difference was this time it wasn't a test, we had a business meeting and it would have been inappropriate to bring Ryan along. About an hour before we were scheduled to leave, the sitter called, said she had a last-minute emergency and couldn't make it. In desperation, I telephoned the Smiths, hoping to get Loretta's home telephone number to ask if she could babysit Ryan for the evening.

After a single ring, Loretta answered. "Oh, I didn't think you would be working. I was going to ask the Smiths for your home number."

"I'll give you my telephone number," Loretta laughed, "but it won't do any good to call 'cause I'm here." She gave another chuckle then said, "What'd you want to call me for?"

I explained the problem and asked if she knew of anyone else who was a trustworthy babysitter. Without a moment's hesitation she suggested I bring Ryan over to the Smith's house where she'd watch him along with the other kids. It was little wonder I took to Loretta as I did, she was a lot like Ryan, easy to like and eager to please.

Ryan was not quite two then and struggled with the name Loretta. Somehow it became jumbled when it rolled over his tongue so that the L and the R were transposed, turning Loretta into Roletta—a name that over the years, came to be his and my mark of endearment for her.

Not long after that, Loretta began helping me one afternoon a week, then one became two and two turned into three and eventually I couldn't imagine my days without her. When I called Loretta to ask her recommendation for someone to help paint and fix up our not-so-new office, she recruited her older son. We all worked together and somehow turned that ramshackle little cracker house into a nicely presentable place of business.

The inside of the building was wallpapered with the grass cloth paper left over from our new house, the outside of the building was painted a soft cream color with green trim that was the color of spring grass. Hanging from a wooden post at the edge of the walkway was a shingle that read GREENS+. Jude's desk was an antiquated teacher's desk we found at the used furniture store, mine was a card table. We added a couple of folding chairs, brought my computer from home and began doing business.

Five mornings a week, I dropped Ryan off for day care at Corey's Day Care, where he could swim, play, socialize with the other kids and learn the things he needed to know before entering kindergarten. Of course, there was not a lot Ryan needed to learn. Before he was three, he could recite the alphabet, count to one-hundred, identify every color in the rainbow, name most animals and plants, swim like a fish and climb like a monkey. He was reading before he was five. Fortunately, or unfortunately, he was a lot like I had been as a child, which meant that he was often bored by classroom activities that offered little or no challenge.

When we decided to settle in Vero Beach, part of the reason was that Ryan would be able to attend St. Edward's, a school well known for the quality of their education and the caliber of students they graduated. In the early spring I submitted our application for his enrollment in kindergarten. To qualify for entrance into the school, every child—yes, even those registering for kindergarten—had to undergo a fairly intense interview and pass with flying colors. St. Edward's insisted these interviews be spontaneous so there was no notification of when or where they would take place. Ryan was in his Pre-K class at Corey's Child Care Center the day they came to interview him. Ryan's interview was shorter than most because when the interviewer arrived, Ryan was helping the daycare instructor teach the other children colors and numbers. The interviewer laughed, "Well, I guess there's no question about him being smart enough for St. Edwards," she said and wrote *approved* on the bottom of Ryan's application.

During the year that followed, everything grew—well, everything except our bank account. I worked in the front room of that little shack, answering the telephone, doing paperwork, placing orders and servicing the handful of customers who wandered in. Jude did everything else. What little money we made went to buy things like a file cabinet and chairs for customers to sit on. After our first month of operation, we were able to begin paying rent to Dot Faber, a feat that to us seemed amazing!

When Jude walked into Dot's office and handed her that first rent check, she looked at it and gave a wide grin, "See," she said nodding to herself, "I got a sense for knowing people what's got good in them!"

Ryan, it seemed, grew faster than the business. Surpassing even a proud mother's expectations, he began swimming in competitions when he was only five, and by the time he was eight he was sixth best in the state for his age category. I had to laugh, our son was as competitive as I had been. Offer a challenge and he'd jump at it. In the second grade he began to play soccer; but he didn't just play soccer, he loved it and excelled at it. Jude and I never missed a game and I cheered so loudly, a bystander might have thought I'd wagered a thousand dollars on the game. Without realizing when the transition had taken place, I knew that I'd become the proverbial Soccer Mom. Me, Lani Verner Deauville— the girl who never wanted to get married or have children was now the most devoted mom imaginable and loving every minute of it! And Jude, who never expected to be a father, found the role for which he was intended.

Looking back on the decades of career growth, prestigious awards, and impressive associates, little did I realize that being a Mom would turn out to be perhaps the most rewarding thing I had ever done. I loved Ryan before I knew him, but once he was placed in my arms, my life was changed forever and I found a place in my heart that was larger than anything I'd dreamed possible.

From the time Ryan was an infant I'd sit beside his bed and gently scratch his back while he drifted off to sleep. Then one night when he was a toddler, I decided to add my rendition of the Brahms Lullaby to the nightly ritual. Unfortunately, I have what is possibly the worst singing voice on the planet. They say a mother's song is always soothing to a child, but I beg to differ because after the first verse of Lullaby and Good Night, Ryan lifted his head and said, "Mommy, please don't make those noises." Never had my horrible singing voice been described more appropriately. I suppressed a giggle and returned to simply scratching his back.

Days turned into weeks and weeks into months and gradually the people in town began to stop by our office and ask about GREENS+. Some came because of a referral, others simply because they were curious.

We had been in business for about a year when we added our first employee—Jude's niece, Sheri. She left New Hampshire and moved to Florida to live in the back room of our little office-house and take a job with very little pay. Having Sheri with us meant that I could cut back to working two or three days a week, which, for me, was wonderful. You might think that after all the years of working I would jump at the chance to stay at home and take life a little easier, but instead, I began doing volunteer work at a school with a substantial number of students from other countries. I was charged with helping fourth graders prepare for the FCAT (Florida Comprehensive Achievement Test).

Because I believe that kindergarten lays the foundation for a child's educational life, I also volunteered to help in a kindergarten class. Unfortunately, that teacher employed very 'old school' techniques in working with the children; rewarding good behavior with excessive amounts of candy and then punishing the hyperactivity that followed with time-out in the corner. I explained how the sugary candy was causing the hyperactivity, but my words fell on deaf ears and she continued to do as she had done for decades. I eventually gave up working in that class. We change the things we can change, but sometimes there are things we cannot change and all we can do is move on. *Another IS!*

When I wasn't working with children I continued to do most of the paperwork for what was now Orange Peel Enterprises. Jude ran the business, Sherri answered the phones and we continued to grow. By the third year we were bursting at the seams. We needed more storage space and we needed someone to process, pack and ship the orders. We rented additional storage space in a small building behind our little office, installed air conditioning and hired Andre, our first shipping clerk. Little did we realize, that in time we would see eighteen-wheelers pull up to our little shipping area and carry away cartons to be delivered all across the United States.

Back then Andre's salary and the added storage space rent were more than we could actually afford. We lived on an income that had to stretch to make ends meet because most of our profit went back into the business. The growth was exciting, but it was also costly. The more we sold, the more we had to produce; the more we produced, the more labels and literature we needed to print. It seemed to be one expense after another and while we could do without fancy office furniture and circle around the back room where termite damage weakened the floorboard; we were not willing to compromise on product quality. Our reason for being in this business was not just to make enough money to survive—we could have continued to live very nicely on Jennie's stipend—our reason for being in business was to give people like me the nutrition they needed for better health. I had experienced the difference GREENS+ could make in a person's health and wanted to share it.

Yes, the company grew, but the needs of the business grew even faster. We had contracted with a manufacturer in Montana to do the blending and bottling, plus, we were adding products to the line. Now, in addition to covering our rent, bills and salaries, we had to set aside money for research and development. We were constantly adjusting the formula to improve the taste, consistency and nutritional value. But every change in formulation meant new labels and literature, so it seemed as if the spending never stopped.

After five years of growth that we never dreamed possible, we outgrew our tiny little cracker house in front of Faber Press and began looking for larger space. After all those years of struggling, we had finally turned the corner and were now ready to buy a building, a building that would be the corporate headquarters for Orange Peel Enterprises—*corporate headquarters*, the thought boggled my mind. We needed a building with room for storage, shipping and growth—oh yes, and one that was reasonably affordable. One day Jude came home and announced that he'd found an absolutely perfect building in Vero Beach. That afternoon we drove over to see the building. I had to agree with Jude, it was perfect—but when we turned out of the driveway to leave I noticed the name of the street and knew that it was more than perfect, it was providence. The name of the street was Ponce de Leon Circle—GREENS+ would be a second fountain of youth, or if not youth, a fountain of good health. *A wonderful IS.*

Ryan was eight when we opened that office, but in the blink of eye he grew to be a teenager. He loved soccer and I loved being one of the soccer moms who went from school to school watching the boys play. I loved that Ryan was an outstanding player, but I was even prouder of the fact that he was a clean and fair player. He seldom received the yellow penalty warning card that forced him to leave the game for a few minutes; and only once was he given the red card that got him ejected from the game. Ryan never intentionally fouled someone, but that time after he'd battled for ownership of the ball and passed it to his teammate, Ryan knocked his opponent down and kicked him before he had time to get up. Whistles sounded and he was handed a red penalty card. With one last angry glance at the boy on the ground, he walked off the field. I sat there aghast. That was so unlike Ryan. I couldn't imagine what had caused such an outburst. I steamed about it until the game ended then went over and angrily demanded an explanation.

"Why would you do such a thing?" I asked.

Ryan's head was bowed, his eyes directed to his shoes, "I'd rather not say," he answered.

"Rather not say!" I echoed incongruously, "Well that's just too bad, because I expect you to explain such unsportsmanlike behavior, regardless of what you'd rather not say!"

He stood there for a long time looking down at his feet, then mumbled something so low that I had to ask him to repeat it.

He finally lifted his head to where his eyes met mine and I could see the start of tears dribbling from the corners. "He made an ugly remark about you being in a wheelchair."

"Oh, Ryan honey," I sighed, "that's not worth fighting about..." I went on to say how such comments had to be ignored and the source considered. "That boy," I explained, "was just trying to get back at you because you outplayed him."

"But Mom..."

"No buts, Ryan. That type of behavior is unacceptable. The boy was wrong to say a thing like that, but you were just as wrong to allow him to provoke you into a fight. The only thing you achieved was getting yourself thrown out of the game, which was probably what he wanted in the first place." Although my words chastised Ryan for fighting, my heart felt a swell of pride in knowing that my son loved me so much that he wanted to protect me. *A treasured IS.*

It was during those years that Jude and I discovered a secluded lot on the Saint Sebastian River, a spot that reminded me of the Tomoka Game Preserve. It was everything my heart held dear— water, wilderness, wild animals living alongside one another, and a blissful solitude that offered a universe of freedom. We bought the seven acre property and built a house on it. Most people would have felled the trees and cleared the brush to make way for rolling lawns and manicured gardens. We didn't. For us, seeing the land in its natural state was reality, it was the earth as it was meant to be, it was the beauty of creation. We cleared an area just large enough for the house and the roundabout that circled back to the dirt road. Our dream house began with a sketch I drew on one of Ryan's school tablets, a sheet of yellow paper with blue lines running across the page. The architect turned my sketch into a house plan and construction was soon underway.

When Ryan graduated Junior High, I assumed he would go on to attend Saint Edward's Senior High, but I was wrong.

"Mom," he said, "I'd like to go to Sebastian River High."

"A public school?" I gasped. "Why on earth would you want to do that?" Without giving him time to answer, I continued on, "If you stay at Saint Edwards you're almost assured of getting into an Ivy League college."

"I don't want it that way," he said, "I don't want an Ivy League College to take me just because I graduated from Saint Edwards, I'd rather earn my way into a college that really wants to accept me."

"But the environment at Saint Edwards is so stable, your friends are from good families, they're..." *Good grief! I was beginning to sound like my mother!*

"Mom," Ryan interrupted, "I know all that, and that's precisely why I want to attend Sebastian River. Being at Saint Edwards is like living in a make-believe perfect world, it's not real. How am I supposed to deal with reality if I never have any exposure to it?"

By then I was older and a lot wiser. I knew what the real world was and I was hoping to spare Ryan, but without realizing it, I had instilled in him the same willful determination that I had as a child. I gave in, albeit reluctantly.

Shortly after we moved into our new house, Benny came into our life. I say our, but the truth is that Benny was MY dog. We had a relationship that went beyond words.

Since the new house was in the middle of nowhere, we wanted a guard dog to fend off trespassers should they invade our private paradise and we needed a service dog for me. We got Benny, a German Shepherd trained in Germany and responsive to German commands. With Benny only understanding the commands he'd been taught, I had to learn to speak his language, and I had to do it fast! Once I did, we went everywhere together. When people saw me, they saw Benny right there beside me, gentle as a lamb but always on guard, watching. In time, Benny became my service dog, helping me in so many ways, picking up things that I'd dropped and handing them to me. He became a hand and arm that worked far better than mine did.

One afternoon we were in Walmart when I noticed an elderly woman hobbling along with her walker. She seemed to be watching us. I wheeled myself back to pots and pans and she followed along stopping at can openers. I moved on to spatulas, and she ventured forth to pots and pans. I looked back and gave her a smile; she returned it, then started to speak in the frail voice of an elderly person.

"Today's my birthday," she said, "I'm ninety-four years old." She toddled a bit closer. "I've been afraid of dogs all my life, but I promised myself that before I die, I'd get up enough courage to pet a dog." She inched her way to within an arm's length of Benny. "I've been watching your dog," she said, "and he's got awful kind eyes...do you think he'd be willing to let me pet him?"

"I think he'd be honored to have you pet him," I answered.

She reached a shaky hand down and allowed it to travel across the crown of Benny's head and along his ears. "My goodness," she exclaimed with wonder, "his ears feel like vel-vet."

I heard a sound and glanced down, there was Benny bestowing a big wet kiss on the woman's hand.

She gave me a wide grin and said "He kissed me! I think he likes me."

"Yes Ma'am, he certainly does like you," I answered.

As she turned and thumped her way down the aisle, I heard her mumbling, "I petted a dog today, and he liked me..."

The woman was right, Benny did like her; Benny liked almost everyone and everyone liked Benny. But me, I loved Benny just as I'd loved Duke nearly a lifetime ago.

When Ryan graduated from high school and left home to live in Boynton Beach where he would be close to the Florida Atlantic University Campus, it was Benny who filled a big part of the void left behind.

Over the next few years, life moved along at a nice easy pace. Ryan did well in school, the business continued to grow and we added another building to warehouse our burgeoning line of products. Ryan had a decade ago outgrown his need for a babysitter, but I never outgrew my need for Loretta. Over the years we became so close that when I introduced her to friends, I'd often refer to her as my sister. It often raised eyebrows, because Loretta is a Black woman, not just a Black woman, but a dark-skinned Black woman whereas I'm an olive complected half-Apache. I'd usually follow my introduction with a grin and the comment that we'd had different fathers, which would cause Loretta to start snickering. The two of us had great fun with such an introduction, but after seeing how close we were, I think some people walked away wondering about the truth.

A person like Loretta is who you turn to in times of trouble.

Twenty

On a Friday morning in 2005, my world was turned upside down. I remember it being a Friday, because Loretta wasn't working that day. Ever since I broke my neck, I have needed a caregiver to get me dressed and to help me in and out of bed. Loretta did it Monday through Thursday and Jude did it when she was off. That morning I was still in bed when he got up and went into the bathroom. Moments later I heard a loud crash. "Jude?" I called, but there was no answer. I called his name over and over again, and got nothing but the dead sound of silence.

Using my arms, I dragged myself to the edge of the bed where I could grab the telephone on the nightstand. I phoned Tony, Loretta's son, who was working outside. "Come quick," I yelled, "I think something has happened to Jude!"

Tony was there in a heartbeat and he found Jude lying on the bathroom floor. "Call 911," I said "while I call Loretta to get me up. When the ambulance arrived they moved Jude onto a stretcher and took him to Sebastian River Medical Center.

When Loretta, Benny and I arrived at the hospital, we were told that Jude had suffered a seizure caused by a walnut-sized tumor in his brain.

"How is that possible," I asked, "he was fine one minute and unconscious the next?"

"Sometimes it happens that way," the doctor said and gave no further explanation.

By then Jude had regained consciousness, so we went home—I had work to do. Minutes after we arrived at the house I was on the telephone with Doctor Barth Greene, a neurosurgeon I worked with when I was the Director of the State Vocational Rehabilitation Program. He was the head of neurosurgery at the University of Miami and headed up the Miami Project to Cure Paralysis. After all those years of working with doctors and people with disabilities as well as being disabled myself, I understood medical terminology, knew what to expect, and could comprehend the reality of a given situation. I explained Jude's condition in detail as Doctor Greene listened. When I finished talking, he said, "I want you and Jude to drive down to Miami tomorrow, check into a hotel, go out have a nice dinner, get a good night's sleep and be at Jackson Memorial Hospital early Sunday morning."

"Sunday?" I repeated, knowing that not much is done in hospitals on a Sunday.

"Yes," he answered. "I'll arrange to have people on staff to run the tests I need and if I find what I think I'll find, we'll get the best brain surgeon there is to perform Jude's surgery on Monday morning."

My next call was to Ryan.

Following Doctor Greene's instructions we drove to Miami on Saturday, and when we arrived at Jackson Memorial Sunday morning, Ryan was there waiting for us. The hours of that day seemed to drag on forever as I sat in that small waiting room with Ryan, Loretta and Benny by my side. It was an odd sort of role reversal—for most of my life I had been the one in the hospital and others did the waiting. But after living through that endless afternoon, I can honestly say that waiting for word of your loved one's fate is far more painful than being the patient.

It was close to dinnertime when Doctor Greene walked in with a grim look on his face.

"It's worse than we thought," he said, "You can forget the walnut, Jude's tumor is the size of a grapefruit."

Alarmed, I asked how it was possible that a tumor could grow to such a size without generating any visible symptoms.

"Well," he said hesitantly, "it's in the left frontal lobe, which is the area that would have an effect on a person's ability to think rationally." He hesitated for a moment more, "How is Jude's rationality? Does he think through problems, or address things with rational solutions?"

I could see the corners of both Loretta and Ryan's mouths curling into a smile. Jude was never an overly rational person; he did things spur of the moment, off the top of his head, whatever felt good—it was a part of who he was and part of why we all loved him. "I haven't really seen any change in the rationality of his thinking," I answered honestly.

"Hmmm," Doctor Greene fingered his chin pensively then went on to explain that despite the absence of any visible symptoms, we were looking at a very grave situation. "With a surgery such as this," he said, "we can never predict what the results will be. There's a possibility that he may not live through the surgery. If he does, he may be paralyzed or suffer severe brain damage, and be in a permanently vegetative state. On the other hand, it's minimally possible that the surgeon can go in there and remove the tumor with little noticeable damage to his brain."

I asked the obvious, "What if he doesn't have the surgery."

"As the tumor grows it will destroy his ability to think, speak, talk or move and eventually he will die."

The next morning, we arrived at the hospital early and spent a half-hour with Jude before he was taken to surgery. Jude, always the carefree jokester, eyed the solemn expressions we wore and said, "Hey, no long faces! I'll get this done and be back in time for lunch. Stop worrying…it's all good."

How often I've thought of that statement—it's all good. That's Jude's way of looking at life. Is it always rational? Maybe, maybe not. Is it a great attitude? Definitely! Our relationship has always been like life on a seesaw—my rationality anchors his optimism and his optimism keeps my rationality from weighing us down.

After what seemed to be endless hours in that same gray-walled waiting room, the surgeon walked in wearing a smile. "Well," he said, "I think I got it all!" Of course Jude was still in the recovery room and we had no way of knowing what, if any, side effects there would be.

As it turned out, it WAS all good. By the next day, Jude could move his right arm and leg, both of which were controlled by the area where they had removed the tumor. He was left with some weakness and would never again be the powerhouse he once was. He could no longer lift me or carry me from one place to another; but his thinking, albeit sometimes a bit slower, is as rational as it ever was.

Jude and I had spent our lives caring for one another. My strength compensated for his weakness and his strength carried me through my most difficult times. But when Jude came home from the hospital it seemed as though our roles had been reversed. While he had been my caregiver, I was now his. I sorted and monitored his medications, arranged his doctor visits, and remained watchful of where he was and what he was doing. He was still Jude, not the exact same Jude I had known for so many years, but still Jude and I still loved him enormously.

In those days I often thought of something Maya Angelou once said, 'I've learned that no matter what happens, or how bad it seems today, life does go on, and it will be better tomorrow.'

And, it did get better; although I was needed at the office during the week, on weekends Jude and I took leisurely boat rides on the river, explored trails lined with cypress, oaks, and sabal palms, watched small animals scurry into burrows and mama ducks march toward the water with a line of bright yellow chicks following in her footsteps. Day after day we were rediscovering the wonder of the beautiful property that we had fallen in love with—in short, we were now stopping to smell the roses. The life that I had sometimes taken for granted, had suddenly become tenuous and very precious. Jude and I had all too often hurried through days of doing and rushing and being—we had always taken for granted that tomorrow there would be time enough for relaxing and enjoying life. We now knew that this was tomorrow, and we were determined to make every moment count. In some ways that revelation is almost laughable, because ever since my accident, I thought I had been living every day to the fullest. I guess we all live and learn.

Throughout all those years Benny walked beside me, patiently retrieving the things I dropped and giving me the type of unconditional love most humans fail to comprehend. But in the tenth year he developed liver cancer and it spread to his spine. I loved Benny as I'd loved Duke and did everything humanly possible to keep him alive. But when I saw him struggling through his pain to stand by my side, I knew I was no longer doing this for Benny, I was doing it for me. My heart ached to keep him beside me for one more day, but I knew I'd always want another day, and another, and he'd respond by being there. I, at last, realized it was time for me to do something for Benny.

It was Ryan, who stood beside me as I said my last goodbye to Benny. I held my face to his and told him for what may have been the millionth time how much I loved him. The doctor gave him the shot that would at last bring relief and Benny with those soft and gentle eyes looked up at me as if he were saying *Thanks Mom.*

You might think that losing the use of my legs, arms, and hands was the hardest thing I've ever had to deal with, but I can tell you straight from my heart that it wasn't. Losing a loved one is harder, much harder. I could fight back after the accident, but after losing Benny, I was helpless to do anything but let my heart break into a million little pieces.

On the way home from the vet, I realized it was Election Day. "Ryan," I said, "we've got to stop at the polls so I can vote."

He glanced over with a look of surprise. "You don't feel up to doing that today, do you?"

"I have to, it's my duty." For a brief moment my sorrow was held at bay when I turned to Ryan and said, "You know that I believe—"

I was interrupted by his laughter, "I know, Mom." He smiled at me then repeated the thought I'd drummed into his head, "Voting is not only a right, it's a responsibility. And the great

Andrus Thiers would turn over in his grave if we relinquished that right simply because we were too lazy or too sad to get up and get our butt to the polls."

"You've learned your lesson well," I said with a smile. Then I again reminded him how Andrus Thiers was not only a forefather of the Tiers family, but also one of the signers of the Articles of Confederation which united the states and made us what we are—America.

Let's face it, when a quadriplegic with a big lovable dog at her side shows up to vote, rain or shine, people remember—and everyone at the polling place knew not just me, but also Benny. The moment I came through the door, the greeter asked, "Where's Benny?"

As I've said earlier, Benny went everywhere I went. I was never without him, so it was an oddity to see me there alone. I sadly explained that I had just taken Benny to be euthanized, in order to spare him any more pain and suffering. Almost immediately, the greeter's eyes filled with moisture and he began sniffing back tears. I moved on to the registration table and the woman there asked the same question—"Where's Benny?" I offered her the same explanation and she began to sob as she stretched her arm across the table and took hold of my hand. Seeing her tears caused the woman next to her to ask what was wrong. I explained and then had both women sobbing. The story was passed from person to person until the murmur of sorrow could be heard throughout the entire polling place.

With the sound of sadness trailing behind us, I turned to Ryan and said, "I know everyone loved Benny, but I feel badly that I made all those people cry."

"They weren't crying because of you, Mom," he said, "they were crying with you. They were mourning the loss of Benny. They loved him too."

Ryan then leaned over and did something that has been a part of our life since he was no more than a toddler—a quick kiss, a rub of noses, and a meaningful hug. It was something we did for one another in times of disappointment, heartache or pain. It healed a scraped knee, eased a hurt, and comforted in time of loss.

After losing Benny, it was a long while before I could even consider getting another dog. Then finally after months of mourning, I got Mexx, another dog trained in Germany and shipped across the ocean in a crate labeled with my name and address. Mexx was no Benny. He was fine with me, but to any number of other people, including dear sweet Loretta, he was downright testy. A 100 pound German shepherd can be intimidating to start with, but one with a growl rumbling through his throat and a fierce snarl is something to be feared. I sensed Mexx had experienced something that made him wary of people and for months I tried to calm him, and make him more accepting of other people. In the process, I learned that he had never lived outside of a kennel and had never been socialized. The only thing he knew was to be on guard, and ready for attack. As a police dog that's what he was trained to do. I was determined not to return Mexx to such a life and, realizing that without help I would be unable to change his behavior, I had a skilled trainer fly in to help me retrain my new best friend.

After a week of lessons, and a few more weeks of consistent follow through on what Mexx had learned, he became almost lovable. He no longer growled at people, he learned to play, and followed commands perfectly. We had accomplished what could easily be considered a miracle.

A few days later, I was outside playing with Mexx. The only toy he had was a hard ball attached to the end of a twisted cord that came in the crate with him. I could put my finger through the looped cord and toss the ball, so I threw and he chased. The last time I tossed the ball, he caught it by the cord and joyfully tossed it back into the air himself. When it came down, Mexx with his jaw opened wide leaped into the air to catch it and the ball went straight down into his throat. He tipped his head to the ground, gagging and trying to dislodge the ball. I called him and he came over. If he had raised his head up, I could have grabbed the cord and pulled it from his throat, but poor Mexx was gagging and couldn't lift his head.

I called for Loretta and Jude, but by the time they got there Mexx, in his desperation to dislodge the ball, had chewed off the end of the cord so neither of them could reach it. I coaxed Mexx into the van and Loretta and I took off for the vet's office which was less than a mile away. Driving as fast as I could, without killing anyone, I called the vet's office and told them of the emergency. "Sorry," the receptionist said, "All of the doctors are out just now, there's no one on duty." I asked if there wasn't a technician or an assistant who could help. "I just need someone to reach in and pull the ball out of his throat," I pleaded. I held on and kept driving while she went to check. After a couple of minutes, she came back to the phone and informed me that none of the technicians felt qualified to do it. They were not permitted to touch an animal without a vet on the premises, not even to save a dog's life.

I remembered passing a house on the way to the vet's office. There was always a police car parked in that driveway, so it stood to reason that where there was a police car there would be a policeman, maybe someone who worked nights and was home during the day. The entire time that I drove, the sound of Mexx gagging and struggling for breath filled my ears. When we reached the house, I asked Loretta to run to the door and try to get help. After what seemed like an eternity a sleepy-eyed teenager answered the door. "My mom's a policewoman," he finally said, "but she's in the shower and I'm not going in there after her."

"Ask the boy if he'll come and help us," I screamed from the car.

Loretta asked, but the boy said he wasn't up to doing something like that, he claimed he was afraid of dogs and wouldn't even consider sticking his arm into a German Shepherd's mouth.

By then, Jude had located Loretta's son Tony, who is big, strong and unafraid of anything, and Tony had come in search of us. He saw my van, pulled in behind us and jumped into the back to help—but by then Mexx was no longer breathing. Tony pulled the ball from Mexx's throat and tried doing chest compressions, but it was to no avail, Mexx was gone. It had taken my sweet Mexx forty-five minutes to die an excruciatingly painful death and in all that time I could not find one person willing and capable of helping me. In the fifty-three years since I had my accident, this was the only time my disability ever left me feeling truly helpless.

That evening I sat in my office alone, the spot beside my chair empty, but the memory of Mexx painfully fresh in my mind. I thought back on all those people who so callously refused to help. What value did they place on life? Were they an entity unto themselves and not part of this planet? What value did we, as a nation, place on life? I thought back to my father and the heritage of his people—people driven from the land they'd believed belonged to no one but the Great Spirit. When would it stop? When would we, as a nation of human beings, begin to care about one another and about the creatures and the earth we share?

I wheeled across my office and stopped in front of a document I have hanging on the wall—The Native American Ten Commandments. One by one, I read through them again for perhaps the hundredth time, taking time to ponder each thought and silently wish that one day this would be the way things are...

The Earth is Our Mother, Care for Her.
Honor All of Your Relations.
Open your Heart and Soul to the Great Spirit.
All Life is Sacred, Treat All Beings with Respect.
Take from the Earth what is Necessary and Nothing More.
Do What Needs to be Done for the Good of All.
Give Constant Thanks to the Great Spirit for Each New Day.
Speak the Truth but Only of the Good of Others.
Follow the Rhythms of Nature, Rise and Retire with the Sun.
Enjoy Life's Journey but Leave No Tracks.

These are the commandments that I try to live by. I strive to follow them because they are not just positive rules of life, they are the core of man's humanity to man. I'm certainly not perfect and I am not always successful in my attempts to live this way—but I make every effort to do so. How painfully sad that these guidelines so often fall by the wayside and people can turn their back on a person or animal in need.

I went through several months of mourning Mexx and feeling the weight of helplessness to save him. But a dog has always been an integral part of my life. Since breaking my neck those many years ago, I really require a service dog. Then one day the trainer I worked with called and said, "Lani, I've got just the dog for you—Kaso. He's well-trained, lovable, and as people-oriented as Benny was. There's just one problem, he's coming from the Czech Republic, so the commands he knows are only in Czechoslovakian."

"I don't speak a word of Czech," I laughed, "so this will be an adventure for both of us."

After two days of being in a crate shuttled from plane to plane, Kaso was scheduled to arrive at the Orlando airport and Ryan went with me to pick him up. We took a collar and leash and while Ryan was attending to the customs paperwork, I made my way back to where there were two crates that had arrived on the flight. I headed for the smaller of the two, deciding that the larger crate must contain a Great Dane or a mastiff. An attendant approached me, "Are you here to pick up a dog?" she asked. I answered yes and gave her my name. She smiled, "Your dog is back here," she led me over to the larger crate.

I peered inside and saw two black eyes looking back at me. Kaso was big, dark in color and formidable in appearance. After the aggression I'd seen with Mexx, I had a moment of hesitation, but then stretched my arm out and pushed my fingers through the cage. Either we'd make friends or I'd lose some fingers and those fingers didn't work anyway! Kaso moved forward, nuzzled my hand with his nose and then covered it with kisses. When Ryan joined me, he opened the crate and slid the collar over the dog's head. Kaso immediately dragged Ryan over to where I was sitting, put his front paws up on the arm of my wheelchair, leaned in and covered my face with kisses! Ryan also received an ample supply of affectionate licks. Knowing the loving relationship that I've always had with my animals, Ryan turned to me and laughingly said, "Gee Mom, this one came pre-programmed."

As I work my way through this tale of my life, Kaso is here by my side—loving, sweet, gentle, totally dedicated to me, and tolerant of all people. Love is what I have promised Kaso and love is what he gives me in return, an abundance of love.

The bond I have with Kaso is one of many that I consider life's greatest treasures. Money and material possessions are easily lost, fame is quickly forgotten, but love and kind deeds live on forever—in both heart and mind. Looking at the love in Kaso's eyes, I see reflections of so many others who have shared the meaningful moments of my life—my nephew Lee, I loved him as a child, and as a man he has returned that love a hundredfold. Although he is now nearing retirement age himself, he never forgets my birthday or a holiday, and often he calls just to recapture the childhood memories of sitting astride Dusty's back. Lee remembers my kindness to him, just as I remember the kindness of others to me.

Two of the people who made a huge difference in my life were teachers—people whose goodness of heart far outweighed the meager salary they were paid. The first was Mister Staggers, my sixth grade teacher, who went beyond the call of duty to act as the father figure I so desperately craved. The second was Marcelline Douglas, or as I affectionately came to call her, Mercy Dougall. Although I was only an eighth grader, she trusted me with a teaching assignment normally reserved for seniors, and in doing so, she changed a rebellious teenager into one who willingly accepted responsibility. Teachers like this have made a difference in my life, just as they make a difference in the lives of many other students. Unfortunately, teachers, although they often shape young lives more than we can possibly realize, are the most underpaid and underappreciated people in the workforce. Rather than finagling ways to cut back on school budgets, our children would be better served if schools would strive to find the best-qualified teachers and compensate them accordingly. The comment *it's not the teacher's job to raise your children* is repeated far too often and I, for one, can say that I am glad neither Mr. Staggers nor Ms. Douglas felt that way. It's been over fifty years since I sat in their classrooms and yet I remember these teachers with great fondness. Will the children of today be able to say that?

Children are this country's greatest resource. They are our future. I've traveled many long and arduous roads in my lifetime, faced challenges that I never anticipated and had successes far beyond what I ever expected. But of all of the things I've ever done, the greatest and most rewarding joy of all was that of being a mom.

I say Mom, not Mother, because that's how my relationship with Ryan is. We laugh, we joke around, tease one another about our foibles, and lean on one another when sorrow comes. Jude's carefree personality delights me and enhances my life greatly, but Ryan's soul is so like mine it's as if we are one. He cares about the preservation of this earth, just as I do. He has the same love and respect for creatures of the wild and the pets that populate our life, but in truth, he is much kinder to people than I was at certain times of my life. I don't just love Ryan, I admire and respect him. I admire the competitive spirit that drives him to excel, I admire his commitment to healthy food and exercise. I admire his dedication and discipline and I admire the way he stepped in to take on an ever-increasing amount of responsibility at GREENS+. I take pride in the fact that he doesn't simply like the company; he understands the purpose and purity of each product and is principled enough to reject a product that he wouldn't take himself.

In March of 2011, Ryan was named President of Orange Peel Enterprises. The appointment wasn't in name only. It was a well-earned promotion that came about because he had worked his way through every department of the company, starting with the shipping room. Recently as we watched him speak on television about his vision for the future of our company, it was the proudest moment of my life. I turned to Jude and said, "My life has been one of thousands of mistakes, but one thing I did right was raising a son like Ryan." Jude gave me a smile, nodded, and kissed me.

The life I have led has been nothing short of incredible. I have experienced innumerable joys and sorrows, but the joys have far outweighed the sorrows. It would be an understatement to say that my life has been unusual. I remember one of the things you had to do prior to entering junior college was write a short autobiographical paper. Mine was titled: "How to Live 40 Years in 20." Now into my 70s, I suppose I could say I've lived at least 100 years!

It has been an awesome experience so far...but, tomorrow I plan to ...

Acknowledgements

As I re-traveled the roads of my life, I realized that I am grateful beyond words to the people who have been such an important part of it—the caregivers, teachers, friends, co-workers, my family and the families of those I love—each of them touched my life in a way that made me the person I am today. Although my life has never been what most would consider normal, these wonderful people filled the voids with caring and kindness.

Long before I had grown to adulthood, two teachers both loved and challenged me. Marcie Douglas showed me the meaning of trust when she charged me with a responsibility I was not deserving of and Lester Staggers stepped up to become a father figure to a little girl who was sorely in need of one. Although they are no longer here to enjoy my words of praise, I think they were well aware of my feelings. During those years Mother struggled to make ends meet and in her absence Scott and Dit tried to serve as parents but in truth, they were simply children themselves. Although Mother had a thousand and one shortcomings, she loved me with all her heart. Even when we didn't agree, she supported my endeavors and applauded them with pride. Hers was not an easy life but she gave me the best she had to give. She also gave me Pappy, a man of infinite patience and wisdom, a man who showed me what it means to have a real father. As Pappy taught me about the love of a father, so my nephew Lee showed me the joy of loving a child; I not only loved him, I adored him—and still do.

I owe a huge debt of gratitude to Orthopedic Surgeon Charles Meade for thinking outside the box and performing a surgery that others had not even considered. My life is better for having known Charlie Meade and I am proud to also call him my friend. During those dark days when hope was little more than the flicker of a candle, Ross Bremer was by my side with friendship, honesty and encouragement; there can never be enough words to adequately thank Ross for that.

The pursuit of higher learning can be challenging at best, but for a quadriplegic it is doubly so. At a time when very few universities could offer handicapped access, Dr. Paul Siegel sought me out and convinced me to attend the University of Alabama, despite my flagrant anti-segregationist opinions. He provided me with a wealth of learning opportunities and supported my goals regardless of how controversial, lofty and often radical they were. It was my pleasure to know this man of wisdom and principle. In the early years of my working career, Patti Hughes was my caregiver, she not only helped to make smooth my pathway but also became a loved and trusted friend.

Next I come to the most important people in my life—my family. I include Loretta Schofield in my family because to me she is everything I have ever wanted in a sister, and more. She knows my words before I speak them and is beside me before I can ask for help. She has a listening ear, a loving heart and a ready smile, how can I ever thank her enough for that?

My husband Jude came into my life with a song and brought laughter, lightheartedness and joy that has lasted throughout the years. And, adding to the richness of Jude's love was the love of his family, a family that gathered me into their midst with open arms. Jude and I have seen good times and bad times, but through it all we had each other. We raised a son together and became what I had always wanted—a real family. Ryan is the best of each of us; he has Jude's wonderful people skills and my tenacity. The moment that Ryan was first placed in my arms I knew a love that had no boundaries. He is everything a mother could ever hope for and I am endlessly proud of all he is and does. Now the President of GreensPlus, he is a man to be admired, yet he is still my son—a loving devoted young man who has gone to great lengths to push me into re-telling my life's story. Thank you Ryan, for everything you are and for all you will be.

Lastly, I would be remiss were I not to thank Bette Lee Crosby for retelling my story in such a beautiful fashion. She has created a memoir that captures not only the facts of my life, but also the feelings that were so much a part of it. Our journey together has been one of laughter and friendship, one that I hope readers will enjoy sharing.

Other Books by

Bette Lee Crosby

CRACKS IN THE SIDEWALK

SPARE CHANGE

THE TWELFTH CHILD

Made in the USA
Charleston, SC
19 March 2012